BEYOND
BODY
POSITIVE

Janet Boseovski, PhD
Ashleigh Gallagher, PhD

BEYOND
BODY
POSITIVE

A Mother's Science-Based Guide for
Helping Girls Build a Healthy Body Image

 AMERICAN PSYCHOLOGICAL ASSOCIATION

Published by
APA LifeTools
750 First Street, NE
Washington, DC 20002
https://www.apa.org

Order Department
https://www.apa.org/pubs/books
order@apa.org

Typeset in Sabon by Circle Graphics, Inc., Reisterstown, MD

Printer: Sheridan Books, Chelsea, MI
Cover Designer: Mark Karis

Library of Congress Cataloging-in-Publication Data

Names: Boseovski, Janet, author. | Gallagher, Ashleigh, author.
Title: Beyond body positive : a mother's science-based guide for helping girls build a healthy body image / Janet Boseovski, PhD, and Ashleigh Gallagher, PhD.
Description: Washington, DC : American Psychological Association, [2024] | Series: APA lifetools series | Includes bibliographical references and index.
Identifiers: LCCN 2024019802 (print) | LCCN 2024019803 (ebook) | ISBN 9781433840999 (paperback) | ISBN 9781433841002 (ebook)
Subjects: LCSH: Body image in girls. | Body image in children. | Self-esteem in children. | Mothers and daughters. | Parent and child. | BISAC: SELF-HELP / Eating Disorders & Body Image | PSYCHOLOGY / Developmental / Adolescent
Classification: LCC BF723.B6 B67 2025 (print) | LCC BF723.B6 (ebook) | DDC 155.4/33--dc23/eng/20240804
LC record available at https://lccn.loc.gov/2024019802
LC ebook record available at https://lccn.loc.gov/2024019803

https://doi.org/10.1037/0000427-000

Printed in the United States of America

10 9 8 7 6 5 4 3 2 1

CONTENTS

Contents

ACKNOWLEDGMENTS

We are very grateful to our acquisitions editor, Stevie Davall, and her team for their expert guidance and feedback. Thank you, Stevie, for recognizing the importance of reaching a broad audience with our developmental perspective on body image development in young girls and for guidance in best communicating this perspective. We appreciate the thoughtful input and valuable suggestions for improvement from our development editor, Beth Hatch, as well as the constructive comments from three anonymous reviewers. We are grateful to our copy and academic editor, Gail Gottfried, for her careful attention to logistics, style, and content clarity in the book.

We would like to thank our graduate assistant Julianne Peebles, who led the development of many of the application activities for moms and daughters you see in this book. We thank Dr. Jasmine DeJesus for providing excellent resources on children's picky eating.

Our gratitude also goes to our bright and enthusiastic undergraduate assistants: Kestyn Harris, who explored the literature along with us in our weekly reading group; Gretta Taft, who assisted Julie with the activities, and, along with Ryan Neese and Abigail Cheek, also helped us track down and manage references.

We are very much indebted to the mothers who participated in our focus group sessions. Each of them shared valuable insight, opinions, and examples of issues related to body image in their young daughters. Above all, we wanted this book to be useful to mothers—reliable and relatable. We enjoyed hearing from you, and we are grateful for your perspectives, which undoubtedly strengthened this book.

FROM JANET

My work on this project was supported in part by a research assignment awarded from the University of North Carolina at Greensboro.

I am most grateful to my coauthor and friend, Ashleigh Gallagher, for our own partnership in writing this book. She made the process wholly enjoyable and enriching, even in the inevitably challenging moments that come with the pursuit of big goals.

For years, Paul Silvia suggested that I write a book, planting the seed that it was possible. I appreciate our conversations about writing and the intricate world of book publishing. I am grateful to Sean Wells for many fruitful discussions about health and wellness and for facilitating my personal experience of the connection between physical strength and emotional well-being. I want to recognize the founders of Balance 365, Annie Brees and Jennifer Campbell, for the transformative work that they do to promote healthy body image in women. I thank Lyn Carlisle, Heather Jaynes, Molly Liebel, and Susan Reinecke for providing their insight on the topic of body image and encouraging this work. Thanks also to Ian McDowell for his steady companionship, for bolstering my confidence in my work, and for distracting me with delightfully eclectic stories.

I have the deepest appreciation for Stuart Marcovitch for his unwavering support, for soothing the stress that I unleash on him all too often, and for insisting on infusing joy in my life when I most need it but fail to realize it. I am indebted to my parents, Steve and Stojna

Boseovski, whose sacrifices as Macedonian immigrants in Canada set the foundation for my education and enabled me to pursue issues of intellectual interest throughout my career. This work is part of their legacy.

FROM ASHLEIGH

I dedicate this book to my mother, Pam, and my daughter, Hope, with much love. Writing this book has been the best kind of adventure, and I am very grateful to those who have helped make it such a happy and fulfilling one.

I would like to first thank my coauthor, Janet. Our friendship, shared curiosity for this science, and desire to make it useful for other women have made this such an enjoyable collaboration. Thank you, my friend, for all the hours spent reading, discussing, and writing together.

I am thankful for the kind and gracious support from friends who have centered and steadied me over the course of this project. Wendi Galinski, your daily kindnesses have given me strength when I wasn't sure I had it, and Rich Galinski, thank you for your always sound advice. David Lagos, I have been so encouraged by your keen insights, timely wit, and thoughtful words, and I am thankful for them, my friend. John Seta and Cathy Seta, you are not only mentors to me but also dear friends; thank you for all your wise guidance and for cheering me on throughout this project. My gratitude goes to many other friends who shared their time and thoughts on this topic with me as well, including Carrie Friesen (along with Emma), Chloe Galinski, Darcy Louzao, Kim Moore, Ashlyn Swartout, and Leigh Watson (along with Clara).

Finally, I am most grateful for the constant and loving support I have felt from my family throughout the writing of this book. My mother, Pam Payne, and father, A. R. Haire, are not only beloved parents but also my treasured friends. I love you both; thank you for all the ways you guide me still. To my husband, Patrick, and our daughter, Hope, I love you dearly. Patrick, thank you for your notes of encouragement, the cups of coffee, and always believing in my work. Hope, you inspire me daily; watching you grow and develop into the strong and lovely person you are today has been an incomparable joy. Throughout the writing of this book, you, dear, were always on my mind.

BEYOND
BODY
POSITIVE

HELPING HER RESIST THE PRESSURE FOR PERFECTION

For most women, not a day goes by when we are spared from messages that focus on what we currently look like or what we should look like. Whether these messages take the form of comments about our bodies from a family member or a friend, hearing about the latest celebrity fad diet on television, or seeing an ad for waist trainers as we scroll through our social media feeds, the input is widespread. This kind of messaging begins very early in life, is difficult to avoid, and can have a strong and long-lasting effect on how we see ourselves.

When you look at yourself in the mirror, what sorts of things do you think? And when your daughter or loved one looks in the mirror, what do you hope she thinks? How women and girls think and feel about their bodies is an important issue—for themselves and the people close to them. Odds are that you, having picked up this book, are thinking about the importance of a healthy body image. If you have ever struggled with your own body image, you are in good company. Body dissatisfaction, preoccupation with imperfections, feelings of inadequacy, desires to change the body— most adult women in the United States admit to these body image concerns, and as women ourselves, we can relate. The numbers are telling: 90% of young women in their 20s are dissatisfied with their bodies (Runfola et al., 2013)! Unfortunately, statistics indicate that the dissatisfaction continues for women as they age, hovering around 90% in young and middle adulthood and finally lessening somewhat in late adulthood: At ages 75 and older, "only" 72% of women are dissatisfied with their bodies.

Your decision to choose this book—among hundreds of other titles—reveals that you are focusing now on the body image of a girl you love: your daughter or another special girl in your life. Your concern for her is well founded. Psychological research shows that like adult women, girls as young as 5 years of age express body dissatisfaction. Dissatisfaction with our bodies has become so routine that it may even seem unusual for women and girls not to be critical about some feature of their physical appearance. This routine dissatisfaction is called *normative discontent*—so routine it has become the norm! The consequences of this dissatisfaction include everything from temporary discomforts of feeling self-conscious and experiencing dissatisfaction or other negative emotions to deep patterns of low self-esteem, dysfunction in relationships, and even physical and mental illnesses.

Think about the first time you discussed body image with an adult; for most girls, this conversation is likely to happen in health or sexual education classes in preadolescence. For some girls, it happens only informally, in conversations with friends. Although some great resources are out there, most available books about girls' body image are marketed largely as tools for preteens or teens. Unfortunately, science indicates that by the time girls have reached adolescence, ideas about body image are already largely entrenched, and unhealthy thought patterns are well in place. A more effective approach is to begin an ongoing dialogue with girls early, as they develop, and to "inoculate" them against the harmful messages that society sends about body image with information that is tailored to their developmental level.

ABOUT THIS BOOK

In recent years, body image has become a popular topic of discussion, and we encounter many opinions and ideas about how to "do" body image everywhere we turn. Celebrities, social media influencers, and advertisement campaigns give plenty of advice on how we should feel about our bodies. Among the many messages we hear, however, some are confusing, contradictory, or even downright false. How can we filter out truth from all the noise? This is exactly where science-based guidance can help.

Body image has been an important focus of scientific study for at least 40 years, but the first studies date back even earlier, to the first half of the 20th century. In that time, a lot of scientific evidence has accumulated on how and why women view their bodies the way they do. Throughout this book, we bring you the most relevant findings for your daughter's body image development because the scientific method is our best tool for uncovering the truth about these issues. Unlike other sources on this topic, science is not merely opinion, common sense, or good advice; it is not anchored in personal anecdotes or persuasive messaging. The process of science is time consuming and complex, but it yields the clarity and confidence necessary for making wise and well-informed decisions. And let's face it: When it comes to our daughters' body image, we want to get it right!

As a developmental psychologist (Janet) and a social psychologist (Ashleigh), we are eager to share with you research from our fields. We have spent a lot of time with children, both as researchers in the laboratory and in the real world. You can count on the recommendations in this book because they are drawn from thousands of research studies, and they are tailored to girls at specific developmental levels. Of course, personal experience is important too, so in addition to our own experiences in mother–daughter relationships, we have worked with moms of daughters in our community in focus group settings to bring you practical and useful recommendations. Applying science to this topic is also personal for us. We are women too: graduates of girlhood and working our way through the milestones of adulthood.

Science indicates that childhood is an ideal time to begin building a healthy body image. Unfortunately, not many resources out there are based in developmental science. For this reason, we have written this book specifically for mothers of 3- to 10-year-old girls. You may have noticed that other guidebooks on this topic focus solely on what moms can say to their girls (e.g., "How to teach your child to love her body") or are written for preteens or teens to read independently (e.g., "Why you should love your body!"). Those books make some good points. But research suggests that the formation of body image is relational at its core—that is, it is forged in the daily interactions, example setting, and imitations that go on between moms and daughters. From this perspective, an important relational aspect is missing from these other resources. The findings from child development, social, and body image research all suggest that building healthy body image effectively takes the form of a partnership between mother and daughter starting early in life.

TAKING A PARTNERSHIP APPROACH

As social and developmental scientists, we are calling for a different approach to healthy body image construction. In this framework, the mother–daughter relationship is the cornerstone for the mutual construction of healthy body image—in both you and her. As we discuss throughout the book, research clearly indicates that your body image is linked with hers. A girl's body image is built through her experience of social interactions. It may be natural to think of her body image as only a personal, internal characteristic she possesses, but it is better understood as the product of an ongoing collaboration between your daughter and her social world. You are her first and most enduring partner in this social world; and, in her childhood years, you will be her primary reference or **attachment figure**. According to attachment theory (Ainsworth & Bowlby, 1991), children's ideas about themselves and others, and what they can expect from the world around them, are heavily influenced by their attachment figures. But as your daughter grows into her own independent person, her social world will increasingly fill with other influences. The time to lay the groundwork of mother–daughter partnership is now.

> **Attachment figure:** a person with whom a child has a close bond, usually a caregiver.

Throughout this book, the science we share will give you the tools for building developmentally appropriate, collaborative dialogue with your daughter about body image, beginning in early childhood. It is important to note that your own body image development and hers are evolving continuously. For example, the way you feel about your body prepartum, postpartum, midlife, and in menopause can be very different, and your feelings at a given time can, in turn, affect how you think about and engage in discussions with your daughter about body image. When it comes to women's body image, this is truly the partnership of a lifetime.

How can you be successful in this role, partnering with your daughter? Although there is no single way to raise your daughter successfully, most scientists agree that aiming to set clear rules and boundaries, showing warmth and compassion, and allowing for open communication and collaborative problem solving are fruitful approaches. This combination of behaviors is called *authoritative parenting*, and we refer to it in various sections of the book. But as you read, keep in mind that parenting is dynamic and that parents use different types of strategies depending on their goals, their child's needs, and the context. These strategies can also vary by culture, socioeconomic status, and ethnic/racial identity. Overall, however, components of authoritative parenting are typically linked with positive outcomes (Lansford, 2022).

One theme that we emphasize throughout this book is that although you play a vital role in helping your daughter construct a healthy body image, the full responsibility for her body image does not rest on your efforts alone. Our perspective is rooted in **developmental systems theory** (Bronfenbrenner & Morris, 2007), particularly the idea that you are one of many influences on your daughter's body image and the strength of your influence will vary over time and across situations. She will also rely on other sources of information, and it is developmentally appropriate for her to do so. Yet anyone who has experienced the mother–daughter relationship (as a daughter, or as a daughter and a mother) understands that it can be complex and unpredictable. Some interactions between you and your daughter are harmonious, and some are disastrous, especially in the years approaching adolescence. For some moms, it may be daunting to think of the large role you play in your daughter's body image development. After all, it is a difficult task all the time to model a healthy body image for your daughter—especially when you have your own feelings about your body and its changes and fluctuations. Although this book provides a lot of guidance specifically for you, just remember that her body image isn't solely influenced by you.

> **Developmental systems theory:** the view that development occurs not just within the individual but as a result of our experiences in a large set of systems—from the immediate environment that we share with parents and peers to indirect influences at the cultural level. These influences can interact with each other, and their impact varies over time (Bronfenbrenner & Morris, 2007).

Science reveals the three most important social influences in body image development: family, peers, and media exposure. Indeed,

Dr. Susan Paxton, a leader in the study of body image, has suggested that body dissatisfaction prevention efforts in young children should consider an ecological approach that includes multiple influences (Paxton & Damiano, 2017). This recommendation is consistent with the developmental systems approach that we described. Among these other sources of information are a girl's social experiences, feedback from and comparisons with her peers, and media participation. A girl's actual biological or anatomical characteristics—body weight, stature, symmetry, and how these characteristics measure up against the norms set by our culture—also matter for body image. So does the timing of puberty, such as whether it happens at the same time as her peers or at a different time. Personality characteristics and individual differences are important as well (e.g., she might be anxious relative to her peers, or, relatively laid-back or optimistic). Our approach considers all these pieces and brings helpful insight from science to enable you and your daughter to handle them successfully.

BEYOND BODY POSITIVITY

Our perspective goes beyond body positivity. In recent years, body positivity has been strongly emphasized as a central feature of healthy body image. A positive body image involves holding favorable opinions of the body, acceptance of the body regardless of imperfections, respect of the body in the ways we treat it, and rejection of unrealistic standards promoted by media. Because positive body image is associated with such powerful outcomes, our book incorporates what is known from positive psychology research along with what is known about the destructive effects of negative body image.

That said, we choose to take a balanced, body-healthy perspective that goes beyond body positivity. It seems to us that many popular sources (e.g., celebrities, social media influencers) advocating for body positivity have placed less emphasis on the part of the positive body image definition that involves respect for the body (Tylka, 2011; Tylka & Wood-Barcalow, 2015b). Many of the currently available guides for girls who are beginning to think about their bodies place a heavy emphasis on positive regard for the body and neglect other components of body respect. Although it is true that all women and girls should enforce kind and respectful evaluations of their bodies, it is our impression that the health-focused component of respect has not been fully appreciated and has become lost in the shuffle. Excess negativity about the body is unquestionably damaging, but exclusive positivity about the body may not be making the most of what the positive body image research suggests either.

In this book, we emphasize a health–behavior approach to body image. In doing so, we hope to shift the focus from centering on how the body is judged (as positive or negative) to the importance of prioritizing health behaviors and a focus on self-concept development. You may have heard the phrase "form over function." A body-healthy approach is one in which function is more important than form. When you have a body-healthy image, your thoughts and feelings about your body are determined chiefly by indicators of good health and proper functioning of your body, rather than based on judgments about its appearance. Teaching girls to see the strengths of their body, to accept their bodies despite imperfections, and to ignore harmful cultural messages about their bodies helps to build crucial components of their healthy body image. In this book, we also incorporate ways that girls can attend to their bodies' needs in healthy, constructive, and balanced ways, using **self-regulation** principles to be responsive to and responsible toward their bodies.

> **Self-regulation:** being aware of and managing your thoughts, feelings, and behaviors. This skill can be learned and practiced throughout the lifespan (Vohs & Baumeister, 2016).

WHAT THE BOOK DOES NOT COVER

This book speaks to the most frequent or typical developmental experiences of girls, and so we do not cover some topics of special interest here. Because we are not clinicians (that is, physicians, clinical psychologists, or counselors), this book does not speak to clinical populations and cannot be used to diagnose or treat disorders (associated with eating or otherwise). Disorders related to body image are exceptional problems that deserve careful attention from trained professionals. If you think you or your daughter may be at risk for a body image or eating disorder, we suggest you seek personalized support. We have included some recommended resources at the end of this chapter to inform next steps.

We also recognize that fathers, other parents, siblings, grandparents, and any other members of your daughter's family can influence her body image development; further, we realize that not all families are the same. When we say "family," it is with the awareness that families come in different sizes and compositions. The research presented in this book, however, samples what many consider to be "traditional" families, and the reason is twofold. First, nearly all the research specifically focused on children's body image development involves this type of family structure. Second, when other family structures have been studied alongside the traditional structure, few differences are found in children's developmental processes or outcomes. As just one example, a family's specific parent composition is less important to children's developmental outcomes than the quality of parenting (e.g., Farr, 2017). It seems likely, then, that much of the information we present here will apply to all types of families.

Women belong to different social groups and differ in race, ethnicity, and socioeconomic status. Our coverage in this book is limited to what scientists have studied, and they have infrequently focused on diverse groups of women; most of the research has focused on White women and girls of middle to upper socioeconomic status. Research shows that despite some important differences, the key influences on body image are common among White, Black, Latina and Asian women: family, peers, and media (Burke et al., 2021). These key influences differ in how they affect these groups. In Chapter 2, we discuss some cultural considerations that may be personally relevant to you and your daughter.

Finally, our book does not speak to the experiences of children with gender incongruence. At present, very little research has addressed body image development in these children, and we simply do not have enough knowledge to speak conclusively about their experiences. It would be inappropriate to assume identical developmental trajectories in children who have exceptional gender identity experiences. Nonetheless, the general science-based tips in our book will likely apply to body image development in all young children (such as our health–behavior approach).

THE STRUCTURE OF THE BOOK

In Chapters 1 and 2, we explore your perceptions of your own body and consider some factors that may have shaped the way you currently feel about your body. Every woman is unique, and although there are certainly different "profiles" of body image concerns (Baker et al., 2023), we hope that this information helps you to clarify your own body image and highlights any body image issues you might want to address for yourself. Throughout these chapters, we highlight how your body image perception and expression affects your daughter. We refer you to several questionnaires and encourage you to complete the sample questions provided. If you are interested in completing any of the questionnaires to obtain maximal personal insight, which we encourage, please contact us directly via email (Janet: jjboseov@uncg.edu and Ashleigh: adhaire@uncg.edu) to receive a supplementary packet.

In Chapter 3, we explore the body positivity framework and discuss how our body-healthy perspective differs in important ways. From there, in Chapters 4, 5, and 6 we describe body image development in early, middle, and late childhood respectively so you can tailor your discussions with your daughter in a developmentally appropriate way. These divisions by age are simply guidelines; you know your daughter best, so feel free to determine the best starting point based on your knowledge about your daughter's developmental level, regardless of her age. Because each childhood chapter provides valuable insight into child development, we suggest you read all the chapters, even if you're starting when your daughter is older than 3 or 4 years. And note that it's not too late to start, even if your daughter is already in late childhood.

We have aimed to provide you with useful, practical guidance. Throughout the book, we present helpful body image building tools that you can put into practice. In the Appendix, we offer a variety of activities for building healthy body image, some for moms to do on their own and some for moms and daughters to enjoy together. The joint activities have been designed to support the application of various themes, such as healthy thoughts and feelings, body respect, self-concept building, food literacy, and physical literacy. You can choose from these activities according to your and your daughter's needs. Finally, if you want to know more about a particular topic covered in the book, please check out the Recommended Resources section at the end of each chapter. We provide some excellent references that offer an even more in-depth look into the science of girls' and women's body image.

Let's get started!

RECOMMENDED RESOURCES

- The National Eating Disorders Association: https://www.nationaleatingdisorders.org
- The American Psychological Association information about eating disorders: https://www.apa.org/topics/eating-disorders

CHAPTER 1

HOW WOMEN THINK AND FEEL ABOUT THEIR BODIES

It is the first day back from the winter holiday, and Kate heads to the office kitchen to fuel up on coffee. There, she walks into a lively conversation happening between several of her female coworkers. *Oh, good!* she thinks, *I can't wait to hear about their holidays.*

"Hey Kate! We were just catching up—how was your holiday?" her teammate Liz asks.

"It was so nice!" Kate says. "We kept things simple this year, and it was great to relax!"

"Well, I feel like I need a vacation from my vacation," Jada laughs. "We traveled and visited both of our families."

"Us too," says Liz, "and with all the big meals and baked goodies, I gained like 10 pounds! I guess it's time for the New Year diet."

"Oh, no way!" exclaims Jada. "You look great. On the other hand, I had trouble fitting into these clothes this morning, so I know I need to cut back!"

Does this scene sound familiar? Perhaps you have witnessed or participated in a conversation like this one. In gender and body image research, this curious form of conversational one-upmanship as to who gained the most weight over the holiday is a type of conversation called **fat talk** (Nichter & Vuckovic, 1994). It is a common pattern of friendly interaction that shows up much more often in female friendships than in male friendships. And women who are generally dissatisfied with their bodies are especially likely to start and maintain these conversations. So are women who are in the habit of comparing themselves with others (Ambwani et al., 2017).

> **Fat talk:** a type of conversation in which a person expresses verbally their dissatisfaction with body fat, shape, or weight (Tucker et al., 2007).

Like Jada in the conversation that opens the chapter, you may have found yourself attempting to help a friend feel better by pointing out your own flaws; or maybe you have felt some obligation to join in the fat talk so that you don't ruin the vibe. In fact, research confirms that women feel pressure to engage in fat talk with their friends (Martz et al., 2009). Although this form of conversation may seem harmless on its surface, science shows that fat talk is damaging to women's views of themselves (Shannon & Mills, 2015). We know that fat talk can harm women's relationships, too. It appears to be somewhat customary in small doses, but it is clearly off-putting in excessive amounts. For example, research shows women are less fond of other women who engage in fat talk, and prefer that women speak about themselves in positive terms (Ambwani et al., 2017). Fat talk can be problematic in romantic and sexual relationships as well, and people (men, especially) take it as an indicator of both overall relationship and sexual dysfunction (Sandoval et al., 2022). No matter how well-intentioned it may seem, fat talk ultimately makes everyone feel worse. Besides, there is so much more to women's lives than talking about their bodies and weight. The energy and effort that we spend on it robs us of richer lives.

Fat talk is just one of the many everyday experiences you might have had that is related to your body image. In this chapter, we aim to build on what you already know about your own body image by adding insights from science. Specifically, we discuss how women tend to think and feel about their bodies. As you become more aware of how and why you feel the way you do about your body, you will find opportunities to set straight negative or unhelpful body attitudes.

Healthy Body Image Building Tool

 As we noted earlier, fat-talk conversations are common, but they offer a prime opportunity to work proactively toward healthy body image by changing the topic and the tone of the conversation. In fact, people rate the "challenger" of fat talk as more socially appealing than the "maintainer" of fat talk (Ambwani et al., 2017). Next time you find yourself in one of these conversations, you may want to give fat talk a good-natured challenge— after all, you will be doing yourself and your friends a favor. To keep it nonconfrontational, you could say something like, "Everyone eats a little differently around the holidays—special foods are part of it! Isn't being in the moment with everyone more important than fretting about weight?"

Not only is the information in this chapter important for us as women, but it also foreshadows how the average girl will likely view her body when she becomes an adult. You can think of it as the possible future of a young girl's currently developing body image. Science is no crystal ball, of course, and it is not possible to know with certainty the future of any specific girl. The results of these studies can, however, tell us accurately and reliably what has been true for most women and girls in the past. By relying on this type of evidence as the source (rather than individual opinions or anecdotes), you can be sure you have a truthful blueprint for gaining insight into your own body image, and this insight is critical for enabling you to be a healthy partner to your daughter in her development.

As you make your way through this chapter, keep in mind that what you are reading is true of women on average, as a group. In Chapter 2, we highlight specific, individual characteristics of women that are related to body image issues to help you fit these general findings to yourself more personally. Although we examine the components of body image issues and concerns individually in these chapters, researchers have noted that women have many different body image concern profiles; women do not all share the same types or amounts of thoughts and behavior patterns related to their bodies (Baker et al., 2023). Taken together, however, these two chapters will give you a solid foundation for understanding your own body image and ways to have a healthier one.

HOW SCIENTISTS STUDY BODY IMAGE

What do we mean by the term *body image*, anyway? The first thing to know is that body image is made up of multiple components. This point is important—so often in public discussion the topic is oversimplified, and oversimplifying body image hides some powerful ways of improving it.

According to Dr. Thomas Cash (2012), an eminent scholar in the field, body image involves (a) the assessments we make of our body's features (e.g., its size, shape, and beauty); (b) our feelings about those features (including positive, neutral, and negative feelings); and (c) our investment in these assessments and evaluations—in other words, how big a deal these attitudes toward our body are in the overall view we hold of ourselves.

Because body image has several components, women have a wide range of experience with their body images. Some women assess their bodies fairly accurately (e.g., "Compared with other women, I am tall"), and other women assess their bodies in distorted or unrealistic ways (e.g., "My body is so misshapen"). Some women celebrate their bodies, and other women dislike or possibly feel shame about their bodies. Some women place a heavy importance on their body's features in daily life, and some do not.

Healthy Body Image Building Tool

 Pause for a moment to consider how you currently think and feel about your body. Do those thoughts and feelings affect choices you make in everyday life? To help you learn more about your body image attitudes, we have provided some sample questions from self-questionnaires in Table 1.1; each questionnaire represented has been validated by research, meaning that it accurately measures what it is intended to measure. These self-questionnaires are not diagnostic in a clinical sense, but they will help you build self-awareness and clarity of your own body image. To draw fully accurate conclusions about yourself from these questionnaires, you would need to complete the whole questionnaire. If you would like to complete any of the questionnaires in full, you can find some of them freely available on the internet, or you can email us (jjboseov@uncg.edu or adhaire@uncg.edu), and we will provide you with a copy for your personal use. After thinking over some of these self-assessment questions, consider the following question: Are there facets of your self-image that could be healthier than they currently are?

You have probably noticed that body image is not always consistent. Our body attitudes can fluctuate with various situations, moods, or major life events we are experiencing. Are there situations in which body image concerns are especially likely to pop up for you? Or periods of time? Scientists have studied both enduring and transient types of body dissatisfaction, which are referred to as **trait body dissatisfaction** and **state body dissatisfaction**, respectively (Cash et al., 2002).

TABLE 1.1. Sample Adapted Questions From Scientifically Validated Questionnaires

Questionnaire	Sample questions to consider
Body Image Quality of Life Inventory (Cash & Fleming, 2002) *Greater agreement with these items indicates greater impact of body image issues on quality of life.*	How and how much do your feelings about your appearance affect: • My experiences when I meet new people • My day-to-day emotions • My daily "grooming" activities • My willingness to do things that might call attention to my appearance • My interactions with people of my own sex • My interactions with people of the other sex
Body Image-Acceptance and Action Questionnaire (Sandoz et al., 2013) *"True" statements indicate less psychological flexibility in thinking.*	Please rate the truth of each statement as it applies to you: • I shut down when I feel bad about my body shape or weight. • When I start thinking about the size and shape of my body, it's hard to do anything else. • To control my life, I need to control my weight. • My relationships would be better if my body weight and/or shape did not bother me. • Before I can make any serious plans, I have to feel better about my body. • Worrying about my body takes up too much of my time.

TABLE 1.1. Sample Adapted Questions From Scientifically Validated Questionnaires (*Continued*)

Questionnaire	Sample questions to consider
Body Image Ideals Questionnaire (Cash & Szymanski, 1995) *Higher discrepancy between perceived actual and ideal body characteristics indicates greater body dissatisfaction. Similarly, greater importance placed on a body aspect indicates greater body dissatisfaction.*	For each of the following, please think about your personal ideal (how you wish or prefer to be), and then evaluate how well your body resembles or matches this ideal. Then, go back through the same attributes, and indicate the strength or importance you place on each attribute and its ideal: • Height • Skin complexion • Facial features • Body proportions • Muscle tone and definition • Chest size
Rosenberg Self-Esteem Scale (Rosenberg, 1965) *Greater agreement indicates higher self-esteem.*	For each of the following statements, record if you strongly agree, agree, disagree, or strongly disagree: • On the whole, I am satisfied with myself. • I feel that I have a number of good qualities. • I am able to do things as well as most other people. • I take a positive attitude toward myself. • I feel that I am a person of worth.

(continues)

TABLE 1.1. Sample Adapted Questions From Scientifically Validated Questionnaires (*Continued*)

Questionnaire	Sample questions to consider
Ten-Item Personality Inventory (Gosling et al., 2003) *Greater agreement indicates higher levels of each of the Big 5 traits respectively: extraversion, neuroticism, conscientiousness, openness to new experience, and agreeableness.*	To what extent do you agree or disagree with the following statements: I see myself as • Extraverted, enthusiastic • Critical, quarrelsome • Dependable, self-disciplined • Open to new experiences, complex • Reserved, quiet
Big Three Perfectionism Scale–Short Form (Feher et al., 2020) *Greater agreement indicates higher levels of perfectionism.*	Please indicate how much you agree with the following statements: • Striving to be as perfect as possible makes me feel worthwhile. • When I notice that I have made a mistake, I feel ashamed. • I feel dissatisfied with other people, even when I know they are trying their best. • My opinion of myself is tied to being perfect. • People are disappointed in me whenever I don't do something perfectly. • I am highly critical of other people's imperfections.

TABLE 1.1. Sample Adapted Questions From Scientifically Validated Questionnaires (*Continued*)

Questionnaire	Sample questions to consider
Iowa-Netherlands Comparison Orientation Measure (Gibbons & Buunk, 1999) *Greater agreement indicates higher tendency to compare oneself with others.*	Indicate how much you agree with each statement: • I often compare how I am doing socially (e.g., social skills, popularity) with other people. • I often try to find out what others think who face similar problems as I face. • I often like to talk with others about mutual opinions and experiences. • I often compare myself with others with respect to what I have accomplished in life. • If I want to find out how well I have done something, I compare what I have done with how others have done. • I often like to talk with others about mutual opinions and experiences.

(continues)

TABLE 1.1. Sample Adapted Questions From Scientifically Validated Questionnaires (*Continued*)

Questionnaire	Sample questions to consider
Physical Appearance Comparison Scale–Revised (Schaefer & Thompson, 2014) *Higher frequency of these behaviors indicates higher tendency to compare oneself with others on physical appearance.*	Indicate how often you make these kinds of comparisons: • When I am at a party, I compare my body shape to the body shape of others. • When I am out in public, I compare my physical appearance to the appearance of others. • When I am shopping for clothes, I compare my body fat to the body fat of others. • When I am with a group of friends, I compare my weight to the weight of others.
Objectified Body Consciousness Scale (McKinley & Hyde, 1996) *Greater agreement indicates higher levels of body surveillance, body shame, and controllability of appearance.*	Indicate how much you agree with the following statements: • I often worry about whether the clothes I am wearing make me look good. • I would be ashamed for people to know what I really weigh. • I think a person can look pretty much how they want to if they are willing to work at it. • During the day, I think about how I look many times. • When I can't control my weight, I feel like something must be wrong with me. • I can weigh what I'm supposed to when I try hard enough.

TABLE 1.1. Sample Adapted Questions From Scientifically Validated Questionnaires (Continued)

Questionnaire	Sample questions to consider

Appearance-Based Rejection Sensitivity Scale (L.E. Park, 2007)
 	
Greater concern of diminished attractiveness and greater expectation of partner's diminished interest indicate greater rejection sensitivity.
	• You are trying on clothes at a department store and notice that you are a few pounds heavier than last week. In this scenario:
	  – How concerned or anxious would you be that others might be less attracted to you because of your physical appearance?
	  – How likely do you think it is that others would find you less attractive?
	• During dinner at a restaurant, you notice your date looking at an attractive person across the room.
	  – How concerned or anxious would you be that your date would be less interested in you because of the way you looked?
	  – How likely do you think it is that your date would be less interested in you because of the way you looked?

(continues)

TABLE 1.1. Sample Adapted Questions From Scientifically Validated Questionnaires (Continued)

Questionnaire	Sample questions to consider
Self-Monitoring Scale (Snyder & Gangestad, 1986) *True responses indicate self-monitoring tendencies.*	Consider whether the following statements are true or false for you. • I would probably make a good actor. • In different situations and with different people, I often act like very different persons. • I may deceive people by being friendly when I really dislike them. • I'm not always the person I appear to be. • I guess I put on a show to impress or entertain others.
Self-Compassion Scale (Neff, 2003) *Greater frequency of unmarked items indicates higher levels of self-compassion; greater frequency of items marked with an asterisk (*) indicates lower levels of self-compassion.*	For each item, indicate how often you behave in the stated manner: • When I'm going through a very hard time, I give myself the caring and tenderness I need. • I'm disapproving and judgmental about my own flaws and inadequacies.* • When things are going badly for me, I see the difficulties as part of life that everyone goes through. • When I'm feeling down, I tend to feel like most other people are probably happier than I am.* • When something upsets me, I try to keep my emotions in balance. • When I'm feeling down, I tend to obsess and fixate on everything that's wrong.*

TABLE 1.1. Sample Adapted Questions From Scientifically Validated Questionnaires (Continued)

Questionnaire	Sample questions to consider
Body Compassion Scale (Altman et al., 2020) *More frequently engaging in the unmarked behaviors indicates greater compassion for the body; more frequently engaging in behaviors marked with an asterisk (*) indicates lower compassion for the body.*	Please indicate how often you believe or behave in each of the stated manners: • When I wish some aspect of my body looked different, it feels like no one else understands my struggle.* • When I feel out of shape, I try to remind myself that most people feel this way at some point. • When I think about my body's inadequacies, it tends to make me feel more separate and cut off from other people.* • When I am frustrated with some aspect of my appearance, I try to remind myself that most people feel this way at some time. • I am accepting of my looks just the way they are. • I am tolerant of my body's flaws and inadequacies.

(continues)

TABLE 1.1. Sample Adapted Questions From Scientifically Validated Questionnaires (*Continued*)

Questionnaire	Sample questions to consider
Body Appreciation Scale-2 (Tylka & Wood-Barcalow, 2015a) *More often engaging in these behaviors indicates greater body appreciation.*	Please indicate whether each statement is true about you never, seldom, sometimes, often, or always: • I appreciate the different and unique characteristics of my body. • I feel like I am beautiful even if I am different from media images of attractive people (e.g., models, actresses/actors). • I feel love for my body. • My behavior reveals my positive attitude toward my body; for example, I hold my head high and smile.
Functionality Appreciation Scale (Alleva et al., 2017) *Greater agreement indicates higher appreciation for the body's functionality.*	Please rate your agreement with each of the items below: • I appreciate my body for what it is capable of doing. • I am grateful that my body enables me to engage in activities that I enjoy or find important. • I appreciate that my body allows me to communicate and interact with others. • I feel that my body does so much for me.

Trait body dissatisfaction: body dissatisfaction that is relatively stable and enduring. Women with trait body dissatisfaction tend to feel dissatisfied with their bodies, regardless of time or situation.

State body dissatisfaction: body dissatisfaction that fluctuates based on the environmental context, current mood, or other situational factors.

HALLMARKS OF BODY DISSATISFACTION

How does body dissatisfaction show up in women's thinking? Whether the dissatisfaction is enduring (trait) or transient (state), research has identified two major drivers of dissatisfaction: *social comparison* and *self-objectification*.

Social Comparison

When we wonder how our bodies are measuring up to others' standards, we do not have to look very far to find out; we can just look all around us. What are our friends posting on social media? What do our favorite actresses and influencers look like? What products do they wear, what defines their beauty, and how do they brand themselves? Comparing ourselves to our peers is a natural social process, and one we all do. In fact, scientists have described social comparison as a basic drive—as humans, we cannot seem to get away from the fundamental tendency to compare ourselves to others. Social comparison theory (Festinger, 1954) says that when we want to find out how we stack up, we often look to other people to find out that information.

You may have heard the saying "beauty is in the eye of the beholder." Although some things are regarded as beautiful by nearly everyone, there is also a good deal of variety in what people find beautiful. So, to determine if she is pretty, a girl compares herself to relevant people. She must get this information from comparison to other people, because "pretty" is a relative term for which no universal metric exists. When we compare ourselves to others, who do we choose? The people to whom your daughter compares herself probably are her friends but can also be people she wishes to emulate, such as a singer she admires or an athlete who inspires her. To the extent that many of the photos a girl sees are selected, filtered, or in some other way edited to be consistent with an idealized female form, she may conclude—in error—that she falls short in the comparison and may experience both negative feelings and a diminished self-worth as a result.

Social scientists have shown that when young women spend time looking at cultural "thin ideals" (e.g., unrealistically thin fashion models), they become less satisfied with their own bodies. These theories and findings likely ring true in your own experiences, and you can probably think of times you have compared yourself to other women in moments of self-doubt or insecurity. It is important for us to understand that decades of these and other aspects of body image socialization have affected us in ways that will, in turn, have an impact on our daughters.

Self-Objectification

One harmful way of thinking that characterizes negative body image is a process called self-objectification. The term comes from objectification theory (Fredrickson & Roberts, 1997), which suggests that when a woman's body becomes the focus of someone's attention, critical analysis, or evaluation, the woman is being viewed psychologically speaking as an object rather than as a person. As girls become increasingly aware of how their culture equates their worth with the appearance of their body or its sexual value, they begin to adopt an outsider perspective on how they look. They anticipate the impression made by their features, figure, makeup, or clothing, and they adjust themselves to meet standards they believe are expected or desired.

Objectifying someone can lead to bad behaviors in which the observer disregards, disrespects, or even dehumanizes her as a person. You may recall feeling objectified before, and if so, you are not alone. Objectification comes from a variety of sources—people we know well and those we do not know at all. Research indicates that objectification happens often to girls, and by the time they reach adulthood, they may internalize this behavior, coming to adopt, value, or think about observers' perspectives on their bodies automatically. In other words, some of our thoughts and behaviors come so quickly to us that we aren't even aware of them, or we don't think to question them even if they are untrue or unhealthy. These thoughts and behaviors are often the result of habits we developed or things we have heard over time. For example, they might include checking the mirror, sucking in our stomachs, or adjusting our body position to try to meet others' real or imagined standards. Conversely, they may include avoidance behaviors, such as wearing baggy clothing to hide one's body or avoiding mirrors. It is well documented that women who self-objectify are more likely to suffer the damaging mental and physical experiences of depression, anxiety, interference with relationships or activities, and unhealthy eating and exercise patterns. Active questioning of our own thoughts can help us to break these patterns.

WHO STRUGGLES MOST WITH BODY IMAGE ATTITUDES?

Body image is a construct that applies to everyone, of course; all of us have thoughts and feelings about our bodies. Because the topic affects everyone, it can become a problem for anyone. But there are personal characteristics especially associated with developing body dissatisfaction, too. Chapter 3 delves into some of the personal characteristics related to women's body image. Yet despite individual differences among women, scientists have known for years that the most significant predictor of who holds these negative body attitudes is gender.

As we noted previously, most women report dissatisfaction with their bodies in all stages of life. As a group, women think more frequently about their bodies, and they judge their bodies more negatively than men do. We also know that women are especially invested in their body attitudes. Body image takes up more space in women's overall self-concept and affects their behaviors—toward both themselves and others—more than it does for men. The size of the gap between women's and men's body dissatisfaction has changed somewhat over time (which we discuss later in the chapter); overall, though, research is clear that women are more vulnerable to poor body image (e.g., Quittkat et al., 2019).

This point does not diminish the issues men have with their own body image, which are also very important. Men experience cultural pressures for muscularity, so it makes sense that the most frequently studied type of body dissatisfaction among men is how muscular their bodies are (or are not); at its most extreme form, this dissatisfaction can result in a psychological disorder called **muscle dysmorphia**. On the other hand, media representations of men's bodies have idealized a lean male body as well, so men certainly experience their own pressures to fit culturally idealized images. Analysis across more than 100 studies shows that muscularity-oriented and thinness-oriented dissatisfaction with the body have remained fairly stable for men over time (Karazsia et al., 2017). Interestingly, body shame in men has shown an uptick in recent years. There is no doubt that men's body image concerns are an important issue in their own right. The Recommended

Resources section at the end of this chapter includes references for research on men's body image.

> **Muscle dysmorphia:** a form of body dysmorphia in which a person has a distorted view of, and dissatisfaction with, their body's muscularity (American Psychological Association [APA], n.d.).

Unlike men, however, women are met with culturally idealized images of the female body everywhere they go. Encounters with these idealized (and often objectified) depictions of women are practically unavoidable; they show up in traditional media, social media, advertisements, and even the filtered photos of friends. As we discuss in this chapter, women's appearance affects nearly every aspect of their life experience, so the sociocultural pressures applied to them are relentless.

WHY DOES BODY IMAGE MATTER SO MUCH TO WOMEN?

Why don't women just "stop worrying" about their bodies? Unrealistic expectations for women's bodies are everywhere, and yet strangely, women are often blamed for caring too much about how their bodies look. But the data on the many ways a woman's body affects her life experiences do not lie—body dissatisfaction is a serious issue. These findings are heavy and discouraging, but please see them as a call to action: If we want our girls to have a healthy body image, it is up to us to help them build it.

One reason women focus on their bodies is that they have learned from experience that others' views of their bodies are very consequential for them. You probably know someone whose appearance has worked for her in life. People who conform to the cultural ideals for beauty, color, size, weight, and youthfulness enjoy privileges across many social situations. Perhaps you have thought that some women just seem to have it easier because of their appearance. The data suggest that you may well be correct.

Bias and discrimination are real experiences that can be measured by observing people's behaviors, judgments, and decisions. *Lookism*—a preference for pretty (Cavico et al., 2012)—is a complex issue. For example, beauty can work for you or against you in criminal justice interactions; size bias can happen to people who are larger and smaller, shorter and taller than the cultural ideals; and age bias can work against both young and old in the workplace. It really depends on the specific context and circumstances, but a great deal of research suggests that women who conform to cultural appearance standards typically benefit from social advantages (Batres & Shiramizu, 2023).

Beauty Bias

Social science has catalogued the benefits of physical attractiveness and its **halo effect** on judgments of character and personality. Women who are attractive on the outside are, by and large, assumed to possess desirable internal qualities as well. For example, people judge photos of attractive faces as more trustworthy than photos of less attractive faces, and this judgment happens quickly and without awareness (Todorov et al., 2009). Other research indicates that physical attractiveness affects how intellectually competent, socially competent, and mentally stable we think someone is. Attractive people are perceived to be more qualified for many jobs, especially when it comes to stereotypically female jobs such as a nurse or secretary. Social psychologists refer to this as the *what is beautiful is good* stereotype (Dion et al., 1972), and it is well established: A woman's beauty is associated with how favorably others perceive her personality in 45 countries studied across 11 world regions (Batres &

Shiramizu, 2023). This finding is probably no surprise to you. That said, the *beauty-is-beastly effect* (Heilman & Saruwatari, 1979) can be seen in some situations. For example, when women are applying for high status, typically masculine jobs, beauty can penalize them.

> **Halo effect:** a bias in thinking in which evaluating one characteristic of a person positively leads to evaluating them positively on other unrelated characteristics (APA, n.d.).

Beauty not only affects judgments of our character; it also affects important life outcomes. Attractive people are more likely than less attractive people to be interviewed, hired, promoted, and paid higher wages for jobs (e.g., earning on average 10–15% more over their lifetime), and this advantage is especially true for women (Langlois et al., 2000). Attractive people (especially women) receive more money in charitable donations (Raihani & Smith, 2015); attractive waitresses receive higher tips (Parrett, 2015); and attractive female professors receive better evaluations of their teaching from students (Riniolo et al., 2006). In the criminal justice system, data show that likelihood of arrest and conviction is lower for attractive women (Beaver et al., 2019), and other research shows that if convicted, attractive women receive sentences shorter than those for less attractive women (Stewart, 1985). Legal scholar Deborah Rhode (2010) examined this and other compelling evidence for the beauty bias and its legal implications for women (see the Recommended Resources section at the end of this chapter for more information).

Weight Bias

People who do not conform to cultural ideals of weight are often penalized in social and professional interactions because of **weight bias**. Employment, health care, education, and interpersonal relationship opportunities are all limited by prejudicial attitudes toward people of higher weight (Puhl & Heuer, 2009). With nearly 42% of all

Americans living with obesity, you probably know someone who has experienced this bias (Centers for Disease Control, 2022b). Women, especially, are harmed by the psychological consequences and social injustice of weight bias and discriminatory practices, perhaps because they are likely to internalize the bias (Boswell & White, 2015). We note that evidence suggests that people of especially low weight also face weight bias, so this is not exclusive to larger bodies.

> **Weight bias:** the negative weight-related attitudes about and behaviors toward individuals who are overweight, obese, or low weight (Alberga et al., 2016).

Age Bias

Bias can operate both ways when it comes to age: People can be penalized for either their relative youthfulness or older age. The negative stigma associated with older age is more well documented in research, however. Overall, younger faces are judged to be more attractive than older faces, and judgments of women's attractiveness are more affected by middle age than judgments of men are (Maestripieri et al., 2014). Age affects the perceived physical attractiveness and sexual desirability of women more than of men, whose desirability is buffered in part by the increasing social status and wealth that age can bring them. To make matters worse, women are often doubly penalized in relationships and in the workplace, where **ageism** can be bundled with lookism. Although people are usually unaware of these biases, they have a significant, negative impact on women.

> **Ageism:** behaviors/attitudes showing prejudice against older adults, negatively stereotyping them (e.g., as unhealthy, helpless, or incompetent), and discriminating against them, especially in employment and health care (APA, n.d.).

This section started with a question: When it comes to women's body image, why don't women just "stop worrying?" As you can see from science, unfortunately, the answer is not simply a matter of thinking more positively. Rather, women have adapted to this way of being from an early age, as it has been sustained and encouraged by others in their social lives and surrounding culture. Women learn from experience (either direct or indirect) that they are often valued and judged based on how they appear, even before their actual competencies or other characteristics are known.

Given these high-stakes cultural prescriptions for the female body, it is no wonder that body image satisfaction matters for women's psychological well-being or that women are especially invested in the topic (Murnen, 2011). In the next section, we share how poor body image affects women's thoughts, feelings, and behaviors.

HOW DOES NEGATIVE BODY IMAGE HURT YOUR WELL-BEING?

Think back to the postholiday coworker conversation that opened this chapter. Kate may not have been thinking about her body or weight before this conversation, but after this conversation she likely was! Most women have experienced these types of pop-up opportunities that can trigger body image concerns in daily social life; however, you may not have had opportunity to reflect on exactly how these experiences affect you. In the next section, we detail some specific ways negative body image hurts women's well-being.

Negative Body Image Directs Our Thinking

In psychological science, the term **cognition** is used to describe our thought life. Being caught up in a special memory, worriedly imagining possible outcomes of a choice that must be made—you have a whole internal world in your mind that processes and stores information uniquely and to which only you are privy. As many women know, body image concerns can affect our thought life quite negatively. One way it affects us is that it filters the type of information we think about.

> **Cognition:** mental processes of knowing and awareness including perceiving, remembering, reasoning, judging, imagining, and problem solving (APA, n.d.).

Negative Body Image Affects the Types of Information We Think About

Negative thoughts about the self guide the judgments and decisions we make socially, the things we pay attention to, and the ways we see ourselves and other people. And negative body attitudes feed into the overall way we think about ourselves as well—women who have a negative body image are more likely to have their self-identity anchored strongly in physical appearance (Vartanian, 2009). This tendency is especially true if they do not have a strong self-definition and they internalize cultural standards.

Another type of thinking women do is taking outsiders' perspectives on their own bodies. Women are more likely to anticipate others' perspectives on their body and adjust accordingly, which often involves a type of objectified self-consciousness (McKinley, 2006). Because others' opinions of their bodies are important for them, women monitor their body's size or shape fluctuations, a behavior called "body surveillance," which involves checking for compliance with societal standards.

Negative Body Image Affects How Much We Think About Information

Even as women manage the everyday tasks and responsibilities involved in our various roles as mothers, wives, employees, community members, and caregivers, we manage to spend a lot of thought on how our bodies are perceived. Yet we can think about our bodies too much, and to our harm. We need to be especially careful to avoid **rumination** about our bodies. Having thoughts that circle back to recurrent insecurities, doubts, or fears about the body and getting on a negative train of thought that will not seem to stop are fairly common experiences. Women even coruminate, sharing these obsessive thought patterns with each other! Women with perfectionistic tendencies and women who have greater body image concerns are more likely than other women to ruminate (Rudiger & Winstead, 2013). This habit can be toxic: Left unchecked, it can be a precursor to mental illnesses, including anxiety, depression, and eating disorders.

> Rumination: obsessive thinking in which repeated thoughts or themes become so excessive that they interfere with our ability to think about other things (APA, n.d.).

Healthy Body Image Building Tool

 Stop the negative thought train in its tracks! If you find yourself obsessing about your body, you do not have to give in to the vicious rumination cycle. Brand et al. (2018) found that vigorous exercise reduced ruminative thoughts. Other evidence-based strategies include getting outside, meditating, distracting yourself (by engaging in an engrossing activity), and challenging the accuracy of the thoughts (and replacing them with more rational ones). Taking charge of your thought life is a powerful tool for building a healthy body image.

NEGATIVE BODY IMAGE DISTORTS THE INFORMATION WE THINK ABOUT

Unsurprisingly, the thoughts women think about their bodies are not always accurate. Have you ever attempted to talk a friend out of a negative belief she holds about her appearance—something she is convinced is true but you don't see? Research shows that women misjudge (i.e., overestimate) their body size and report a wide gap between the body they want and the body they have (MacNeill & Best, 2015). Not only do women wish for a lower body weight, but they also wish they could change specific body features; further, they do not tend to show psychological flexibility and instead judge their bodies harshly and have difficulty accepting themselves as they are (Linardon et al., 2021). Some women avoid viewing or thinking about their bodies altogether, for example by refusing to weigh themselves or avoiding looking in the mirror. Although these avoidant behaviors can be adaptive in some circumstances, researchers have pointed out that they can backfire in that they do not allow women to confront their own unrealistic perceptions of their bodies (Trottier et al., 2015).

Negative Body Image Has an Unhealthy Relationship With Social Comparison

Although the numbers vary across studies, it is well established that women engage in social comparison frequently (Leahey et al., 2007; Sahlan et al., 2021). Data from nearly 200 studies clearly show that social comparison of physical appearance is strongly related to body dissatisfaction for women (Myers & Crowther, 2009). When social comparisons of appearance happen, unfortunately, women often respond in ways that do not make them feel better about themselves. For example, when women are exposed to attractive celebrities' and attractive peers' social media posts, social comparison increases (in this case, comparing upward) and results in both bad mood and body dissatisfaction (Brown & Tiggemann, 2016).

Research suggests that when people are motivated to feel better about themselves, their social comparisons can be strategically guided to protect their self-views (Helgeson & Mickelson, 1995). For example, they may compare themselves to someone who is less than they are in some regard and, in so doing, feel better about themselves. One reason for the connection between social comparison and body dissatisfaction may be that women as a group do not use social comparison as a means for **self-enhancement**, such as making comparisons that are in their favor, as much as they could (Voges et al., 2019).

> **Self-enhancement:** strategic behaviors that increase self-esteem. These behaviors can be conscious or unconscious (APA, n.d.).

Healthy Body Image Building Tool

 Take a look at your social media use for a week. Jot down how much time you spend on social networking sites and how you feel after. What information (if any) did you encounter that made you feel happy, interested, or encouraged? What information (if any) led to bad feelings about yourself? Did any information make you feel bad about your own appearance or cause you to compare yourself to another woman's appearance? If so, consider reducing your exposure to that content. Research indicates that social media exposure that results in social comparison (especially about our bodies' appearance) has few benefits and quite a few harms (McComb et al., 2023).

Negative Body Image Has an Impact on Our Feelings and Moods

In science, **affect** is the term used to describe our emotional experiences, including positive and negative feelings, intense and mild feelings, and brief and prolonged feelings (APA, n.d.). Affect covers a wide range of emotional experiences—large and small, fleeting and lasting. Research is clear that negative body image is related to toxic feelings about ourselves and others. And, because a chief function of emotions is communication between us and other people, negative feelings about our bodies can interfere with our relationships.

> **Affect:** emotions or feelings. Affect can be positive or negative, simple or complex, and it includes emotions as well as moods (APA, n.d.).

As a group, women are vulnerable to **shame** about their bodies and distressed by what they perceive as their bodies' dishonorable or inappropriate failures. This shame is often tied to objectified self-consciousness (Manago et al., 2015). Women living in larger bodies are especially likely to feel body shame because of the social stigma and the comments they hear about their bodies from close others (Carter et al., 2021). And when it comes to food, women experience both shame and **guilt** (Else-Quest et al., 2012). These emotional experiences are serious, and unsurprisingly, they have serious consequences for self-esteem (i.e., a woman's enduring sense of her own value or worth).

> **Shame:** a distressing, self-conscious emotion that results when we feel our behavior is dishonorable or inappropriate. When we feel the behavior will be publicly judged, shame often leads to social withdrawal (APA, n.d.).
>
> **Guilt:** a self-conscious emotion in which we are pained by the thought of having done something wrong, often paired with a readiness to remedy the wrong (APA, n.d.).

Negative Body Image Affects How We Behave

Poor body image affects how women treat their own bodies, how they behave toward others, and how they act in various social situations (as with the fat talk example at the beginning of this chapter).

Across the science literature, the strongest indicator that a woman will have poor body image is high body mass index (BMI), so researchers know that a woman's overall size is an important component of her body image (Frederick et al., 2022). Women who have body image concerns are more likely to be chronic dieters, repeatedly restricting their eating. Ironically, chronic dieting is itself predictive of overeating (Gingras et al., 2004). Not only is chronic dieting unhealthy; it simply does not achieve the long-term goals most women are hoping it does. Of course, taken to the extreme, restricted eating is a precursor to, and a feature of, several psychological disorders.

Finally, concerns about appearance affect the leisure activities women pursue. Evidence suggests that the leisure activities we choose to (or choose not to) participate in are often limited by concerns about our appearance. These limits include not participating in fun activities, experiencing less enjoyment of those activities when we do participate, and taking part in physical activities solely for the sake of weight loss (Liechty et al., 2006).

Healthy Body Image Building Tool

 Can you think of a time when you structured your activities around a body insecurity? The beach may come to mind! Comedian duo Kristen Hensley and Jen Smedley (at https://www.imomsohard.com/) have a hilarious video poking fun at the difference between what dads get to wear to the beach and what moms are expected to wear. One line particularly resonates: "I do *not* feel confident in a swimsuit *at all*, but I'm not going to let that get in the way of me building a moat!" Next time you find yourself limiting an activity because you fear the way your body will appear, challenge yourself to override that fear and do what you enjoy instead. If you are interested in getting a better idea of how much body concerns affect your quality of life, see the sample items from the Body Image Quality of Life Inventory (Cash & Fleming, 2002) in Table 1.1.

HOW ADULT EXPERIENCES AFFECT BODY IMAGE

Life experiences that matter for how women see their bodies include events such as marriage, divorce, remarriage, pregnancy, health changes, menopause, and retirement. According to body image science, important adult experiences like these are related to body changes in weight, skin, hair, muscle tone, and capability. Pause for a moment to reflect on your experience of adulthood thus far. In your experience, have any body changes accompanied these or other important events? In Chapters 4 through 6, we discuss important developmental considerations for girls' timepoints in childhood. Although changes in adults may not be as stark as they are for children, it is similarly useful to consider where you are in the adulthood experience, how your age is related to specific body image issues, and how these aspects might influence your interactions with your daughter. Developmentalists often differ in the specific age ranges they define, but generally, you can think of adults as being in one of several phases—early adulthood (roughly age 18–30 years), middle adulthood (roughly age 31–59), and later adulthood (roughly age 60+).

Early Adulthood

Body image research indicates that women in early adulthood report high levels of body dissatisfaction (Runfola et al., 2013). On the one hand, this dissatisfaction is not surprising, given other insecurities and uncertainties that come with increased independence and responsibility. On the other hand, it is quite surprising when one considers that youthfulness itself is fairly central to many definitions of beauty.

Young adult women report being concerned primarily with their physical appearance, especially the attractiveness of their faces as well as the weight and shape of their bodies. Their new adult status offers exciting new social roles arising from careers, marriage, and parenthood; the evidence indicates that body image concerns are linked with these new social roles. For example, women who experience pregnancy face strong cultural pressure to bounce back postpartum to the body they had before the baby. One mom we spoke with mentioned the frustratingly mixed messages of a popular pregnancy book—both urging mom to eat well for the baby but also reminding her to beware of gaining excessive weight that she would need to shed postpartum! The cultural expectation seems to be that while parenthood will change your life, it should not change your body. Indeed, it is very common for women to express dissatisfaction with their postpartum bodies compared with their prepartum bodies, and this finding holds across racial groups (Boyington et al., 2007).

Middle Adulthood

In middle age, most women report the emergence of an added body concern—preserving youthful appearance. Research indicates that women in this age range become a little less focused on beauty alone than they were formerly, especially women in the later part of this range (e.g., Slevec & Tiggemann, 2011). Instead, they are more concerned with the prevailing cultural emphasis on beauty and youth. Women in middle age report being concerned with diminishing the effects of aging and losing weight gained since early adulthood (Clarke, 2002). Although evidence suggests that middle-aged women accept somewhat heavier weight as satisfactory, data also indicate that weight is a very common concern.

Late Adulthood

Unsurprisingly, as women move into late adulthood, body concerns begin to focus more on health and functioning. For women in these later years, research indicates that appearance matters somewhat less than before because of the inevitable physical effects of aging

(Robert-McComb & Massey-Stokes, 2014). Older women feel more accepting of their bodies and are less invested in their physical appearance than young women are. Overall, experience and perspective seem to lessen body discontent somewhat; nonetheless, dissatisfaction with one's body persists.

HOW FAMILY MEMBERS AFFECT BODY IMAGE

Many moms and daughters build healthy body image in the broad family context in which they live and interact daily. And not all families look the same—they come in a wide variety. For example, families differ in socioeconomic level, size, whether the household is single or double parented, gender composition (e.g., same-sex siblings, same-sex parents), whether siblings are present, and whether the family is blended or unblended; these are just a few of the ways families differ.

Some of these factors do not appear to be related to body image development. For example, although we do not have direct evidence addressing body image development, we know that children of same-sex and different-sex parents do not differ in psychological functioning generally (Farr et al., 2019), and parenting styles of same-sex couples do not differ significantly from different-sex couples (Kranz, 2023). Based on these findings, we have no reason to believe that girls' body image development would differ based on the genders of their parents. For other factors, such as socioeconomic status, the findings are not straightforward enough to draw strong conclusions.

Although family living arrangements certainly play a very influential role in how family members interact, few studies have looked at the specific impact of family composition on girls' body image development, and there is not a great deal of science to inform our discussion on this point. In the following sections, we highlight several conclusions that can be drawn from the available research.

Fathers

Researchers have noted that science has rarely focused on fathers' influence on daughters' body image, despite the plentiful science on mothers' influence. Siegel and colleagues (2021) reported that fathers can help build positive body image through conversations with their daughters but can also be damaging to their daughters' body image when they are emotionally distant, make negative comments about their daughters' weight, or parent with authoritarian behaviors. We know from other research that fathers who place especially high value on attractiveness and thinness are more likely to have daughters who engage in unhealthy dieting and disordered eating behaviors (Dixon et al., 2003). Based on interviews with fathers, Siegel and colleagues (2021) reported that fathers find it challenging to discuss body image issues with their daughters, seeing barriers that make effective communication challenging as well as negative cultural influences on women's body image that are hard to counter. An important way moms can help build healthy body image is by supporting and engaging fathers in conversations with girls that may be otherwise challenging for dads; it is our hope that the information in this book will be helpful to moms in informing and structuring those conversations. Also, many of the healthy body image building tips that we provide throughout the book can be used by fathers as well as mothers (e.g., healthy role modeling for eating and exercise, avoiding excessive appearance-based comments).

Siblings

Sibling relationships are complicated, and, even as adults, they can be integral to our identity and daily lives. It should not be surprising that science finds that siblings have considerable impact on the development of both body image and disordered eating patterns (e.g., Nerini et al., 2016). Siblings serve as a source of social information as well as information about oneself; of course, the precise influence they have on a developing girl depends on several factors, including gender, age, proximity, and family dynamics.

The ways in which siblings typically impact a girl's attitudes toward her own body differ between sisters and brothers. Sisters tend to be important for two reasons. First, they model body image attitudes; some research shows that sisters can be as important as mothers in shaping a young woman's body attitudes (Coomber & King, 2008). Second, sisters affect women's body image through social comparison. In adulthood, women compare their bodies with their sisters more than with their mothers, and these social comparisons are related to body dissatisfaction and a drive for thinness (Lev-Ari et al., 2014).

Siblings can certainly be supportive and encouraging, but one way they can hurt the development of healthy body image in girls is to make body-related comments. Such comments are a primary way brothers can affect body image. Research results regarding positive body-related comments (e.g., compliments), are mixed, but the evidence is clear that negative comments are very harmful for the developing body image (Nerini et al., 2016). Teasing girls about appearance, weight, or shape is extremely damaging (we discuss this topic at length in Chapters 4 through 6). In general, we can say that young women who report having had siblings who teased them are more likely to be dissatisfied with their bodies, especially when the teasing was centered on weight and shape as opposed to general appearance (Nerini et al., 2016).

Although this book focuses on healthy body image development in daughters, many of our tips can be applied to sons and male siblings. Moms should monitor the dialogue between brothers and sisters about weight and body image. Although you are the key influence on your daughter's body image development, developing other family members' sensitivity to the importance of body-healthy attitudes and behaviors is important for success.

EFFECTS OF CULTURE ON BODY IMAGE

Outside of the home, cultural environment also affects developing body image. We use the term "culture" here to refer to one's enduring environment or context in a very broad sense. When we refer to cross-cultural differences or similarities, it is important to remember that they can exist in different areas of the world (e.g., different countries) or within a single country (e.g., within the United States), region (e.g., the Northeast United States), or local community. We consider race, ethnicity, socioeconomic status, and sexual orientation, as well as the intersection of these factors, as personal identities that are part of culture and culturally relevant; as such, these factors intersect with others to determine how we see ourselves and how we are seen by others. For people who are part of minority groups, dominant cultural forces can further affect these impressions of the self and others.

An unfortunate aspect of much of the science presented in this chapter is that it heavily sampled what researchers call WEIRD participants; in other words, the people who were studied were from Western (W), educated (E), industrialized (I), rich (R), and democratic (D) populations (Henrich et al., 2010). For this reason, most of the research mentioned up to this point represents the macrosystem of WEIRD women best and offers less information about women from non-WEIRD backgrounds. Much of the research on girls' body image presented in Chapters 4, 5, and 6 also relies on WEIRD samples because this is the science currently available to us. Even within Western cultures such as the United States, which is the main focus of much of the research presented in this book, relatively little attention has been paid to cultural variations in race, ethnicity, and the body image experiences of people of color, individuals from diverse socioeconomic backgrounds, and individuals who identify as a sexual minority. Thus, we should be cautious about **generalizing** the findings of a study to people who are very different from the people who were studied.

> **Generalizing:** taking some facts that are relevant in a particular situation or context and broadly or universally applying these facts to a different situation or context.

Is the conclusion, then, that the information covered in this book applies only to women and girls similar to those who have participated in the studies cited, who tend to be White and of middle to high socioeconomic status? Based on recent research that has started to expand the study of body image to different racial and ethnic groups, we are confident that this conclusion is unwarranted. Although we must respect and appreciate differences between groups, we also know from the available data that in the United States, the experience of body image in White, Asian, Black, and Latina women tends to be more similar than different (Burke et al., 2021). Family, peers, the media—all these factors affect women's body image, regardless of background, but the impact, intensity, and timing of these influences differs for individual women in important ways.

In the next sections, we describe some persistent body image commonalities across many cultures, followed by some differences in experience that are specific to groups of women. We also offer suggestions for how moms and daughters can incorporate cultural awareness into their own partnerships for healthy body image.

Common Themes in Women's Body Image Across Cultures and Time

Two major points stand out when one looks across culture at the research on women's body image. The first point is that women's body image issues are not new. The science on body image dates to the early 20th century, but this time period is only recent history. How do we know that body image concerns have been around for a long time? One measure used today, *appearance-fixing*, can provide a little insight. Appearance-fixing refers to a spectrum of behaviors that serve as coping mechanisms for dealing with threats to body image (Cash, 2001; Cash et al., 2005). Some are benign behaviors that most of us participate in, such as wearing makeup and altering hair color or hairstyle. For researchers, appearance-fixing also includes behaviors such as concealing or correcting what one believes to be physical flaws (e.g., skin-bleaching, cosmetic surgery). For women who are especially dissatisfied with their bodies, appearance-fixing behaviors can become more extreme over time and potentially harmful (Walker & Murray, 2012).

As we discussed earlier in Chapter 1, women's physical attractiveness is highly valued in U.S. culture, and cross-cultural research indicates that physical attractiveness confers benefits in other cultures as well (e.g., Shaffer et al., 2000). It is probably not surprising, then, that women have long been concerned with their appearance. Available evidence from ancient civilizations all over the world indicates that even long ago, women used appearance-fixing cosmetics, for instance. Professional cosmetic makers produced eyeshadows, rouge, and foundation in ancient Egypt; paint for lips, cheeks, and eyes have been found in Sumerian tombs in the Indus Valley civilization; and face paints were used in ancient East Asia (Russell, 2011). Footbinding, a practice designed to keep the feet at a desirable, small size, was normative in Chinese women by 1650, although evidence suggests the practice started much earlier (Gamble, 1943). We can infer from examples such as these that women have long attended to the appearance of the face and managed perceptions of their bodies. Archaeological evidence from 5,000 years and across many ancient civilizations demonstrates women's attempts to beautify—to improve their appearance to meet the collectively held beauty ideals of their times.

Body image concerns affect women of many ethnic and cultural backgrounds, so the problem is not unique to American culture—it is widespread. Women's dissatisfaction with some aspect of their bodies is a common problem across Western and, increasingly, non-Western cultures (Bakhshi, 2011). As we noted, much of the evidence surveyed earlier in this chapter has been collected from women of English-speaking countries (such as the United States, Canada, the United Kingdom, and Australia). However, there is also ample evidence of body dissatisfaction in women from East Asian cultures such as Japan (e.g., Chisuwa & O'Dea, 2010), China (e.g., Luo et al., 2005), and Korea (e.g., Lin & Raval, 2020; Noh et al., 2018). South Asian women's body dissatisfaction and body concerns have been documented as well (Goel et al., 2021; Mishra et al., 2023).

Different Cultures, Different Body Image Issues

Despite women's cross-culturally shared concern for how their bodies are perceived, science suggests numerous cultural differences in specific body ideals and concerns. In this section, we review some of the most common cultural differences in women's specific body concerns.

Concerns About Body Shape and Size

Often, women's dissatisfaction with their appearance centers on the size or shape of their bodies, although not always (Edmonds, 2012). As we noted earlier, research shows that American and other Western cultures have promoted a thin ideal and that the pressure of this unrealistic ideal is an important driving factor in women's dissatisfaction with their bodies (Grabe et al., 2008). And yet, important differences remain in how much size matters to women. Research by Rodgers and colleagues (2023), for example, found that in non-English-speaking

European countries, overall rates of body image concerns are slightly lower than those in English-speaking cultures.

Another study examined the impact of viewing thin-ideal images on women from the United Kingdom and Turkey (Ozbek et al., 2023), and interesting cultural differences emerged. At the outset (and before viewing any images), women from Turkey reported higher body satisfaction, greater **body image flexibility,** and less fear of negative evaluation than the women from the United Kingdom. After viewing the thin-ideal images, both groups of women felt less satisfied with their bodies, but the negative impact was stronger on the women from the United Kingdom. The researchers concluded that Turkish women were less affected by thin-ideal images because they show greater body image flexibility than women from the United Kingdom. Indeed, a strong body of research indicates that body image flexibility is beneficial in several ways. Not only do women with greater body image flexibility have fewer body image problems and more positive attitudes toward their bodies, but they also have fewer psychological problems overall (Linardon et al., 2021).

> **Body image flexibility:** the experience of having thoughts or feelings about the body that one does not act on, try to change, or avoid but instead responding adaptively to these thoughts and feelings (Sandoz et al., 2013).

Even within the same country (i.e., the United States), racial and ethnic differences are evident in attitudes toward body shape and size. It is well documented that Black women report more positive views of their bodies than White women do, despite having larger bodies on average (e.g., Grabe & Hyde, 2006). Black women engage in fewer appearance-fixing behaviors than White women do (Cash et al., 2005) and also express less body dissatisfaction than either

White or Latina women (Grabe & Hyde, 2006). One possible reason is that Black women and girls show a lower drive for thinness than White women and the bodies they consider ideal are larger than the body ideals of either White or Latina women. Other reasons could be that Black men tend to prefer larger female bodies than White men do and that historic marginalization has led Black women to reject White beauty ideals. Grabe and Hyde's (2006) meta-analysis of body dissatisfaction among ethnic subgroups of American women showed a small but significant difference between Black and White women that decreased with age but no significant differences among White, Asian American, and Latina women.

Interesting differences between specific subgroups of Latinas reinforce that even within these subgroups, no two women are exactly alike. In one study, Cuban, Puerto Rican, and White women all had similar levels of body dissatisfaction, but Mexican women had higher levels of body dissatisfaction than White women did (Quiñones et al., 2022).

There are also interesting differences among Asian women. Kennedy and colleagues (2004) found that women of Chinese descent reported greater body dissatisfaction than Indo-Asian women. Other reviews have concluded that women from India do not experience pressures for thinness to the same degree as other Asian women (Bakhshi, 2011). Both Indo-Asian and Chinese women reported greater dissatisfaction with their bodies than did women of European descent (Kennedy et al., 2004). Reviewing the available evidence across Asian countries, Kawamura (2012) concluded that women from Singapore, Hong Kong, and Japan are the least satisfied with their bodies, and Filipinas were generally the most satisfied with their bodies.

If you are interested in learning more about cultural variations in body image concerns and their effects on mental health, see the Recommended Resources section at the end of the chapter, which includes Rodgers and colleagues' (2023) excellent and comprehensive book on this topic.

Healthy Body Image Building Tool

 The thin ideal is alive and well in the world, and exposure to it can be damaging for our self-views. Consider how much you have internalized the thin ideal. One effective, evidence-based strategy for protecting yourself against the thin ideal is to grow in body image flexibility. Increasing your body image flexibility involves learning to tolerate intrusive, negative thoughts about yourself without quickly attempting to change those thoughts, responding to them judgmentally, or allowing them to guide actions. A person with body image flexibility instead chooses self-compassion and moves on from negative thoughts, realizing those thoughts need not define who she is and take over her emotions and behaviors. This skill can be challenging, especially because culture often urges women to focus on their bodies and appearance (increasing the likelihood of negative self-evaluations), but research indicates that practicing flexibility will pay off (Linardon et al., 2021)—increasing body image flexibility has been shown to be an effective strategy for decreasing body image issues, weight concerns, and symptoms of eating disorders (Merwin et al., 2023). To learn more about your own body image flexibility, see the sample items from the Body Image Acceptance and Action Questionnaire (Sandoz et al., 2013) in Table 1.1.

CONCERNS ABOUT SKIN

Another body image concern for women is the color of their skin. **Colorism** is a term for prejudice and discrimination based on one's skin tone (Norwood & Foreman, 2014). Importantly, the term refers to negative attitudes and behaviors within a racial or ethnic group and contrasts with racism, which involves negative attitudes and behaviors between racial or ethnic groups. Colorism is not a new problem, and it is not limited to one group of people, although it has certainly been much more salient and consequential for people of color, both historically and currently. Preference for lighter skin tones over darker skin tones shows considerable consistency across time and culture.

> **Colorism:** the prejudicial or preferential treatment of a person based on the tone of their skin (Norwood & Foreman, 2014).

In their review of the ubiquitousness of colorism, Norwood and Foreman (2014) presented evidence not only that ancient Greeks and Romans preferred lighter skin tones, as evidenced by their attempts to lighten their skin tones, but that lighter skin tone has historically been privileged in Latin America, Asia, and Africa as well (although there are some notable variations in this trend pre- and postcolonization). In the United States, where color and race have been sources of conflict and vehicles for discrimination and dehumanization from the start, legal progress on the topic has not eliminated the basic social power and privilege of lighter skin. Indeed, in writing this book, we recognize our dominant culture privilege, and our sincere intention is to present some of the science on these matters without presumptions or judgment.

It is not surprising, then, that lighter skin tone is especially valued in minority subgroups within the United States. Interviews with African American women, for example, reveal that colorism is keenly felt and psychologically distressing. Hall (2017) interviewed women who self-identified as light, medium, dark, or very dark complexioned. Darker skinned women reported teasing and bullying within their own community as well as the psychological distress of not conforming to the lighter skin ideal.

For women of Asian descent, skin tone is also a particular focal point of body dissatisfaction. Because of the premium placed on lighter skin throughout Asian countries dating back before the modern era (Norwood & Foreman, 2014), women in many Asian countries deal with the pressure of the lighter skin ideal. East Asian women frequently report skin tone is an important focal point of body dissatisfaction; South Asian women living in Canada report feeling pressure to meet a cultural ideal of having a thin body, light skin, and long hair.

CONCERNS ABOUT HAIR

Other examples of common body image focal points for women are hair, eyes, and nose. When it comes to these features, many women feel the pressure to live up to Eurocentric beauty ideals promoted by media. As one example, U.S. media representations, in particular, associate women's blonde hair with youthful sex appeal and physical attractiveness (Rich & Cash, 1993). African American women experience the pressures of not matching the Eurocentric ideals regarding hair (Patton, 2006), and research shows that many Black girls report bullying and teasing about their hair (Henning et al., 2022). Mbilishaka and colleagues (2020) found that hair texture, length, and style were aspects of natural hair that particularly attracted teasing. And the hair product industry benefits from this body concern: Black women spend about three times as much money on their hair as White women do (Wilson & Russell, 1996).

BOOSTING RESILIENCE BY BUILDING A STRONG ETHNIC AND RACIAL IDENTITY

Consider to what extent these cultural factors affect you and your daughter. For some women, cultural considerations may play a relatively small role in body image. For others, they will be substantial. If you are part of an ethnic or racial minority group, you may feel that you do not conform to the norms of the dominant culture. Or, you may have specific feelings about being underrepresented in the mainstream media—and these feelings can be positive or negative.

Research shows that one protective factor for body image and body image development relates to social identity and the self-concept, which we talk about quite extensively in this book: cultivating a strong **racial or ethnic identity**. According to Phinney and Ong (2007), racial and ethnic identities offer a sense of belonging to a group and a desire to learn about that group. They consist of values, attitudes, and behaviors, and they can provide a buffer for dealing with discrimination.

> **Racial or ethnic identity:** an individual's sense of being defined, in part, by membership in a particular racial or ethnic group. The strength of this sense depends on the extent to which an individual has processed and internalized the psychological, sociopolitical, cultural, and other contextual factors related to membership in the group (Phinney & Ong, 2007).

Ethnic identity can be important for well-being because it creates a sense of belongingness in a group. Although the evidence is mixed, some research supports the protective effect of a strong ethnic identity on body image specifically. In a study with southern African American adolescents (Turnage, 2004), girls with high ethnic identity achievement reported more positive appearance evaluations than girls with low ethnic identity achievement. In another study with African American women, stronger ethnic identity was associated with lower internalization of the thin ideal (Rogers Wood & Petrie, 2010).

As noted earlier in this chapter, overall, Latinas experience similar rates of body image disturbances as White women (Grabe & Hyde, 2006). But for these women, body image can be complicated by their exceptionally strong ties to their families, or what is known as **familism**. Because the family is such a central influence on girls and women, messages that they convey about body image—positive or negative—may be particularly impactful. Indeed, researchers have found that negative body comments from fathers, mothers, and sisters are related to body image shame (Rivero et al., 2022).

> **Familism:** an important value for many Latinas emphasizing obligations to one's family and strong interdependence and connectedness among family members (Burke et al., 2021).

Issues related to ethnic and racial identity apply to many different groups and people. In our examples, we have noted particular points of relevance for some minority groups. But family composition is a complicated thing (e.g., multiracial families). The complex intersections of our social identities and their impact on how we feel about our bodies is a sensitive topic. The goal of discussions with your daughter is to bring awareness to any negative influences so that they can be discussed openly. We have noted that a strong ethnic identity can be protective of body image, and in this case, fostering a strong ethnic identity may be helpful if it is a value that resonates with you and your family. If you receive mixed messages about your body—if messages from the broad culture differ from those of your ethnic or racial group—a different strategy may be warranted. It is a losing battle to attempt to fit conflicting body ideals, and it is unhealthy to have even more body ideals with which to contend, for reasons we have already discussed. In Chapter 3, we discuss the merits of taking a body-neutrality approach to handling these pressures.

Because the development of body image is a complex, multilevel process, it is not possible to describe all the specific cultural, subcultural, or social identity influences that affect you and your daughter personally. The goal for this chapter is to encourage you to critically examine the type and extent of macrosystem influences contributing to your and your daughter's body attitudes and to talk about these factors openly. When we feel the sting of not living up to some socially constructed body ideal, it is healthy to remember and teach our daughters to remember to examine the social contexts in which they are immersed and that often go unnoticed if we are not intentional about it. Equipped with this awareness and keeping our personal values in mind, we need not accept or internalize those ideas if they are not working for us.

PUTTING IT ALL TOGETHER: PRACTICAL TIPS FOR MOMS

In this chapter, we have reviewed some consequences of negative body image and offered science-based tips to help you reflect on your own body image and how it might become healthier. Here we summarize several general practices that will be helpful for pursuing healthier body image. Although these tips are for moms, they will equip you to be a healthy partner to your daughter in her development as well.

- **Build self-awareness of your own body image.** One option is to complete one or more of the suggested body image questionnaires in Table 1.1.
- **Self-reflect on your body image.** For example, identify strengths and areas for change in how you view your body or others' bodies.
- **Practice self-compassion.** Extend to yourself the same kindness you would extend to a close friend or loved one who has body concerns.
- **Consider the important role of culture in defining body image.** For example, examine the body ideals in your own culture and the ways in which they differ from the body ideals in other cultures.

In the Appendix, we provide companion activities to help you reflect on important concepts in this chapter if you are interested in doing so. These supplemental activities are meant to be helpful and insightful—to complete if you would like. We don't intend them as work!

- Activity 1: Who Am I Now? Exploring Past, Present, and Future Selves

Recommended Resources

Cash, T. F. (2012). *Encyclopedia of body image and human appearance.* Academic Press.

Cash, T. F., & Smolak, L. (Eds.). (2011). *Body image: A handbook of science, practice, and prevention* (2nd ed.). Guilford Press.

Gill, R. (2008). Body talk: Negotiating body image and masculinity. In S. Riley, M. Burns, H. Frith, S. Wiggins, & P. Markula (Eds.), *Critical bodies* (pp. 101–116). Palgrave Macmillan.

Kenny, E., & Nichols, E. (2017). *Beauty around the world: A cultural encyclopedia.* Bloomsbury.

Rhode, D. L. (2010). *The beauty bias: The injustice of appearance in life and law.* Oxford University Press.

Rodgers, R., Laveway, K., Campos, P., & de Carvalho, P. (2023). *Body image as a global mental health concern.* Cambridge Prisms: Global Mental Health. https://doi.org/10.1017/gmh.2023.2

CHAPTER 2

UNDERSTANDING YOURSELF TO HELP HER BUILD A BETTER BODY IMAGE

Arriving a few minutes late at the shopping center, Alex enters the coffee shop and immediately spots her friends ordering at the counter and hurries over to place her order. After the week she had at work and all her kids' afterschool activities, she is hoping to relax a bit with friends. Coffee and pastries in hand, they sink into the comfy chairs and start planning which stores they hope to hit before the morning is finished. "Hey, has anyone decided what to wear to the reunion cocktail party yet?" Miriam excitedly asks the group.

"Wow, that's two months away, I can't even plan next weekend," Kayla laughs.

"I know, but this is our 20th reunion and *everyone's* going to be there—it's a big one," Miriam replies.

"Really? Everybody's coming?" Alex asks.

"Oh yeah, I've been keeping track on my socials. I think I've found the perfect dress too," Miriam nods excitedly.

"Well, I'll wear something nice," Kayla shrugs, "but I'm not going to overthink it."

Alex has thought about it, but she just keeps pushing the thoughts out of her mind. Honestly the whole thing makes her a little anxious (she hasn't seen these people in years!), and she wants to make the right impression. "I wish I had your confidence," she smiles at Miriam.

"Well, you should—you look great!" Kayla reassures her, "I know . . . we'll help you—let's shop for the perfect dress today! Who knows? Maybe even I'll find something."

Have you had an experience like this—three friends, each with her own unique take on the same situation? We have a lot in common as women, but when it comes down to it, each of us is unique. Some of these differences are especially important to consider when thinking about body image. In Chapter 1, we explored the research on women's body image and examined the social and psychological costs of negative body image that many women experience. We reviewed common experiences shared by many or most women as well as differences based on cultural or familial factors. But as we explained in Chapter 1, even women with the same cultural or familial backgrounds can have very different body images. How is that? Much like the friends in the example that opens this chapter, women have personal qualities that affect the way they think about issues related to body image. Examining these characteristics is useful because they provide clues about ways we can potentially improve our body image. It's not always easy but doing this work will likely help you to think and feel better about your body; awareness of your own thoughts about your body will also help you nurture a positive body image in your daughter.

Table 2.1 presents a list of some evidence-based clues to improving body image. The following sections describe these characteristics in detail, as well as several others, and offer some concrete practices and tips.

NURTURE A MULTIFACETED SELF-CONCEPT

Body image is housed in the **self-concept**, which is essentially your sense of who you are. The self-concept works hard for us, taking an active and central role in our overall psychological functioning.

TABLE 2.1. Some Personal Characteristics You Can Work on to Promote a Healthy Body Image

Goal	Sample practices to help you achieve the goal
Nurture a multifaceted self-concept	Add new social identities, social roles, or knowledge to your self-concept (Emery et al., 2015)
	Include aspects of those close to you in your own identity, and try novel activities together (Aron et al., 2000)
Maintain healthy levels of self-esteem	Spend time with people who provide you with acceptance and positive regard (Vonk, 2006)
	Practice mindfulness meditation and build relaxation skills (Niveau et al., 2021)
Increase self-efficacy	Break down big goals into smaller subgoals and take note of your achievements on them (Bandura & Schunk, 1981)
	Push through reluctance to try something intimidating (such as committing to exercise), and make yourself do it (Funder, 2019)
Increase self-compassion	View yourself from the perspective of a loving friend (Neff, 2011)
	Resist harsh self-judgments by reminding yourself you are still worthy (Adams & Leary, 2007)
Increase autonomy	Spend time doing things that enhance your sense of competency (Deci & Ryan, 2000)

(continues)

TABLE 2.1. Some Personal Characteristics You Can Work on to Promote a Healthy Body Image (*Continued*)

Goal	Sample practices to help you achieve the goal
Reduce self-discrepancy	Practice mindfulness meditation
	Reevaluate unrealistic ideals
	Build trait-like curiosity (Ivtzan et al., 2011)
Reduce neurotic behaviors	Practice mindfulness meditation (Hanley et al., 2019)
	Track and refute maladaptive thoughts (Jorm, 1989)
Reduce perfectionism behaviors	Attempt to find some positive aspect of perceived failures (Stoeber & Janssen, 2011)
	Practice self-compassion (Neff, 2011)
Reduce appearance monitoring, rejection sensitivity, anxiety of social evaluations	Emphasize the importance of other facets of the self-concept
	Practice self-compassion, and remind yourself that everyone feels this way sometimes
Reduce authoritarian behaviors	Practice open-mindedness (Berggren et al., 2019)
	Engage in critical thinking about issues (Tam et al., 2008)
Reduce social comparison	Practice intentionally resisting comparisons with others
	Practice gratitude when envy arises (Mao et al., 2021)

For example, it filters and processes incoming information, organizes all our self-knowledge, aids us in setting and managing goals, and provides us with a cohesive sense of identity. In short, it helps us make sense of the world (Oyserman et al., 2012). To be sure, body image is only one part of our self-concept, but it is an important part. As we noted in Chapter 1, body image occupies more proportional "space" in women's views of themselves than it does in men.

> **Self-concept:** the part of the mind that stores descriptions of and feelings about a person's physical and psychological characteristics, roles, relationships, and social identities (American Psychological Association [APA], n.d.).

Healthy Body Image Building Tool

What is your self-concept like? To know more about it, pause for a moment to complete the Twenty Statements Test (TST; Kuhn & McPartland, 1954) used often by researchers. Simply jot down 20 different responses to the question "Who am I?" beginning each response with the words "I am _____." The TST is a widely used measure in psychological and sociological sciences, and it reveals some of the most significant contents of your self-concept (according to you). Looking over your responses, you may see descriptors of your occupation (e.g., "I am an accountant"), your social roles (e.g., "I am a mom"), or your personality characteristics (e.g., "I am outgoing"). You may even see descriptors that are relevant to your body image, such as "I am tall" or "I am athletic." There are certainly no right or wrong answers to this test; instead, researchers are usually looking for themes in the statements. For example, were more of your responses personal descriptors or descriptors of your social relationships? Were more of your responses descriptors of your physical body or your psychological attributes? The specific way scientists analyze the themes in your responses depends on their research questions; for the purpose of building self-awareness, you can simply observe how often appearance-related statements show up on your list.

The amount of space body image occupies in one's self-concept is an important individual difference among women. Researchers have known for some time that a woman's self-concept can create either a buffer against or a vulnerability to the internalization of cultural ideals about appearance (Vartanian, 2009). What is different about the women whose self-concept buffers them from appearance culture? We must be careful not to oversimplify here—people are complex, and there could be many differences between these women. But psychological science suggests that one important difference is that these women have an **expandable self** (Walton et al., 2012).

> **Expandable self:** the ability to view oneself as multifaceted, defined by many different attributes and qualities rather than only a few primary ones (Walton et al., 2012).

According to Walton and colleagues (2012), threat situations tend to narrow the self-concept, and a person with a narrowed self-concept simply has few coping resources from which to draw. In Chapter 1, we detailed the heavy cultural emphasis on and value of youth, thinness, and beauty; no doubt, at times, these pressures can seem threatening. When we feel these cultural pressures, something like anticipating a reunion with people we have not seen in 20 years can narrow our focus to appearance concerns. By building a self-concept that is founded on a diverse array of personal and social characteristics, we establish a psychologically protective layer so that when appearance concerns arise, they do not take hold, take over, or set in. An expanded sense of self helps us keep perspective on appearance concerns, seeing them as only one facet of the whole person who has developed over the last 20 years.

If you completed the TST, take a quick look back at your results. Could some responses be replaced with non–appearance-related features of yourself? Identifying those is a great first step in choosing to de-emphasize the importance of appearance (and the accompanying appearance-related concerns) in your self-concept. You know your self-concept better than anyone, and you get to define yourself the way you want and by the qualities that are important to you. You can actively manage these qualities as well.

Overall, research suggests that women are likelier to have healthier body image when their self-concepts are not heavily dominated by body and appearance themes. Of course, there is no incorrect way of "doing" your self-concept—it is yours, and its contents make you the unique person you are. However, one powerful way you can model healthy body image for your daughter is to show her a self-concept that is founded on all the other, and perhaps more important, aspects of who you are: your wit, your compassion, your problem-solving skills, your creativity, your athletic prowess (we could go on and on!). Consider the values that best represent how you want to live. Think about the everyday decisions you make and the behaviors that correspond to these values. By emphasizing these non–appearance-related qualities in your self-definition, you will teach her to do the same for herself.

MAINTAIN HEALTHY LEVELS OF SELF-ESTEEM

No doubt you are very familiar with the concept of **self-esteem**. Across social science literature, self-esteem has been studied as an indicator of well-being for a long time. Theories about why it is so connected with mental health may differ (e.g., Leary & Baumeister, 2000; Pyszczynski et al., 2004), but researchers agree that feeling generally worthy, or good about who you are, is an important component of mental health in Western cultures. A person's individual self is such a fundamental part of the Western way of being that it is almost assumed by all that we should try to maintain healthy self-esteem ourselves and foster it in our girls. Note, however, that this view of the self is not necessarily the case in other cultures, such as East Asian cultures, where the self-concept is defined much more relationally (Markus & Kitayama, 1991).

> **Self-esteem:** one's evaluation of their self-concept; specifically, how positively someone feels about who they are, ranging from relatively low positivity to relatively high positivity (APA, n.d.).

The relationship between low self-esteem and negative body image is well-documented; this relationship is particularly strong for women who have less clarity about their self-concept and those who internalize sociocultural standards for bodies more (O'Dea, 2012). The link between self-esteem and positive body image has been observed across multiple European countries, indicating that the connection between these characteristics is stable and strong.

Healthy Body Image Building Tool

 You probably already have a good feel for your level of self-esteem. If you would like more clarity about it, you can find some sample items from the Rosenberg Self-Esteem Scale (Rosenberg, 1965) in Table 1.1. If you are interested in improving your level of self-esteem, research including more than 100 intervention studies has identified effective strategies (Niveau et al., 2021); the most effective strategies are cognitive–behavioral strategies. If your self-esteem is very low, you might consider consulting with a mental health professional who specializes in this type of therapy. Cognitive behavior therapies (CBTs) are among the most time-sensitive and science-supported strategies for improving mental health. A core feature of the CBT approach is to help you change distorted or irrational thoughts about yourself into more reasonable ones. As we noted in Chapter 1, poor body image can certainly distort your thoughts. Learning to challenge those thoughts and replace them with more accurate (and less toxic) thoughts is a skill that can boost not only self-esteem but mental health more generally. If you would prefer to work on your self-esteem at home and by yourself, see the Recommended Resources section at the end of this chapter for a great workbook you can use to guide your efforts toward healthier thoughts.

INCREASE SELF-EFFICACY

Our thoughts about who we are (self-concept) and our feelings about that self (self-esteem) yield expectations about what we are able or not able to achieve or accomplish. This belief about the self is known as **self-efficacy** (Bandura, 1997), and it can differ from one woman to the next. Some of us may have self-efficacy about running a marathon, whereas others may have very little self-efficacy in that domain. Some women feel confident in their ability to cope with challenging situations, whereas others feel very ineffective in handling life challenges.

> **Self-efficacy:** a person's confidence of success in specific situations or in their capability to perform specific behaviors (Bandura, 1997).

In health science, self-efficacy is a very important personal characteristic. As personality expert David Funder (2019) has pointed out, self-efficacy often defines what we will or will not attempt. If a woman does not feel she has a reasonable chance of improving a health condition, for example, she is not very likely to attempt to change her behaviors. Someone who feels capable of thinking optimistically is likely to make an effort to see the glass as half full. Strengthening self-efficacy is important because it is a demonstrated pathway for psychological and behavioral change.

Broadening our minds about our capabilities enables us to set goals and to keep track of how we are pursuing those goals; building self-efficacy empowers us to do the hard work of physical or psychological change. This science-based insight is one we can pass on to our girls: We limit ourselves by what we do or do not expect from ourselves. Further, we can build or revise our beliefs about what we are able to accomplish. When we attempt to do challenging things, we will not always be successful, but sometimes we will! Over time, attempting challenges and taking note of successes will build self-efficacy. We also know from research that self-esteem and self-efficacy go hand in hand. In fact, Bandura (1991) maintained that self-esteem is changeable by increasing self-efficacy, and a good deal of science supports that claim. Indeed, Funder (1999) wrote "the best way to raise self-esteem is through accomplishments that increase it legitimately" (p. 560).

Of course, not every attempt to change your body image will be successful. We want to be clear that we do not take a **healthism** perspective. There are always multiple causes for physical conditions or features related to body image (including both nature and nurture). Often enough, the causes lie largely outside a person's control, and narrow standards, overcontrolling behaviors, and blame are not very helpful to anyone. We believe, however, that if a woman desires to change something about herself, she should be empowered to set achievable goals and pursue them confidently, and psychological science can help with this endeavor.

> **Healthism:** a hyperfocus on physical health paired with evaluation of what the individual has or has not done to maintain physical health or avoid disease (often ignoring external factors; Jiménez-Loaisa et al., 2020).

Research indicates that interventions that build self-efficacy are effective in changing people's intentions and behaviors (Sheeran et al., 2016). For example, having a high level of self-efficacy is related to healthy behaviors such as eating a healthy diet and losing weight among patients with obesity (Gallagher, Yancy, Denissen, et al., 2013; Gallagher, Yancy, Jeffreys, et al., 2013). Self-efficacy about one's body is also related to body image. For example, low self-efficacy is related to unhealthy body attitudes and behaviors as well as body image disorders and eating disorders (Kinsaul et al., 2014), and people with low self-efficacy about eating and weight are more vulnerable to an unhealthy preoccupation with weight (Valutis et al., 2009).

Healthy Body Image Building Tool

 Because self-efficacy facilitates personal change, increasing it is a great way to fortify physical and psychological health. It is easy to say, "Think about yourself differently," but it is another thing to do that authentically. How do you learn to think differently about your capabilities? One type of psychotherapy, *motivational interviewing* (Miller & Rollnick, 2002), is a scientifically supported route for behavior change, and one of its key components is building self-efficacy. If you want to learn to build your own self-efficacy and model confidence for your daughter, consider practicing some exercises from the motivational interviewing approach. In the Recommended Resources section at the end of this chapter, we recommend a great workbook authored by a motivational interviewing expert that will help you build self-efficacy skills.

REDUCE SELF-DISCREPANCY

So far, we have considered self-concept and how we feel about it. If you are like us, however, your self-concept does not always match up with what you wish it were or what you feel it ought to be. The gap between your actual self and other possible versions of the self is what psychological scientists refer to as **self-discrepancy**. As you can probably imagine, self-discrepancy does not feel nice! Self-discrepancy theory (Higgins et al., 1985) focuses on two types of other possible selves: the "ought" self, which is concerned with living up to perceived obligations, and the "ideal" self, which involves fulfilling the best version of the self. Falling short of either of these possible selves can result in negative feelings (e.g., anxiety and depression symptoms).

> **Self-discrepancy:** a disjoint between aspects of your self-concept, specifically, your actual self and your "ought" self as well as your "ideal" self (Higgins et al., 1985).

A person's actual/ideal discrepancy is the gap most often examined in body image literature because the ideal self reflects the internalization of cultural ideals (Vartanian, 2012). How about you? Do you have an ideal self that differs from your actual self? You can check out the sample items from the Body Image Quality of Life Inventory (Cash & Szymanski, 1995) in Table 1.1 to help you think about your body ideals. Pause to reflect on any discrepancies between your ideal and actual self and the ways in which these discrepancies might fuel body concerns. Are any unrealistic or toxic cultural ideals hanging out in your ideal self and, if so, can they be revised? One way to address toxic ideals is to make them less important to you. Practice reminding yourself of the ways these ideals are unrealistic and artificial as well as the good reasons you have for prioritizing other self-goals (e.g., pursuing the healthful functioning of your body or interesting hobbies and personal goals instead).

INCREASE AUTONOMY

Women also differ from one another in the ways they think about their basic connectedness to other people. At our core, we all need to be in relationships and feel belongingness with others; psychological scientists describe this need as a fundamental human need (Baumeister & Leary, 1995). But women can differ widely in the amount of connectedness with other people they need or want. Think for a moment about your own friends. You can probably identify some who prefer to share and connect frequently as well as those who prefer more solitude and space.

Research shows that women who need or want a strong connectedness with others—that is, people who are low in **autonomy**—are more likely to be *people-pleasers*. A desire to make others happy is generally a healthy and positive characteristic, but as one scientist noted (Funder, 2019), our biggest strengths can also be our greatest weaknesses. Pressure to please others and a strong desire to be liked may increase a person's sensitivity to social cues (L. Clark & Tiggemann, 2008). Given this increased social sensitivity, it is no surprise that women low in autonomy are especially susceptible to social influences (Noom et al., 2001). As discussed in Chapter 1, appearance-related social influences abound in women's daily lives, many of them toxic. Women who are especially sensitive to social cues may find it more difficult to tune out the toxicity.

> **Autonomy:** a person's sense of independence and self-determination and their experience that their actions are driven by their own choices rather than by pressure from others (APA, n.d.).

REDUCE NEUROTIC BEHAVIORS

One personality characteristic that has strong and clear implications for body image is **neuroticism**. Although it is not without its benefits, neuroticism is usually to a person's disadvantage, both psychologically and socially. People who have high levels of neuroticism are more attuned to negative information, experience more negative emotions, and fluctuate emotionally more than people with lower levels. They are also more vulnerable to depression and anxiety symptoms as well as mental illness. Systematic reviews of the literature (e.g., Allen & Walter, 2016) have shown conclusively that high neuroticism is associated with more negative experiences regardless of gender, culture, and body weight (Allen & Robson, 2020). Thankfully, however, personality is not set in stone.

> **Neuroticism:** one of the five primary dimensions of personality, characterized by a chronic level of emotional instability and proneness to psychological distress (APA, n.d.).

Healthy Body Image Building Tool

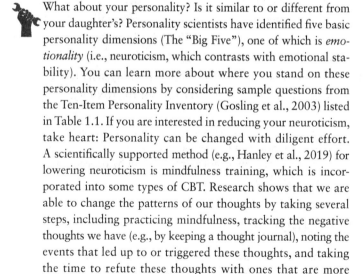 What about your personality? Is it similar to or different from your daughter's? Personality scientists have identified five basic personality dimensions (The "Big Five"), one of which is *emotionality* (i.e., neuroticism, which contrasts with emotional stability). You can learn more about where you stand on these personality dimensions by considering sample questions from the Ten-Item Personality Inventory (Gosling et al., 2003) listed in Table 1.1. If you are interested in reducing your neuroticism, take heart: Personality can be changed with diligent effort. A scientifically supported method (e.g., Hanley et al., 2019) for lowering neuroticism is mindfulness training, which is incorporated into some types of CBT. Research shows that we are able to change the patterns of our thoughts by taking several steps, including practicing mindfulness, tracking the negative thoughts we have (e.g., by keeping a thought journal), noting the events that led up to or triggered these thoughts, and taking the time to refute these thoughts with ones that are more neutral or positive. See the Recommended Resources section at the end of the chapter for an excellent at-home workbook (D. A. Clark & Leahy, 2020) you can use to practice restructuring negative thoughts.

REDUCE BEHAVIORS THAT REFLECT PERFECTIONISM

We opened this chapter with a scenario many of us have faced—trying to find the right apparel for a special occasion. For perfectionists, a task like this one may be especially challenging. You probably know someone who tends toward perfectionism, or you may show this pattern of behavior yourself. Although this term is used casually in everyday conversations, scientists have identified some precise characteristics of perfectionism, and these characteristics have implications for body image. Setting excessively high standards for yourself along with being highly self-critical are key features of *neurotic perfectionism* (Frost et al., 1990), and this type of perfectionism is related to body dissatisfaction (Wade & Tiggemann, 2013). Women who have perfectionist tendencies and are dissatisfied with their bodies have special cause for concern: This combination is especially predictive of disordered eating symptoms (Boone & Soenens, 2015). If you are interested in assessing your perfectionistic tendencies, consider some of the sample questions from the Big Three Perfectionism Scale–Short Form (Feher et al., 2020) in Table 1.1.

REDUCE AUTHORITARIAN BEHAVIORS

Authoritarianism is another body-image-related characteristic that can differentiate women from one another. Some people believe rules, morals, and societal norms should be followed without question or challenge, and they expect others to do the same; these people are described as having an **authoritarian personality**. Authoritarianism is related to body attitudes and how we interact with other adults. Women who tend toward strict rule following are more likely to endorse, accept, and participate in cultural prescriptions for women's bodies—even damaging ones. For example, some scientists (Crandall & Biernat, 1990) have made the case that antifat attitudes are a part of an underlying ideology that reflects an authoritarian view of the world. Indeed, authoritarianism is linked with an antifat prejudice (e.g., O'Brien et al., 2013). Because Western culture teaches its "rules" (such as the thin ideal) for women's bodies so clearly and forcefully, compliance with social norms that support the thin ideal is very important to people who show authoritarian tendencies.

> **Authoritarian personality:** "a personality pattern character-ized by strict adherence to highly simplified conventional values, an attitude of great deference to authority figures while demanding subservience from those regarded as lower in status, and hostility toward people who deviate from conventional moral prescriptions" (APA, n.d.).

Authoritarianism can also affect how adults interact with chil-dren, as anyone who has ever heard a parent answer, "Because I said so!" can readily attest. Occasional interchanges like this happen in every parent–child relationship, and certainly do not, on their own, indicate a pattern of authoritarianism. In some cases, however, parents require unquestioning obedience and strictly enforce rule adherence without any exceptions; in parenting patterns in which unquestioning obedience is the top priority, authoritarianism is at work. This aspect of ourselves can be modified and, with our daughters, it is a change worth making—considerable evidence shows that parental authoritarian behaviors are typically ineffective and can be damaging to children.

REDUCE SOCIAL COMPARISON

Social comparison, a psychological process that involves learning information about ourselves by comparing ourselves to others (Festinger, 1954), plays a huge role in body image concerns. Sometimes we intentionally compare ourselves to others, but because appearance concerns are so well learned and ingrained for women, social comparisons are often automatic and unintentional, although not without consequence. Social comparison has already been discussed at length in the Introduction; it is reintroduced only briefly here to highlight that some women engage in social comparison more than others do. Women who compare less are more likely to have healthier body image than those who compare more, and science suggests that social comparison is a habit we want to avoid modeling for girls.

Healthy Body Image Building Tool

 In Chapter 1, we recommended intentionally taking distance from online content that makes you feel bad about your body or appearance. Distancing is important because psychological science shows that the cumulative effects of appearance-based social comparisons are psychologically damaging. Take a moment to reflect on your own tendency to socially compare. To learn more about your social comparison tendencies, answer the sample questions from the Iowa-Netherlands Comparison Orientation Measure (INCOM), which is a social comparison orientation scale developed by Gibbons and Buunk (1999), as well as the Physical Appearance Comparison Scale–Revised (Schaefer & Thompson, 2014); both are in Table 1.1. Responding intentionally to social comparisons that make you feel bad is a great way to build healthy body image in yourself and to model it for your daughter. Helpful recommendations come from research by Mao et al. (2021), which shows that exercising gratitude inhibits envy. There are multiple ways to practice gratitude. In the Recommended Resources section at the end of the chapter, we provide a book recommendation (Emmons, 2007) that provides evidence-based tips for practicing gratitude.

REDUCE THE IMPORTANCE OF PERSONAL APPEARANCE

Some women place a high value on appearance and have formed core beliefs about themselves around the meaning, importance, and effects of their appearance on their daily life experiences (Cash & Labarge, 1996; Cash et al., 2004). These women tend to have a relatively large investment in their appearance as a part of their self-worth; body image scientists describe women who engage in this tendency as **appearance schematic** (Cash & Labarge, 1996).

> Appearance schematic: the degree to which a person is aware of the cultural attitudes toward appearance and the degree to which an individual person internalizes those cultural attitudes (Cash & Labarge, 1996).

Awareness of these cultural attitudes is hard to avoid, especially in the age of social media, but women can control, to some extent, the degree to which they internalize or embody these ideals. Internalization of cultural standards is a complex process. Social media use certainly plays a role. A meta-analysis of available studies showed a small to medium-sized relationship between social media use and internalization of the thin ideal (Mingoia et al., 2017). But social media is only one factor, of course. Other sociocultural pressures toward a thin ideal play a role as well, coming from family, friends, dating partners, or other types of media (Stice & Agras, 1998). The role of social media in forming women's body ideals has received much attention both in popular culture and by researchers, and we examine it more closely in Chapter 3.

Take just a moment to identify some sources that may pressure you, personally, toward unrealistic appearance ideals. Several strategies that may help women not to overvalue appearance are discussed in the next sections.

Reduce Personal "Fear of Fat"

Sometimes the pressures toward sociocultural ideals are so great that women experience anxiety about the consequences of violating the standards. In Chapter 1, we reviewed some of the very real consequences affecting women socially, financially, and in other important ways. Seeing a gap between actual and ideal selves can cause women to experience negative emotions. An example of a negative emotion is a personal fear of fat (Crandall, 1994), such as gaining weight or becoming obese. For many women, this fear causes anxiety and drives some potentially problematic behaviors such as overly controlling food intake. The negative consequences can extend to daughters as well. We discuss these consequences in Chapters 4 through 6.

Healthy Body Image Building Tool

 Do you ever feel as if you are being watched? No worries. It is only the little girl in your house! But she is noticing the things you do and the foods you do not eat. No pressure, right? One of the questionnaires referenced in Table 1.1, the Objectified Body Consciousness Scale (McKinley & Hyde, 1996), is made up of three different types of questions: those measuring feelings of body shame, those measuring the behaviors of body surveillance, and those measuring beliefs about how controllable appearance actually is. Think back to the last week. Can you remember expressing any of these feelings or beliefs about yourself out loud? Were there any times you did something different than the rest of the family because you were keeping yourself in check?

Reduce Appearance Rejection Sensitivity

Being in tune with others' perceptions of us can both help and hurt us. When others deny us their interest, acceptance, or approval, we experience rejection. No one enjoys rejection; it is an unpleasant, even painful experience. But some people take rejection harder than others. In fact, people who are especially sensitive to rejection (Downey & Feldman, 1996) are so worried at the prospect of possible rejection, they may behave in ways that create a self-fulfilling prophecy: Their fear-driven behaviors meant to maintain the relationship actually drive their partners away (Funder, 1999).

Based on all the evidence that many cultures value appearance and that many women internalize the ideals they see held up by media sources, it may come as no surprise to you that women are especially likely to fear appearance-based rejection (N. Park et al., 2009). Women who show high levels of appearance rejection sensitivity experience intense fear of being rejected by a close other because of some aspect of their appearance. If you are curious about your level of appearance rejection sensitivity, consider the sample scenarios from the Appearance-Based Rejection Sensitivity Scale (L. E. Park, 2007) in Table 1.1.

Reduce Appearance Monitoring

Women also respond to appearance concerns by engaging in a type of **self-monitoring**. Although all people engage in self-monitoring at times, it is habitual for some women. If we are to be successful in our careers and relationships, we must have some degree of self-awareness and a basic willingness to meet the unique demands of our contexts. Most women probably do not pay excessive attention to their appearance when headed to the gym for a workout; getting ready to go to work or to a social meetup afterward is a different matter. Of course, the degree to which women attend to their appearance in either of these contexts can differ significantly from one woman to the next. Body image research shows that physical appearance (one's own as well as others') is more important to women who have a high tendency to self-monitor than to those who have less of this tendency (Sullivan & Harnish, 1990). If you would like to assess the degree to which you engage in self-monitoring, consider the sample questions from the Self-Monitoring Scale (Snyder & Gangestad, 1986) in Table 1.1.

> **Self-monitoring:** sensitivity to social cues and a corresponding willingness to adjust oneself in accommodation to those cues (Snyder, 1987).

Self-monitoring one's physical appearance involves behaviors that are fairly easy to spot: checking oneself in the mirror, attempts to "fix" appearance in some way, and attending closely to others' appearances. Some women monitor aspects of their bodies continuously, engaging in a type of **body surveillance** (Fredrickson & Roberts, 1997; Moradi & Huang, 2008). Again, social media plays an important role, and we discuss how in Chapters 4 through 6. Besides, all that self-monitoring is costly in that it uses up valuable cognitive resources (Winn & Cornelius, 2020) that could be used in other ways.

> **Body surveillance:** the act of keeping a close eye on physical attributes such as weight to make sure to stay within the socially acceptable boundaries and norms and taking action to correct deviations (Fredrickson & Roberts, 1997).

Reduce Anxiety About Social Evaluations of Appearance

It is never a fun experience to be negatively evaluated by others. A healthy concern for the way that others view us is a natural aspect of human social behavior, and anticipating the impressions we make on others is something we all do. Like the friends in the opening vignette of this chapter, many of us have had the experience of not knowing what to wear to an event, so we seek the counsel of our friends, partners, or even the department store salesperson. After all, there are many ways to err in the eyes of others—too formal, too casual, age inappropriate, unflattering, and the list goes on! But some of us agonize more than others over decisions like these because of a heightened fear of others' negative evaluations of our appearance.

INCREASE COMPASSION TOWARD OUR OWN BODIES

In your daily interactions and friendships with other women, you have likely met some who are forgiving, accepting, or protective of their bodies as well as some who are very self-critical about their bodies. When thinking about the aspects of our bodies that we do not like or that we wish were different, it may be harder for some people to simply "like" ourselves more. Body image researchers have developed tools to distinguish between people who are more self-critical and those who are more self-compassionate (J. S. Mills et al., 2022). Their findings indicate that people who have negative body image tend to struggle more generally with self-critical thoughts; the good news is that self-compassion is a known buffer against poor body image, which makes it a great start for evidence-based change.

Self-compassion (also mentioned in Chapter 1) involves taking a noncritical perspective on ourselves, including personal aspects that we see as inadequate or faulty—similar to how a loving friend might view us. If you have heard a friend talk harshly about some aspect of her body, you may have found yourself wishing she could be kinder to herself and that she could see herself the way you do. In practicing self-compassion, we take the perspective of a loving friend toward ourselves—a perspective that forgives imperfections and emphasizes that, just like all humans, we deserve our own compassion.

Healthy Body Image Building Tool

 Research has shown that developing self-compassion is related to having a healthier body image. According to scientists (e.g., Neff, 2011), this process entails several steps: extending kindness rather than criticism to yourself, keeping your negative thoughts and feelings about yourself in balance by acknowledging them but not overindulging them, and understanding your own experience as one that is also experienced by everyone (i.e., you are not alone in experiencing that thought). You can increase self-compassion through intentional behaviors (more on this in Chapter 3). If you are curious to know where you stand on self-compassion generally, we have included some sample questions from the Self-Compassion Scale (Neff, 2003) in Table 1.1. We have also included some questions from the Body Compassion Scale (Altman et al., 2020), which measures self-compassion about your body.

MAINTAIN A HEALTHY LEVEL OF PHYSICAL ACTIVITY

One important way to build a healthy body image and model it for our daughters is to foster healthy body movement attitudes and behaviors. Based on an analysis of more than 100 studies, Hausenblas and Fallon (2006) concluded that exercise is indeed related to building better body image. Although the effect of exercise on body image is small compared to some other factors (e.g., the negative impact of unrealistic media representations of women's bodies), science consistently shows exercise is good for body image. In their analysis, Hausenblas and Fallon found that exercisers had more positive body images than nonexercisers and that special programs designed to improve body image that involved exercise were more effective in improving body image than programs that did not involve exercise. Interestingly, the researchers also found that the positive effect of exercise on body image is greater for younger women than for older women. More generally, exercise and physical activity have many benefits for mental health, beyond their influence on body image (Landers & Arent, 2007).

What types of exercise should women pursue? Ultimately, women and girls should choose the activities they most enjoy—these will be the most intrinsically motivating. In truth, all types of physical movement have their benefits, but some research indicates that sports participation increases both self-esteem and self-efficacy in women (Elavsky, 2010). Other research shows that, compared to some of the more aesthetic (e.g., ballet) types of physical movement, sports participation is related to lower levels of body shame and unhealthy eating patterns (Slater & Tiggemann, 2006, 2011). Beyond body image, some research has found that women who participate in sports have higher life satisfaction and are more likely to thrive psychologically than those who do not (Ghosh & Periasamy, 2019). Ultimately, you know best which type of physical activity is right for you. Practicing a sport or activity together with your daughter is just one way for you and your daughter to spend time together building healthy bodies and healthy body images.

PUTTING IT ALL TOGETHER: PRACTICAL TIPS FOR MOMS

In this chapter, we examined some personal characteristics that are associated with women's body image. These characteristics provide clues to evidence-based changes that you can make in your habits that will help both you and your girl. We touch on these healthy habits throughout the book, provide supplemental activities to put them into practice in the Appendix, and summarize them here.

To benefit yourself and your daughter, you may focus on developing the following healthy habits for healthy body image:

- **Develop a well-rounded self-concept.** For example, you can deprioritize the importance of appearance, focus on body functionality, and gain insight on and nurture other aspects of your identity.

- **Practice mindfulness about your thoughts.** You might notice and refute harmful patterns, such as perfectionism tendencies, appearance monitoring, and apprehension of social evaluation.
- **Practice compassion toward yourself and others.** Remind yourself that everyone experiences insecurity at times and that despite imperfections, you are still fundamentally worthy of love and respect.
- **Resist social comparisons to other women's bodies.** Strategies can include engaging with social media in responsible and intentional ways as well as opting out of fat talk.

We provide companion activities to help you reflect on important concepts in this chapter if you are interested in doing so. These supplemental activities are meant to be helpful or insightful; they are completely optional, of course!

- Activity 2: Perspective Taking & Taking Charge: Exploring the Unfamiliar

Recommended Resources

Clark, D. A., & Leahy, R. L. (2020). *The negative thoughts workbook: CBT skills to overcome the repetitive worry, shame, and rumination that drive anxiety and depression.* New Harbinger Publications.

Emmons, R. A. (2007). *Thanks! How the new science of gratitude can make you happier.* Houghton Mifflin Harcourt.

CHAPTER 3

BEYOND BODY POSITIVE: OUR APPROACH TO A BETTER BODY IMAGE

Maria is waiting for her daughter in the school pick-up line. She arrived 15 minutes early, but already the line has extended out to the neighborhood street, so she knows she is in for a wait. Making the best of it, she shifts the car into park, grabs her phone, and uses the opportunity to see what is going on in the world. Casually scrolling through her social media feed, Maria sees her friend triumphantly modeling some super expensive, hard-to-find workout leggings she scored at a consignment shop. Maria shakes her head and laughs, "That was a lucky find!" She sees an article on a formerly overweight celebrity she admires who recently looks much thinner but is now under fire for losing too much weight, and she feels a flash of empathy for the woman. She likes a post from a fitness influencer she follows but she wonders if that level of fitness is even attainable in real life. Turning to email, an ad from a size-inclusive activewear retailer displays images of models with larger bodies practicing yoga; Maria remembers a meme she saw recently that reminds her that she is enough. She is not so sure she believes that she is, however. "I guess I ought to work on that," she thinks. Looking up, she sees that the line has started moving, and she quickly puts the phone down to catch up.

Body messaging is everywhere we turn. Not only do beauty culture norms dictate how we should look, but plenty of well-intentioned influential people are simultaneously advising us to ignore these standards altogether—the mixed messages can be overwhelming! In recent years, the concept of body positivity has become an extremely popular social movement (e.g., #bodypositivity, #bopo)—so popular, in fact, it almost needs no introduction. Intuitively, feeling good about your body seems to be an admirable and uncontroversial goal; after all, as discussed in Chapter 1, it is abundantly clear that we need to seriously remodel women's body image. But what is the best way to tackle this project? The body positivity movement has been a popular source of guidance for many women, but what impact does this movement actually have on women's feelings about themselves? Is building a healthy body image the same as pursuing an unconditionally positive outlook on our bodies and hoping our daughters will do the same, as some in the body positive movement would have us do? Can mere positivity really be the answer? The best place to look is science.

As discussed in Chapters 1 and 2, a great deal of evidence suggests that body image concerns are deeply ingrained in who women are. Our body concerns intersect with many other aspects of our self-concept and are embedded in our thoughts, feelings, and behaviors; they are housed in our personalities and in the different meanings we make of life events, large and small. Because body image concerns are so deeply rooted, disentangling from them is complicated and requires a plan. "Be positive about my body? Sure, I want to, but how do I do that?" Like Maria in the opening vignette, many women find themselves a little unsure or unconvinced about some of the assumptions built into body positivity messaging. "What about how others think about my body? Is it okay that I want acceptance, admiration, or affection from others who matter to me?" Or, "I wish we could focus on something other than my appearance—it isn't the core of who I am." Or, "Doesn't my health come first? Should I really silence all my body concerns if my doctor says I have risk factors for serious illness and mortality?" Many women have experienced thoughts like these and, truth be told, as women ourselves, we sometimes are stressed by body negativity as well as by trying to stay body positive.

In this chapter, we consider what it means to be body positive, what science says about positive body image, and we present our own perspective on healthy body image. We begin by identifying the origins of the body positivity movement. We then discuss how scientists define positive body image and highlight some key findings about its impact on women, carefully considering what these findings mean for our girls. Finally, we discuss in detail our perspective, which emphasizes women's body autonomy, functionality, and health as well as the importance of balancing the overall priority of body image so that it is not disproportionately privileged relative to other aspects of self-concept. Along the way, we discuss some practical next steps for incorporating science into your daily lives and inspiring your girls to do the same.

To be honest, the opposing viewpoints and strong emotions around the topic of body positivity made this chapter surprisingly challenging to write; with so many stakeholders, it seems likely that some will take issue with nearly anything we could write about the topic. In keeping with the theme of this book, however, our goal in this chapter is to bring you the science on body positivity and positive body image, with no special motive outside of the facts and drawing informed guidance from them.

ORIGINS OF THE BODY POSITIVE MOVEMENT

Although the body positivity movement has been very prominent in recent years, it is not new. It began in the 1960s—a time of enormous cultural change in the United States—when people who had been historically marginalized began to assert their civil rights. In 1969, nonprofit groups (the first being the National Association to Advance Fat Acceptance [NAAFA]) organized to bring awareness to, and end discrimination against, people with heavier bodies. Early on, the goal was to increase "fat acceptance" and protect the rights of people with diverse body sizes and shapes (i.e., "fat rights" or "fat justice").

In the 1990s and early 2000s, the meaning of the term body positivity expanded to include acceptance of, and appreciation for, a wide array of body differences, including differences of shape, size, skin color, and ability. The arrival of computerized social networking and social media platforms played an important role in spreading the message of body acceptance to a much larger audience and fostered the development of both activist and special interest groups. In the 2010s and 2020s, the body-positivity movement has become a powerful sociocultural influence (Rodgers et al., 2022). A quick internet search of "body positive" turns up countless blogs, advertising and social media campaigns, "expert" interviews, popular press books, official organizations (e.g., Association for Size Diversity and Health, The Body Positive), and academic journal articles. In popular culture, body positivity is a common topic of conversation, debate, and social identity.

As the body positivity social movement began making its mark on culture in the 2010s, it became clear that body positivity is more complex than it may at first appear. It is tied to strong emotions and issues that are especially important to various groups of people. Pointing back to the original fat acceptance movement in the 1960s (which also celebrated Black and Queer bodies), some people believe the topic should focus especially on the experiences of historically marginalized bodies to right social injustices. Other people are especially passionate about promoting body positivity for its psychological benefits. They believe that the body positivity movement is key for bringing about positive body image, well-being, and, more generally, a healthy way of living—one that rejects diet culture and unrealistic cultural ideals, for example. According to this perspective, body positivity is a public health issue and, as such, is important to all.

Some people are skeptical of the body positive movement; they doubt that it can deliver what it promises. For example, they note that declaring body positivity does not necessarily translate to having a positive body image. Other critics are not sure that body positivity is the best alternative for negative body image. For example, some are concerned that body positivity still focuses excessively on the body. Some critics suggest that body positivity can potentially encourage obesity and other health problems. Still others are concerned that body positive content often does not feature truly diverse representations of women's bodies. Finally, some simply ignore the body positivity movement; instead, they embrace diet culture just as generations before them have, complying with the current diet or fitness fads.

Healthy Body Image Building Tool

Pause for a moment to consider the body positive movement and what it means to you. How often do you come across this content on social media, and do you actively seek it out? When you encounter body positive messaging, do you feel inspired by this movement, skeptical of it, neutral toward it, or even a little pressured by it? There are no right or wrong answers to this question. Pause to reflect on your goals for your body image and your hopes for your daughter's. Do some aspects of the body positivity movement ring true for you, and are there any that do not? Building a healthy body image is not one size fits all, and that applies to body positivity as well. A key feature of our approach, presented later in this chapter, is that you get to decide how to pursue the healthiest body image for yourself.

BODY POSITIVITY VERSUS POSITIVE BODY IMAGE: POPULAR AND SCIENTIFIC DEFINITIONS

As previously discussed, the body positive social movement has different emphases and applications; similarly, the popular meaning of the phrase *positive body image* differs according to whom you ask. Some use positive body image to mean positive evaluations, such as acceptance of our bodies, approval of our bodies, or even celebration of their imperfections. Others use the term to indicate a liberation from body evaluations altogether. To many, body positivity broadly represents an inclusive perspective that accepts all body types, broadens the definitions of beauty, and rejects sociocultural expectations for women's bodies (Tiggemann, 2015). Still others use the term more specifically, such as to mean enhancement of one's natural appearance or caring for and protecting oneself from toxic external influences.

Body image researchers (e.g., Rodgers et al., 2022) draw a distinction between **body positivity** (attitudes consistent with the social movement) and having a **positive body image** (a woman's personal experience of attitudes toward her own body). Often, these concepts overlap with one another, but sometimes they do not; for example, a woman could be very much in favor of body positivity while harboring a less-than-positive body image.

Body image scientist Tracy Tylka and her colleagues have studied the topic of positive body image extensively, and they describe it as acceptance, appreciation, love, care, and respect for the body regardless of one's assessment of its appearance or functionality (Tylka & Wood-Barcalow, 2015b). According to this definition, a woman does not need to feel especially positive about her body all the time to be body positive. Rather, the most important feature is that despite fluctuations in her feelings, she continues to navigate multiple feelings with care, appreciation, and respect (Wood-Barcalow et al., 2010).

Body positivity: a popular term with varying definitions, such as acceptance, approval, or celebration of one's own body; acceptance, approval, or celebration of all bodies; or freedom from body evaluations altogether.

Positive body image: a specific term used in research meaning acceptance, appreciation, love, care, and respect for the body regardless of how you feel about its appearance or functionality (Tylka & Wood-Barcalow, 2015b).

Healthy Body Image Building Tool

Again, we invite you to consider your feelings about the body positive social movement. When it comes to your own body specifically, how positive are you? If you are interested in learning about your own positive body image, you can answer some sample questions from the Body Appreciation Scale-2 (Tylka & Wood-Barcalow, 2015a), which we have included in Table 1.1. After looking these over, take a moment to reflect on what you value and want for your own body image. Remember that there are no right or wrong answers. If any items on this questionnaire inspire you to set a new goal for your self-attitudes, science provides some insight for success. You can set yourself up for achieving your self-change goals by generating specific if–then plans to implement when you catch yourself getting off track (Gollwitzer & Sheeran, 2006). For example, if you decided you wanted to build respect for your body, one way you could set yourself up for success at reaching this goal would be to implement a plan for familiar trouble spots. So, "If I criticize the way some part of my body looks, I will name something I appreciate about my body and what it can do."

Several body image researchers point out that the definition of positive body image may not simply be the absence of negative body image. They argue that women who have a positive body image differ from those with negative or even neutral body images. Indeed, some research suggests that women with a positive body image have a greater sense of well-being than those with a more neutral body image (Tylka & Wood-Barcalow, 2015a). Tiggemann and colleagues have researched one specific component of positive body image, body appreciation, in women of various ages and social identities (e.g., race, education, involvement in athletics) and concluded that the psychological benefits of body appreciation and positive body image go beyond the mere absence of body dissatisfaction or negative body image (Tiggemann, 2015; Tiggemann & McCourt, 2013).

Plenty of evidence suggests that positive body image is important for psychological well-being and, by extension, physical health. Women with positive body image also tend to have high self-compassion and high self-esteem. They experience more positive emotions, such as happiness, are more optimistic, and report higher life satisfaction (Tylka, 2019); well-being indicators such as these are known to influence health and longevity (e.g., Diener & Chan, 2011). In Chapter 1, we made the case that the multifaceted nature of negative body image makes it a challenge for women; positive body image is also complex (Wood-Barcalow et al., 2024). This complexity suggests that it is far easier to build positive body image than it is to undo negative body image (Tiggemann, 2015). The central feature of our own perspective, and the chief reason for this book, is that the evidence clearly suggests that building healthy body image is best done developmentally. Chapters 4, 5, and 6 of this book give you tools to help you and your daughter partner to build healthy body image as she grows.

DOES BODY POSITIVE CONTENT ACTUALLY HAVE AN IMPACT ON BODY IMAGE?

Because we take a developmental-systems perspective (described in the Introduction of this book), we understand women's psychological experiences as the result of a very complex process that involves multiple factors at multiple levels. Adult women with positive body image have the self-views they do because of many interacting factors, and it would be inaccurate and oversimplistic to conclude that any one factor is responsible for their body image. The more precise question, then, is "Is the body positivity movement one of the factors that contributes to positive body image?"

The guiding assumption of the social movement, is, of course, that body positivity content supports and elevates a woman's view of her body (Rodgers et al., 2022), and many people rely on it to do so. As Rodgers and her colleagues noted, however, social media is often self-generated content, and anyone can post anything and label it as body positive. The label alone does not necessarily make it helpful for your body image specifically. For this reason, we turn to science to see if the body positivity movement is effectively contributing to women's healthy self-views.

Is Body Positive Content Really Body Positive?

The answer to this question is yes and no. First, the good news: A recent Instagram content analysis (Cohen et al., 2019) examined Instagram posts with the hashtag #bopo (i.e., a common abbreviation for body positivity) to determine how frequently the messaging supported the central tenets of body positivity, including defining beauty broadly, accepting or loving one's body, experiencing inner positivity, filtering and buffering the toxic effects of unrealistic images, investing in body care, and body appreciation. Cohen's team found that 80% of the posts they examined explicitly promoted at least one major theme that is central to body positive messaging. Similarly, a separate analysis of Instagram #bodypositivity posts by Lazuka and colleagues (2020) found that most posts supported one or several key themes of body positivity (e.g., 73% of posts messaged the theme of inner positivity).

The bad news is that some body positive content bears mixed messages, sometimes directly conflicting with body positivity themes or is otherwise problematic because of some conflicts of interest. Body image researchers have observed two primary tensions for body positive content, its body-centeredness and the degree of its commercialization (Rodgers et al., 2022). For example, Cohen and colleagues (2019) found that 41% of the #bopo content they examined on Instagram had an appearance-focused theme. As noted in Chapter 2, women who are especially invested in their appearance are at risk for poor body image (Jarry et al., 2019). Further, meta-analysis shows across multiple studies that images that push appearance ideals can affect women's body image in several damaging ways (de Valle et al., 2021).

Another problematic finding noted in these content analyses is that so-called body positive content often contains directly contradictory messages to the main themes of body positivity. Examples of these contradictions include posts that feature women in objectifying (or sexualized) ways, simultaneously promote the thin ideal, and disproportionately feature White and young women as well as women who generally conform to appearance-culture norms. Lazuka et al.'s (2020) analysis showed that only a minority of the body positive posts they examined featured women with larger bodies, which is not an accurate representation of the actual U.S. population. Lastly, several researchers have noted that many posts are motivated by commercialism, which calls into question the authenticity of their motivations and can hinder their benefit (Brathwaite & DeAndrea, 2022).

What about your own experiences of #bopo or other body positive content? Have you witnessed these tensions (or others) in the online content you have seen? We have encountered some of this content ourselves and have observed that it sometimes misses the mark of promoting "unconditional body acceptance," as noted by Rodgers et al. (2022, p. 370). With baggage like this, it is fair to ask whether women truly benefit psychologically from body positive content.

Does Body Positive Messaging Actually Help Body Image?

The body image science to date is fairly encouraging on this question. Based on the available evidence, it appears that body positive messaging does indeed have some real psychological benefits for women. For example, body image scientist Rachel Cohen and her colleagues (2019) found that participants who briefly viewed #bopo content on Instagram experienced boosts in their mood, satisfaction with their bodies, and increased feelings of body appreciation.

In fact, quite a few studies have shown that body esteem, body acceptance, body appreciation, body satisfaction, and even positive mood increase immediately after exposure to #bopo content. Initially, most studies that investigated the relationship between body positivity content and women's body image were *correlational*, meaning they only tell us about a relationship between body positivity and women's body image and cannot determine whether that relationship is a cause-and-effect one. These studies typically find small or medium-sized relationships between body positivity content exposure and positive body image. But it is impossible to rule out from these studies that women who already have a positive body image in the first place are more likely to be the ones who seek it out and in turn be affirmed and encouraged by it. Another limitation of this correlational research is that it is also possible (and likely) that other factors also impact participants' positive body image.

Experimental studies that measure the cause-and-effect relationship between body-positivity content and women's body image are beginning to accumulate, however, and once again, the evidence is mixed. Some studies have shown a limited impact of #bopo content on body image, but they did not measure impact past the immediate viewing of the content. One experiment showed that although #bopo increased positive mood, decreased negative mood, and increased body appreciation, it also increased self-objectification (Cohen et al., 2019). And then there are the fitspiration (#fitspo) images you may have encountered in your social scrolling. Research indicates that viewing fitspiration images can be harmful, as they increase both body dissatisfaction and bad mood (Tiggemann & Zaccardo, 2015).

Recently, however, Fardouly and colleagues (2023) showed that women exposed to body-positive content on Facebook three times daily for 2 weeks showed decreases in body dissatisfaction as well as appearance social comparisons across those 14 days; these decreases were still evident a month later, which is certainly good news. Interestingly, Fardouly and colleagues' experiment did not show an increase in self-objectification due to viewing body positive content, as the Cohen and colleagues (2019) experiment did. Unfortunately, women did not show increases in positive mood or body appreciation across the 2 weeks (Fardouly et al., 2023). Of course, we need to be cautious in drawing conclusions—this is only one study, and other findings differ. Perhaps a better route would be to spend time engaging with online content focused on things other than appearance or your body, more generally.

Healthy Body Image Building Tool

 Ever get the urge to pass a little time wading into celebrity culture? When print magazines were still popular, we both read fashion magazines, and one of us subscribed to a celebrity news magazine. Next time you are tempted to indulge in some celebrity culture, consider also taking a look at the Instagram account of Celeste Barber (@celestebarber). Her parody images of celebrities (#CelesteChallengeAccepted) are hilarious and wildly popular; one study suggests that when women view her parody posts alongside the celebrity thin-ideal photos, their mood and body satisfaction increase compared to when they view the thin-ideal photos alone (Slater et al., 2019). A good-natured spoof of the lengths women are expected to go to in compliance with body- and appearance-centered culture may do you good, according to this study.

DO THE RESEARCH FINDINGS ON BODY POSITIVE MESSAGING APPLY TO CHILDREN?

When we consider the research already discussed, it is tempting to apply the findings to young children; after all, we certainly want them to have positive attitudes about themselves! At present, unfortunately, very little research addresses the impact of body positivity messaging on developing children, so we cannot responsibly assume that what applies to adult women can or should be applied to children. The reason is that most research on body image has been conducted with college-age women, who have self-concepts that are developmentally different from those of children.

Children's self-concepts develop over the course of several years, and although most children express satisfaction with their bodies in early childhood, some do not—there are individual differences (Tatangelo et al., 2016). Body image has several different aspects, and it is unknown which aspects may be aided by messages about body positivity. Further, we do not know whether body-positive messages are helpful for maintaining or developing a healthy body image, and we do not know whether these messages can help to transform a negative body image to a more positive body image. As we noted previously, positive body image is not merely the opposite of negative body image—they are separate entities, and both are multi-faceted, but it is not clear at this point how exactly they develop.

Although it may seem that encouraging children to feel highly positive about their bodies could do no harm, some research suggests we should be cautious about being overly positive, particularly when we are trying to help children with their self-esteem. In a study by Brummelman and colleagues (2017), parents' inflated or excessive praise given to children while they were attempting to solve mathematics problems was associated with decreases in their children's self-esteem. This finding does not suggest that we should never praise our children and, to be sure, moderate amounts of realistic praise are a wonderful thing! The takeaway here is that we need to resist the tendency to apply what we know about adults directly to children without considering children's development on the whole. In Chapters 4 through 6, we look at the important ways children's cognitive and social abilities are still developing and the implications for how they think about their bodies.

BEYOND BODY POSITIVITY: FUNCTIONAL APPRECIATION AND BODY NEUTRALITY

For more than 10 years now, evidence has been mounting that when it comes to their bodies, it is better for women to concentrate on function rather than form. Body image experts have highlighted **functionality appreciation** as an important characteristic; although related to positive body image, functionality appreciation is distinct. This construct comes from the broad research on the topic of *body functionality*, a person's attitude about their body's physiological and psychological abilities (Alleva & Tylka, 2021). The thinking goes that focusing on what our bodies can do, rather than how they appear, is an important way to buffer ourselves from the harsh evaluations that result from comparing ourselves with unrealistic body ideals. Body appreciation has important psychological benefits, such as helping us to build a sense of agency and to develop social identities related to our body functioning; it also has physical benefits because it promotes self-care and participation in enjoyable physical activities that are related to body movement. From this area of body image science, we can draw the conclusion that a woman's appreciation and respect for her body's functioning is another key component for building healthy body image.

> **Functionality appreciation:** appreciation for the body's many capabilities, including physical abilities, internal processes, creative processes, as well as social and communication abilities (Alleva & Tylka, 2021).

Healthy Body Image Building Tool

 When was the last time you took a moment to really appreciate all your body can do? Have you ever had a moment where you were proud of something impressive your body did? Awestruck, even? Running a half marathon and giving birth are two examples that may come to mind. Not to sound trite, but we really are stronger than we know! Whether engaging in extraordinary feats or everyday functions, we owe our bodies a pat on the back and an "attagirl" for the ways they serve us well. In the hustle and bustle of our busy schedules, we can easily forget this, only to be reminded when we are sidelined with an injury or illness. If you are interested in seeing how appreciative you are of your body's functionality, check out some of the sample items from the Functionality Appreciation Scale (Alleva et al., 2017) in Table 1.1. New or renewed appreciation for all our bodies do is a wonderful way to build a healthier body image! If you would like to read more about how you can appreciate the functionality of your body, we recommend checking out the book *More Than a Body: Your Body Is an Instrument, Not an Ornament,* which offers helpful ways women can build resilience against our culture's appearance focus (see the Recommended Resources section at the end of the chapter).

Another social movement growing in influence is **body neutrality.** Similar to the functionality appreciation argument, those promoting body neutrality claim that, whether positive or negative, excessive focus on feelings about the body can be toxic. Currently, there is not enough science to draw strong conclusions about its effect on body image, but the focus on neutrality does represent a pivot away from body positivity.

> **Body neutrality:** a multidimensional view of the body that is realistic, mindful, and flexible; this perspective focuses on the functionality of the body and does not define self-worth by appearance (Pellizzer & Wade, 2023). Note that some researchers (Wood-Barcalow et al., 2024) view body neutrality as one part of positive body image.

Further, some indirect evidence lends insight. For example, one commonly used method in studies of positive body image is to show women photos and then measure their body dissatisfaction levels. In studies that use this method, some women see a photo that supports the cultural thin ideal, some see a photo that is more representative of real women, and some see a photo that does not include people but is simply of nature or some inanimate object (i.e., non–appearance related). Several of the studies have found that in-the-moment body dissatisfaction is lower among women who see the inanimate or non–appearance-related content (Groesz et al., 2002; Salomon & Brown, 2021). This finding provides indirect support that images of bodies, whether positive or negative, stoke some level of body dissatisfaction. Similarly, a review of 35 studies examining the impact of body positive social media content concluded from the evidence that some of the most helpful body positive content did not involve images of other people (Rodgers et al., 2021). This finding may reflect the fact that social comparison is a strong tendency, and even well-intentioned posts can trigger body dissatisfaction by way of unfavorable social comparison. From this area of research on body image, we can draw the conclusion that the most helpful messages about body image may be ones that do not feature photographs of people. Importantly, though, we note that by "neutrality," we do not mean that women should avoid information about their bodies, whether this means getting weighed or looking in the mirror; instead, we mean that women should practice choosing to reduce evaluative thoughts, whether positive or negative. As noted by Dr. Mark Leary, we do not have to give credence to every thought that comes to mind (Leary, 2004).

TRANSLATING THE SCIENCE INTO PRACTICE: OUR PERSPECTIVE

The body-positivity approach has some important strengths and benefits for taking a healthier perspective on one's body—especially when compared to the toxicity of the perpetual diet culture many of us grew up in. The following list presents some key conclusions from the research. These conclusions have become important components of our approach to helping your daughter build a healthy body image.

- Respect for the body is indisputably healthy, so body respect is a key feature of building healthy body image.
- Choosing to reject unrealistic appearance ideals is a vital component of a healthy self-view.
- Surrounding ourselves with people who are accepting of our bodies, limiting our participation in toxic social scripts (such as fat talk), appreciating our best characteristics, and, when possible, choosing to avoid comparing ourselves with other bodies are all unquestionably sound practices for building a healthy body image.
- Appreciating the essential functions of our bodies and adopting neutral body attitudes are helpful and proactive goals.

All told, the body image research on positivity and neutrality offers valuable tools for building healthy body image. But women can do more, and other structural components are needed as well. These components stand out clearly when you think about a little girl you love. What makes this little girl beautiful has little to do with her appearance or body; rather, her beauty is primarily defined by all the personal qualities of who she is. What if she could love herself like that? What if we could love ourselves like that? That is not to say naively that body image does not matter; on the contrary, it is very important for women. *But as women, we have the power individually to make appearance matter less, to lessen its importance just as we automatically and naturally do when we think about her.*

In our view, elevating the importance of other aspects of our self-identity relative to our bodies' appearance and investing in our appearance with proportion and balance are active strategies worth considering for building a healthy self-perspective. Coming alongside our developing girls and encouraging them to implement these same strategies is even better.

Based on the research findings, we build on each of the approaches we have highlighted in this chapter to suggest a new framework for healthy body image. Consistent with research on positive body image, we think it is unreasonable to expect that all women love their bodies, but rather they should foster respect of the body. We agree with the functionality appreciation (Alleva & Tylka, 2021) point that people should appreciate all that their bodies can do, but this continues to focus excessive attention on the body, and the body is only one aspect of the overall self. Perhaps it is time for women to prevent body image from taking up a disproportionate and unhealthy amount of mental space.

Like the neutrality perspective (Pellizzer & Wade, 2023), we suggest deprioritizing the time and attention paid to body appearance and instead redirecting focus to other values, goals, and behaviors. We do not mean, however, that women should neglect their bodies. In our view, taking responsibility for how we treat our bodies is an important aspect of body respect and body functionality appreciation. Regardless of body shape, size, weight, or body mass index, we endorse the development of consistent health behaviors such as getting regular movement, keeping a healthy sleep schedule, managing stress, and eating in a balanced way that is enjoyable and sustainable.

Importantly, we argue that this process should begin early in development to be most effective and that it requires you to partner with your daughter by modeling for her your management of your own healthy body attitudes and behaviors. The earlier you can start the better, but truly it is not too late at any age, during childhood or beyond, to make positive changes! If your daughter is anywhere between 3 and 10 years old, the age-appropriate developmental guidance in Chapters 4 through 6 will give you the tools you need to come alongside your daughter and effectively help her build a healthy body image. In our view, a woman can actively build her own healthy body image. You are the manager. Instead of being merely the passive recipient of cultural influences, you can actively choose cognitive strategies, make decisions, and manage your own physical and psychological best interests. You take in information from peers and culture, medical professionals, and mental health experts; you weigh the pros and cons and decide what is best for you and your body personally. It is a thoughtful and intentional process.

This view suggests that it may be best for one woman to engage with body positivity content, while it may be better for another woman to emphasize the functionality of her body. One woman may find body neutrality messaging to be the right perspective for her well-being; another may decide she wants to change her body's size or shape in a healthy way. One size does not fit all, and no single body image perspective works equally well for all.

Healthy Body Image Building Tool

 Think of yourself in the active role of manager of your own body image; you may want to review the Twenty Statements Test (Kuhn & McPartland, 1954) recommended in Chapter 2. Then, take a moment to craft a brief mission statement for your body image. Many free online sources are available to help you; the point is to articulate what you want your body image to be about (i.e., the specific goals, principles, or values that define it). You may even consider what your vision is for your self-concept and how your body image fits into it. You can articulate a vision statement if you find it helpful.

Taking an active role in managing our self-concept and body image involves making sure one aspect of the self-concept (such as weight or appearance) does not eclipse the importance of all others. It also involves balancing the health decisions for the body that is under one's care and making responsible choices. Considering your own health in a holistic way, you are in charge of drawing conclusions for your own body image— well-informed and with intention.

On a related note, we do not believe that it is fully possible or even advisable to reject all cultural prescriptions for body and health. People have a basic psychological need for belongingness and acceptance. As noted in Chapter 2, we are fundamentally social creatures, and inclusion and acceptance matter to us all, to some more than to others, and that is perfectly normal. Because of the range of individual differences in social motives and concerns, it seems unreasonable to apply a uniform instruction to all women to reject conformity to all social conventions regarding appearance. Social psychological research suggests that there will always be a tension between the desire to reject cultural ideals and the desire to conform to them. It is the role of each woman to determine what is best for her personally, thinking about how best to approach her mutual ambitions of fitting in and maintaining a healthy, individual self, and modeling this approach for her daughter as well.

PUTTING IT ALL TOGETHER: PRACTICAL TIPS FOR MOMS

In this chapter we have presented the essential features of the body positivity perspective, highlighted important research support and limitations of this perspective, and described our own body-healthy approach. Key takeaway points include the following:

- **Practice respect for your body.** One way you can show respect for your body is to acknowledge that you don't always view yourself optimally but you can be intentional about respecting your body in the ways you care for it, think about it, and talk about it.
- **Strive for balance in your health behaviors.** You can both indulge in your favorite foods and intentionally pursue fitness; you can acknowledge current strengths and areas for growth in your health and well-being.
- **Resist excessive focus on and evaluation of appearance and bodies.** You can choose to redirect your thoughts and attention to other important personal and social goals, and you can practice redirecting until it becomes habitual.
- **Take an active role in managing your own body image.** You do not have to passively accept or follow one-size-fits-all recommendations or memes. Rather, you can choose which information you attend to, which standards you adhere to, and which health goals you want to pursue.

In the Appendix, we provide companion activities to help you reflect on important concepts if you are interested in doing so. These supplemental activities are meant to be helpful or insightful; they are completely optional, of course!

- Activity 3: Who Will She Become? Wishes for Your Daughter's Future

Recommended Resources

Hobbs, L. M., & Balentine, A. C. (2023). *The self-compassion workbook for kids: Fun mindfulness activities to build emotional strength and make kindness your superpower.* Instant Help.

Kite, L., & Kite, L. (2021). *More than a body: Your body is an instrument, not an ornament.* Harvest.

CHAPTER 4

YOUR DAUGHTER'S BODY IMAGE IN EARLY CHILDHOOD: AGES 3 THROUGH 4 YEARS

Imagine this interaction between 3-year-old Emily and her mother, Sarah, at lunchtime. Sarah serves Emily one of her regular lunches, along with a glass of milk. But Emily is not interested; she shakes her head and blurts out "Diet!" Sarah springs to attention with surprise and concern, wondering where she has gone so wrong in her parenting that her preschooler is already interested in dieting. Now that she thinks about it, Sarah has noticed that Emily has used the word "fat" to describe people and that Emily sometimes makes comments about her own and others' physical appearance. She also recalls Emily's puzzlement at dinnertime when everyone in the family eats the same thing except for Mommy. Sarah is silent for a few seconds, trying to decide how she should respond, when Emily again declares, "I want a diet!" and points directly at Sarah. Sarah looks down, only to realize that Emily is referring to the can of diet cola that Sarah has been sipping. Sarah feels relieved; Emily is simply curious about the drink that she has seen Mommy sipping many times. And although Sarah is relieved, she begins to wonder, "Does Emily think about her body yet? If so, what does she think?"

   In this chapter, we dig into what is known about development and body image in early childhood, specifically, 3- to 4-year-old girls. We start by covering the major milestones of cognitive, emotional, and social development that describe girls in this age group to show how girls think about key topics related to body image and how to talk with them about these topics in an age-appropriate way. Then, we look at what research has shown about 3- and 4-year-olds' body image and cover the main influences on their body image at this age.

It is important to note that studying young children is messy—it relies on the development of methods that girls will understand, and the measures are often adapted from research with women. Researchers such as Paxton and Damiano (2017) and Smolak (2004) have rightfully encouraged caution in interpreting the findings. No study provides all the answers, but patterns across studies can be used to increase confidence about the findings. And despite questions about the extent to which very young children experience body image problems, we take the stance that any amount is too much.

Next, we discuss your role in your daughter's body image development, along with considering cultural impacts on body image. These considerations will start to make you aware of how outside influences can lead you to experience troublesome thoughts, feelings, and behaviors. Throughout the chapter, we provide healthy body image building tips for you to consider when communicating with your daughter. We end the chapter by directing you toward some collaborative activities and potential talking points with your daughter that will help you establish the groundwork for a healthy body image.

THREE THINGS TO REMEMBER AS YOU READ ABOUT CHILD DEVELOPMENT

One of the most remarkable features of young children is that they are highly perceptive one minute and utterly naïve the next. Taking a moment to unpack the scenario between Emily and Sarah, we highlight three general points about child development that will inform how we approach body image development.

First, as we have already discussed, developmental systems theory describes how individuals—children and adults—are embedded in a large cultural system and set of subsystems (workplace, households) that affect daily life. These systems change in importance at different points in the lifespan; in early childhood, the *microsystem* (i.e., the child's immediate surroundings) is the most influential. And although fathers certainly can and do influence their daughters' body image, you, as her mother, are the main influence on your daughter.

Second, even if it is not terribly surprising, it is worth reminding ourselves that children absorb information from us even when we do not teach them directly and even when we do not want them to do so. Raise your hand if you have ever been embarrassed when your child publicly blurted out a curse word seemingly out of nowhere. Of course, it did not come from nowhere; she heard it from someone around her, and perhaps it was you! This situation is common, so there is no need to fret about it; this type of **observational learning** is a major driver of children's development. Emily's interest in diet cola comes from hearing her mother mention it, seeing her mother drink it, and desiring to imitate her mother's behavior.

> **Observational learning:** learning from observing others and modeling their behavior (Bandura, 1989).

Third, although child development is straightforward in some ways, the vignette that opens the chapter shows that we cannot assume children use or understand words in the same way adults do. To communicate effectively with our girls, we need to understand their developmental level. In the example, Emily referred to diet soda, attempting to mimic her mother's behavior, but she showed no indication that she wanted to go on a diet. Research has shown that before age 5, children do not fully understand the meaning of the word "diet" (Holub et al., 2005). Altogether, the vignette about Emily and Sarah shows the value of taking a scientific perspective on body image. Mothers can meet girls at their developmental level and tailor our discussions and parenting approach so that they are effective.

WHY START IN EARLY CHILDHOOD? AREN'T 3-YEAR-OLDS TOO YOUNG TO LEARN ABOUT BODY IMAGE?

If 3- and 4-year-olds do not even know what "diet" means, why is it so important to start talking about body image at this early age? Aren't children at this age engaged in a carefree world of pretense and fantasy? Yes—they sure are—as any parent with a child who watches Paw Patrol and enacts her own adventures with real or stuffed animals knows. And if you have never really thought about body image as a major concern in children quite this young, you are not alone. Research reveals that parents often think about body image as important in pre-adolescence and adolescence (Hart et al., 2015) and that most parents do not discuss or attempt to influence body image in their preschoolers despite reporting that their children receive multiple messages about weight and body image even at this early age (Liechty et al., 2016). Avoidance of the topic of body image is likely due, in part, to what some scientists call "age of innocence" beliefs—beliefs that we should leave well enough alone during this time and that we need only address an issue if it becomes a problem. But this approach is shortsighted; parents want to prevent problems from starting in the first place.

Young children show specific patterns of thinking, feeling, and behaving that clue you into how you can promote healthy body image development. And it is important to recognize that girls are growing up in a landscape quite different from the one many of their mothers experienced: easy access and increased exposure to television, the internet, and many forms of media culture. All these outside sources come with an abundance of messages targeted toward dieting, exercise, and body image. Have you noticed any body image messages in the television shows that you have watched with your daughter? For example, taking a close look at the Paw Patrol (Dodge et al., 2013–present) team, you may notice that the two girl dog characters have eyelashes, whereas the boy dogs do not. The girl dogs also have lusher hair, and their hair is featured more prominently than the hair of the boy dogs. These differences may seem entirely trivial, but it's important to understand that they communicate subtle nonverbal messages about societal ideals for feminine beauty. One such message may not have impact but imagine the effect of thousands of such messages over the span of childhood.

Young children gain knowledge quickly, and they are open to what they see and hear around them. When children are 3 or 4 years old, the underpinnings of a negative body image are seen mostly in girls' thoughts and feelings about themselves and less so in their behavior. For example, girls may show dissatisfaction with their bodies, but they are highly unlikely to be dieting because parents and other guardians plan, prepare, and serve most of their meals. Even when we shelter 3- and 4-year-olds relative to older children, they still see plenty of thin-ideal models—in toys, television, and movies and in conversations that are about them or that involve them directly. Because body dissatisfaction, weight bias, and negative stereotypes about weight are linked with unhealthy thoughts and behaviors as children get older, it is important to address them early. The next section addresses what is happening in the minds of 3- and 4-year-olds.

COGNITIVE, EMOTIONAL, AND SOCIAL DEVELOPMENT IN EARLY CHILDHOOD

To effectively communicate healthy body messages in an age-appropriate way, it is necessary to understand how 3- and 4-year-old girls think. In this section, we review some of the relevant general milestones of preschoolers' development to help guide interactions with them around body image specifically.

Self-Concept: "Who Am I?"

If someone asked you, as an adult, to describe yourself in a few sentences, what is the first thing you would say (e.g., refer to the Twenty Statements Test in Chapter 2)? One guiding force that shapes how and what we think about ourselves is the self-concept (Collyer et al., 2018; see also Chapter 2). The self-concept is crucial for our health and well-being because it influences how we feel and behave, how we present ourselves to others, and in turn how others view and treat us. An important aspect of the self-concept is that it is dynamic; it can change throughout our lives based on our experiences and interactions with others (Demo, 1992). Young children's self-concept is open to change as their cognitive abilities increase and their social circles and other influences expand over time. Because of this flexibility, early childhood is an excellent time to set the stage for healthy thinking about the self.

By 3 years of age, children have a *categorical self* well in place. They understand that they are their own person and can describe themselves in basic ways, often using new categories they are learning (Collyer et al., 2018). For example, a child might say, "I am a girl. I am 3 years old. I have brown hair." During the early preschool years, children's self-descriptions focus on things that they like or dislike, things that they do (i.e., behaviors), and the way that they look rather than internal qualities such as personality type; these descriptions also change often because children are rapidly absorbing new information and gaining language skills.

Relative to older children, 3- and 4-year-olds generally feel good about themselves, in part because they do not have a realistic sense of their abilities, and they do not yet compare themselves meaningfully to other children. They have not yet been exposed to many of the social and cultural influences that await as they experience more of the world around them. Although this elevated level of positivity makes children sound irrational, it is a good thing developmentally—it enables them to feel capable of building skills (Boseovski, 2010). Likely due to this positivity, some studies have reported only a trivial difference between boys' and girls' liking of their own appearance at this age, with very young girls reporting higher regard for their own appearance than boys in some cases (Marsh et al., 2002). However, with increasing age, girls rapidly begin to express greater body dissatisfaction and lower **body appreciation** than boys. So, it is important to encourage girls to develop a broad self-concept that is not centered wholly on their physical appearance beginning early in life.

> **Body appreciation:** a component of body image that captures positive opinions, acceptance, and respect for the body. Importantly, body appreciation is not the opposite of body dissatisfaction. For example, an individual can have high body dissatisfaction and high body appreciation at the same time (Tylka & Wood-Barcalow, 2015a).

Healthy Body Image Building Tool

 Expand her categorical self. It is perfectly fine to tell little girls that they are pretty and to praise their physical appearance from time to time, but we want to start emphasizing other characteristics often and early in life. Focus on her behaviors, including her hobbies, interests, and accomplishments. Point out her personal characteristics in simple terms that are action oriented (e.g., "You are a great helper!"). You may not feel comfortable asking family members to refrain from commenting on your daughter's physical appearance, and that's okay. If that's the case, consider enlisting them to help you build your daughter's confidence and character by making her interests and achievements a focal point of the conversation. For example, you might say something like "You know, I am trying to build Amy's confidence with numbers right now, and I would love your help. Maybe you could ask her about the counting worksheet that she finished the other day and have her show it to you?" This type of statement provides a nonconfrontational way to direct attention away from her physical appearance and to show family members that you want them to be involved in your daughter's life. Activity 4 in the Appendix, **Walk and Talk With Mother Nature,** allows you to implement some of these ideas about self-concept development.

Gender Identity: Sugar and Spice and Everything Nice?

Girls have a sense of gender identity—most of them relate to other girls and to adult women—that is stable by about 4 years of age (Leaper, 2015). At this age, children tend to embrace **gender essentialism:** They tend to believe that all girls share an underlying quality that makes them girls (Meyer & Gelman, 2016). Gender identity also develops in large part from information that girls receive in the different environments in which they participate, ranging from their homes to the cultures and societies in which they live (i.e., from the microsystem to the macrosystem). Beginning early in life, girls are exposed to social norms and expectations for how they should look. For example, wearing bows and dresses and polishing nails is normative or expected for young girls but less so for boys. Girls also receive messages, whether direct or indirect, about how they should behave and what we expect of them in terms of **gender roles.** For example, whether knowingly or unknowingly, we might scold girls for talking loudly or engaging in horseplay that is deemed perfectly acceptable for boys of the same age, and we might buy them different toys—play kitchens for girls and Legos for boys.

Gender essentialism: the belief that inborn, biological qualities explain the differences between women and men. These qualities are thought to be stable and unchangeable (Meyer & Gelman, 2016).

Gender roles: "the pattern of behavior, personality traits, and attitudes that define gender in a particular culture" (American Psychological Association, n.d.).

The focus on girls' appearance also begins incredibly early; researchers have found that parents use more appearance-related terms to describe their girl infants (e.g., "She's delicate") than their boy infants ("He's strong"; Karraker et al., 1995). These kinds of labels can set up a situation in which we are effectively telling girls that their appearance matters most, and this message may be even more striking for girls who have male siblings. At the same time, we are setting standards for what is considered acceptable, attractive, and feminine. Although these kinds of descriptions may seem harmless, especially in isolation, the use of gender-stereotyped language can affect how children interpret everything from the suitability of colors (Yeung & Wong, 2018) to the suitability of activities for girls as compared to boys (Martin et al., 1995). So, we need to be mindful of what kinds of attitudes and stereotypes we convey about gender that may affect girls' body image development. Moms' behaviors are especially influential on the ideas that girls develop about gender and what is appropriate for girls. For example, girls pay attention to everything from who does the household chores to child care to appearance-based behaviors. Does your home have defined roles for men and boys that are different from the roles for women and girls? These distinct roles are not "right" or "wrong," but importantly, they shape a girl's ideas and expectations about roles she will or should fill when she is older.

Finally, the language used to describe children's behavior or preferences can affect how children view what is appropriate for their gender. In a study with 3-year-olds, researchers found that parents who used generic statements that define people as a group rather than as individuals assumed that those group members were all very similar (Pronovost & Scott, 2022). For instance, when we say that "girls like ballet," we define all girls as a group. This labeling promotes essentialist thinking rather than the consideration of individual differences among girls (Rhodes et al., 2018).

Healthy Body Image Building Tool

 Go beyond traditional gender boundaries. Expose your daughter to a variety of toys and activities; begin to challenge the idea that there are girl toys and boy toys and hobbies. Use descriptions specific to individuals rather than those that suggest that groups of girls or boys are the same (e.g., "This girl likes ballet" instead of "Girls like ballet") and point out the commonalities among genders. Focus on the ways that your daughter shows strength and independence in her behavior and point them out by talking about her behavior. Note that it is perfectly fine if your daughter happens to enjoy traditionally feminine activities—the goal at this age is to show her what is possible and to open her mind to the idea that girls do not need to conform to societal expectations of "sugar and spice." You play a key role in creating your daughter's ideas about gender by the environment you create: your roles, activities, and behaviors as compared to a male partner or spouse (e.g., division of labor, such as laundry and washing dishes; division of child care such as feeding). Consider your behaviors and use chores and other duties as a chance to expand across gender lines. Although these everyday activities may not seem like a big deal now, the messaging can compound over time. To apply some of these ideas, see Activity 5, **Toy Test Lab**, in the Appendix.

Moral Development: When Everything Is Good or Bad

Think for a moment about the many books you have read and movies you have seen with your daughter. In many of them, the heroes are "good" or "nice," and the villains are "bad" or "mean." Few characters can be described as "in between." Correspondingly, the good or nice heroes are typically physically attractive, whereas the bad or mean villains are typically physically unattractive. So, even in children's media, we create a false association between moral goodness and physical attractiveness. If a girl does not perceive herself as physically attractive, which is very common in a climate of social media filters and airbrushing, she may also see herself as a bad person. In fact, one of the first ways that children learn to describe people and things is in broad categories that are largely positive or largely negative (Alvarez et al., 2001; Boseovski & Lee, 2006). And beginning early in life, children have a keen sense of morality (Killen & Smetana, 2015). They understand the basic idea of fairness, label actions correctly as right or wrong, and can identify when they have been bad (when hitting a sibling) or good (when cleaning up their toys). Children also understand that their behavior often has consequences, whether positive or negative.

Categorizing the world makes it easier to absorb information, and the development of a broad moral compass is, of course, a desirable and positive milestone for children. But seeing people and things in the world as exclusively good or bad can also set up children for unhealthy ways of thinking. For example, our daughters may misbehave on occasion, but that does not make them bad people. How does this way of thinking relate to body image development? When we knowingly or unknowingly idealize certain body shapes or sizes as good, we may set up the corresponding belief that other body shapes or sizes are bad, and this is exactly the type of messaging that we want to avoid. As discussed later in the chapter, research has shown that even young children have negative impressions about people who are overweight, and these impressions extend to their personal attributes, such as the assumption that they are lazy. These ideas can become internalized, or applied to themselves over time. These biases are even more likely to happen if these negative impressions come from family members.

Similarly, when we describe food in absolute ways—"That's bad; don't eat it!"—we promote beliefs that could ultimately lead to unhealthy feelings and behaviors. For example, girls may develop the impression that they cannot allow themselves any treats because girls must "be good." For adult women, this way of thinking leads to guilt and shame about eating, and it can result in a cycle of restricting and bingeing behaviors. So, we also need to think about how we talk with our daughters about the properties of food, which is discussed in the next section.

Healthy Body Image Building Tool

 Broaden your use of descriptions beyond positive and negative, and avoid describing people or characteristics of people as wholly good or bad. When talking about bodies and physical appearance, it is important to avoid evaluative terms, verbal tones, and gestures that result in associating positive or negative internal characteristics with specific body shapes or sizes. Instead, point out that bodies are simply different from one another for lots of reasons; there is no better or worse body. See the Appendix for Activity 6, which involves reading the book *Shapesville* with your daughter. This book encourages the appreciation of body diversity, as recommended by Dohnt and Tiggemann (2008).

Thoughts and Feelings About Food: You Are Not What You Eat

It can be difficult to separate our experience with food from our feelings about our bodies. After all, our eating behaviors can affect our body size, physical appearance, and health and well-being. Perhaps even more important, we develop ideas about eating, whether correct or incorrect, that relate to how we feel about our bodies. For example, we might believe that we should eat breakfast every morning to have energy or that it is appropriate to eat certain foods, such as desserts, only on special occasions or not at all so that we do not gain weight. As discussed, for many women, food choices are connected to morality: "I was bad—I had two pieces of chocolate cake!" or "I was good today—I had a salad for lunch." This way of thinking can cause problems because it is associated with guilt and shame around the necessary and enjoyable act of eating, and it sets up the false expectation that we must eat in certain ways to feel worthy. Put simply, we should never tie what we eat to our worth as people.

Because the way we think about food matters to body image and health behavior, it is important to understand how food ideas develop. Our surroundings affect the way that we think about food. Due to the strong influence of the microsystems in which 3- and 4-year-olds are embedded, children are not independent in their food choices at this age and instead rely on what they can access or receive in the home, at their day care, or at preschool. Mothers have been described as the main gatekeepers of their children's access to food (Wijayaratne et al., 2022), and they are the most influential when it comes to diet at this age.

One challenge that parents face with children in the early preschool years is the emergence of picky eating and **food neophobia,** the fear of eating unfamiliar foods, which can affect children's willingness to eat foods that are nutritious and in turn reduce the quality of their diet. If your child engages in picky eating, it may help to know that multiple attempts at introducing new or unfamiliar foods are often necessary to reduce children's reluctance to try these foods. Your reactions can also affect your child's willingness to try a novel food. For example, declaring that a food is yummy, instead of attempting to force a child to eat it, may result in an increased desire for your child to try it. That said, the influence of peers on eating behavior is even stronger than that of adults. In one study, children were more likely to want to try food that a peer ate than one an adult ate, and they preferred food eaten by a same-gender child (Frazier et al., 2012). You might be able to use this kind of information to nudge your child to try new foods (e.g., "Your friend Brianna liked this a lot!"). We realize that these strategies take patience, resources (because it can result in the waste of food that goes untouched), and a whole lot of time that you may not have as a busy parent who is trying to get it all done. Because this topic goes beyond the scope of this book, we encourage you to see your child's pediatrician if challenges with eating are an ongoing concern for you and your daughter. If you are interested in more information about this topic, see the Recommended Resources section at the end of this chapter.

> **Food neophobia:** the fear of eating unfamiliar foods. It can affect diet in terms of both the type and the amount of food that a child eats. See Firme et al. (2023).

In addition to the influence of parents and peers, children receive an abundance of messages about food from the culture, or macro-system. Even toddlers are bombarded with targeted advertising—on television, on the internet, and in public spaces such as playgrounds—that promotes foods that are high in fat, sugar, and sodium (American Psychological Association, 2010). Have you ever noticed the placement of candy in the grocery store? It is often positioned at children's eye level at the checkout, and it can be very difficult to say "no" when you are trying to settle your bill and get out of the store quickly while your child is tugging incessantly at your sleeve.

The Centers for Disease Control and Prevention have emphasized the importance of setting the stage for healthy eating early in life. Childhood obesity rates have increased dramatically over the past several decades, and obesity is associated with numerous health risks (Centers for Disease Control and Prevention, 2022a). Of course, there is substantial variation in healthy body sizes—some people have naturally smaller bodies and others have naturally larger bodies. For this reason, it is important to go beyond metrics such as weight and body mass index (BMI) in considering your child's health profile, as assessed by a trusted health care provider. It is also important to appreciate the premise that a healthy body image does not rely solely on what or how we eat. We are worthwhile regardless of what we eat and regardless of our body shape. That said, it is possible to encourage both healthy eating behaviors and healthy body image if we are intentional about it, particularly if we begin to do so at an early age.

Considering the influence of parents, children's personal feelings and experiences, and the content that children absorb from the media, what do 3- and 4-year-olds actually know about food? Children in this age group have a basic understanding that they need food for growth (Schultz & Danford, 2021). Studies of children's understanding of the nutritional value of food have shown that children can correctly label foods as "healthy" or "junky" (Nguyen & McCullough, 2009) and can classify foods into basic categories (fruits, vegetables). This ability continues to improve with age (DeJesus, Kinzler, & Shutts, 2018).

Although young children can identify what is healthy, they are less able to identify what is unhealthy (Tatlow-Golden et al., 2013). It is also clear that children do not necessarily use their knowledge about what is healthy to consider what kinds of food they should eat. In a study in which researchers designated 3- to 5-year-olds as a doll's "caregiver" who would help the doll to stay healthy, only about one third of the children selected healthy foods for the doll, and over half served soda to the doll on request (Wiseman et al., 2016). This finding may strike you as predictable and more than familiar: Even as adults, we often make choices that we might consider to be less healthy or inconsistent with our nutritional goals despite the best of intentions. For adults, these inconsistencies between what we know we should do and what we actually do can result in negative emotions such as guilt or shame. In contrast, by children at this age, these behaviors are thought to simply reflect age-typical cognitive limitations and do not appear to result in negative emotions.

As girls' knowledge base about food develops, it is important to consider the attitudes that we show them about food. Strong messages about the value of foods as positive or negative begin early (Norton et al., 2023). As noted earlier in the chapter, moralization of foods is something that we want to avoid. Having a healthy body image means that we do not see individual instances of eating for pleasure, rather than nutrition, as good or bad.

Healthy Body Image Building Tool

 Take a neutral stance when you talk about food rather than talking about specific foods as good or bad. Instead, focus on whether the food might be appropriate in terms of timing. Be responsive to your child's satiety cues (i.e., when she reports that she is hungry or full) rather than rigid about how much or how little she should eat. Aim to include a variety of foods in your child's diet so that food with less nutritional value is not off limits (excluding allergies or intolerances, of course). Emphasizing that different foods can be enjoyed and appreciated at different times is protective because it removes the tendency to make a connection between what we eat and how we should feel about our bodies and ourselves more generally. To apply some of these ideas, see Activity 7, **Fun-Filled Foods**, in the Appendix.

Thoughts and Feelings About the Body: A Focus on Function, Not Form

Body image is not just about how we see our physical appearance; it also involves our understanding and appreciation of what our bodies do for us. An important part of building a healthy body image involves understanding the functions of the body. After all, our bodies are here to serve us for the activities and challenges of daily living, not to be treated as decorations. But it is easy to lose sight of this fact in a world in which girls and women are flooded with images of idealized bodies and countless products and plans to get us closer to a supposedly "ideal" body that is sold to us as our main priority in life. Taking a health-behavior approach means we foster behaviors that keep us healthy, strong, and capable of what we need and want to be doing. In turn, this approach fuels a healthy body image.

Even young children are surprisingly savvy about their bodies. They understand that people need food and water to stay alive (Schultz & Danford, 2021). They understand that certain behaviors are important for health, such as avoiding sick people who are contagious (Kalish, 1997) and refusing contaminated food (e.g., rejecting the idea of drinking milk in which a cockroach had been placed; Siegal, 1988). Three- and 4-year-olds know that there are biological limits to what the body can do—people cannot stay awake forever, hang from a tree limb forever, or grow to their preferred height simply because they would like to do so (Schult & Wellman, 1997).

An important part of understanding body functionality is to appreciate the role of movement in keeping our bodies healthy. And although we do not want 3- and 4-year-olds to have formal exercise regimens by any means, we want to pay attention to how they think about movement at this age so that we can promote an appreciation for its importance both for body image and general health. In fact, researchers have identified the preschool years as an ideal time to encourage physical play habits (Wiseman et al., 2016), and health guidelines specify that children in this age group should be active throughout their day when they are not sleeping.

How do children feel about activity and moving their bodies? Although it is difficult to monitor precise patterns of activity at this age, research indicates that as a group, preschoolers are quite sedentary and tend not to participate in vigorous physical activity; additionally, young boys are more active than young girls are (M. Oliver et al., 2007). Some children name physically active behaviors when asked about the kind of things they like to do at home and at school; other children focus on electronic media (Lanigan, 2011). Research also shows that children cannot easily distinguish between active and sedentary behaviors on their own. For example, preschoolers are as likely to name drawing or reading as health-related activities as they are to choose kicking a ball or skipping. Attention to safety and discomfort (cold or rainy weather) may also affect children's impressions about activity and their desire to participate in movement. In one study, children who were asked to select healthy activities for a doll stated that they wanted to protect the doll from rain (Lanigan, 2011). The preference for movement or the reluctance to engage in movement is associated in part with—you guessed it—parents' attitudes and behaviors. In general, children whose parents participate in physical activity are more likely to participate in physical activity themselves (Petersen et al., 2020).

Healthy Body Image Building Tool

Focus on what the body can do in simple ways and talk about how bodies are made for movement. At this early age, most children are not ready to engage in organized sports activities, and this type of structure is not even necessary. Hopping, skipping, using playground equipment, and going for walks as a family all count as activity. Emphasize how good you feel when you move your bodies—make it fun! We recognize that giving your daughter free rein in activities can be scary. What parent has not panicked after seeing their child face-plant after a fall from the monkey bars? Use your judgment—you know your child best—but try to promote safety while avoiding excessive warnings about potential harm from activities that your child enjoys. Consider sharing your appreciation of your body's functionality with your daughter by reading together the children's book *Her Body Can!* by Ady Meschke and Katie Crenshaw. See also Activity 8, **My Miraculous Moving Body**, and Activity 9, **Celebration Station**, in the Appendix.

Body Image

Up to this point, we have covered key developmental milestones in this age group, many of which relate to body image development (such as ideas about one's personal characteristics, how the body works, and what people should eat). We now turn to what is known about girls' emerging body image at this age. It is likely that you have already heard your daughter engage in body talk. Researchers have suggested that children begin to develop a thinness **schema** in early childhood. Girls form ideas about appearance, body weight, and dieting in relation to cultural expectations about what they should look like (Smolak, 2004).

> Schema: a mental framework that we use to filter, organize, and interpret information around us. Schemas determine what we pay attention to, and they develop based on our experience, including what we observe around us and our interactions with other people.

How does this schema show up in the everyday life of preschoolers? You may be surprised (and disheartened) to learn that it is already operating quite powerfully. By 3 years of age, children understand the difference between the words "thin" and "fat," and they associate fatness with negative characteristics such as sadness, illness, and having no friends (Worobey & Worobey, 2014). Research by Peretz-Lange and Kibbe (2024) reveals that preschoolers readily categorize people of the same weight as having similar internal qualities—more so than those of the same race.

Weight bias also extends to the toys with which children play. For example, girls prefer thin dolls over fat dolls. Depending on your age, you may remember the Emme doll. Emme was created as a body-positive "plus-size" doll who had body proportions that were supposed to represent what most women look like in American society. Her appearance was a stark contrast to the famously unachievable proportions of the Barbie doll. The intentions of the creators of Emme were good, but nonetheless Emme did not fare well against Barbie. Girls did not express an interest in playing with Emme. In fact, young girls see thin dolls as prettier, healthier, and as having more friends than an average or chubby doll, and they are more likely to state a preference to be friends with a thin or average doll than a chubby doll (Musher-Eizenman et al., 2004). That said, a good deal of time has passed since researchers conducted these studies. It is possible that girls now have more positive views of dolls such as Emme due in part to societal efforts to promote body positivity, discussed in Chapter 3.

Although children in this age group may not have a particularly good sense of their own body size, a minority of children already show a preference to look thin by 4 years of age! To put it frankly, this desire is highly worrisome. In one study, researchers asked children to select dolls that they would most and least like to look like, and only 20% chose the heaviest figure as most desirable (Musher-Eizenman et al., 2003). Many preschoolers already have some body dissatisfaction, even when their weight is healthy. We know this information based on a particular type of analysis, called a systematic review, that found this pattern across many different studies that looked at children's body size preferences. We also know that body dissatisfaction can predict unhealthy eating behaviors (Tatangelo et al., 2016).

What pushes this early focus on thinness? If we can understand the factors that influence body image at this age, then we have an opportunity to steer our girls in a healthy direction and in ways that are appropriate for their developmental level. Influences fall into three broad categories in a tripartite model: parents (mothers in particular as attachment figures), media, and peers. Peers are influential in some ways at this age, as noted in the earlier discussion of food preferences, but they are not yet major influences on girls' body image. The next sections of the chapter thus focus primarily on maternal and sociocultural influences on the lives of 3- and 4-year-olds.

MANAGING MAJOR INFLUENCES ON YOUR DAUGHTER'S BODY IMAGE IN EARLY CHILDHOOD

As previously discussed, your experiences—from girlhood to womanhood—influence the ways in which you parent your daughter. And you are the key attachment figure in your daughter's life, so she looks to you as a role model. Research has shown that certain tendencies of mothers can affect girls' body image beginning early in life. That said, it is important to understand that this observation is in no way a "blame game" on mothers. You might feel it is your fault if your daughter is already showing signs of a negative body image. It is decidedly not your fault! Mothers have been socialized to accept unhealthy ideas about their bodies and have been expected to conform to unrealistic ideals; it is difficult to overcome a lifetime of these messages. Although it is not your fault, it is your opportunity to do something about it. Being aware of these tendencies allows you to empower yourself to break this pattern for your daughter. To do so, it is important to understand that your attitude about bodies, weight, and appearance affects your daughter's views about the kind of physical appearance that is valued. Several studies have examined the association between mothers' and daughters' views on body image and related issues, such as attitudes and stereotypes about overweight people, associations between weight and personality characteristics, and dieting behavior. These studies inform where we need to direct our energy to promote a healthy body image.

YOUR ATTITUDE TOWARD PEOPLE WHO ARE OVERWEIGHT

Have you ever thought about how you feel about overweight people and what you think about being overweight, whether this characteristic applies to you, your acquaintances, or complete strangers? Do you feel your judgments of the physical appearance or characteristics of people described as fat or overweight are positive, neutral, or negative? Although it may feel uncomfortable, it is important to consider whether and how much we each show fat bias and how we might convey this bias to our daughters. As one researcher puts it, we need to be aware of how our "fear of fat" shows up (Holub et al., 2011, p. 120).

Healthy Body Image Building Tool

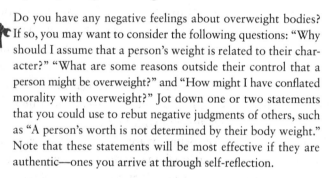

Do you have any negative feelings about overweight bodies? If so, you may want to consider the following questions: "Why should I assume that a person's weight is related to their character?" "What are some reasons outside their control that a person might be overweight?" and "How might I have conflated morality with overweight?" Jot down one or two statements that you could use to rebut negative judgments of others, such as "A person's worth is not determined by their body weight." Note that these statements will be most effective if they are authentic—ones you arrive at through self-reflection.

Because of the negative stigma society places on people with larger than "ideal" bodies, it is reasonable to have concerns about having a daughter who is in a larger body or whom you fear will develop a larger body. The effects of fat bias and discrimination are very painful and very real. Some research suggests that people hold parents responsible for their children's weight (Schwartz & Puhl, 2003), which puts enormous pressure on parents to control or prevent their children from becoming overweight.

Healthy Body Image Building Tool

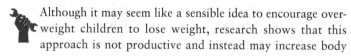

Although it may seem like a sensible idea to encourage overweight children to lose weight, research shows that this approach is not productive and instead may increase body dissatisfaction and the risk of developing an eating disorder (Puhl et al., 2022). Also, because young children grow rapidly and need proper nutrition for optimal development, a diet is inappropriate for your daughter unless it is medically endorsed and supervised by your child's pediatrician. The best approach is to emphasize a well-balanced diet, reduce sedentary behavior, and encourage body movement in a fun, positive way. It is especially effective to model these behaviors and add them to your lifestyle as a family, rather than singling them out only for your child.

YOUR FEAR OF BEING FAT

Mothers' fear of being fat predicts their daughters' negative stereo-types about fat people, which sets the stage for an unhealthy link between one's body size and their characteristics as a person (Holub et al., 2011). As we described previously, girls may begin to internalize the idea that being thin is good and being fat is bad, which may eventually lead to body dissatisfaction (Harriger, 2015). Similarly, mothers more highly concerned about weight—and that is many of us—are likely to have daughters with higher weight concerns (Tatangelo et al., 2016). When mothers idealize the thin body and show what is known as *dietary restraint* (i.e., limiting caloric intake, typically to lose weight), girls are more likely to pair positive characteristics with thin bodies. Again, this line of thinking creates a connection between thinness and goodness.

Although moms do not choose the thin ideal for their daughters when asked to comment on body size, they also do not support over-weight ideals (Musher-Eizenman et al., 2003). If you find yourself having these feelings, you may feel that you are stuck between a rock and a hard place, which is totally understandable. It is difficult to find the balance between shielding girls from diet culture and the lure of the thin ideal and protecting them from the potential health problems and stigma that can be associated with being overweight. As we discussed earlier in this chapter and as an ongoing theme of this book, we emphasize the importance of building body-healthy behaviors from the ground up—early in life—so that they become lifelong habits.

Finally, although somewhat less of a concern in preschoolers in comparison to older children, mothers who are high in *self-surveillance* (i.e., who tend to think a lot about how their bodies look to others) have daughters who are likely to be involved in a teen culture that emphasizes personal grooming, attention to beauty products, and a focus on clothing and appearance (Tiggemann & Slater, 2014).

Healthy Body Image Building Tool

 Body surveillance is discussed in Chapters 2 and 3. How much self-monitoring do you engage in? Does it distract you from what you are trying to do? Is it stressful? Could it be motivated by fatphobia? It can be difficult to quiet down this process, particularly if it has been ongoing for many years, but you can take small steps toward focusing on body functionality instead. What are all the things that your body enables you to do (e.g., hiking up a hill, carrying groceries, pushing your daughter on swings at the park)? Contemporary U.S. culture makes it easy to see our bodies in terms of appearance, but when we start to add up everything our body does for us each day, we grow our appreciation of its functionality and diminish the emphasis on its appearance.

It might feel overwhelming to hear how much your own thoughts and behaviors can affect your daughter's body image even at this early age. But as we discussed in Chapter 2, your awareness of the issues that are specific to you—and these issues are not the same for all moms—is a crucial step toward taking active control over how you approach body image in a healthy way for both you and your daughter moving forward. Also, keep in mind that you are not the only influence on your daughter's body image, and there are many things you can do to structure a body-healthy environment for her. We consider these external influences on girls' body image in the next sections.

Sociocultural Effects on Preschoolers' Body Image

You do not need to be a scientist to observe that culture—what researchers call the macrosystem—influences girls' body image development. Beginning early in childhood, children are bombarded with body-relevant images and messages from many sources, including television, the internet, advertisements, books, and other printed materials. The toys available to children also influence what they think about, what they believe, and how they behave. When it comes to body image, culture is powerful because it communicates (and enforces) norms and expectations for how people should look, even if we do not realize it. Buying into these ideas—such as the message that there is an ideal body we all need to aspire to—is associated with a negative body image. But whether these ideas take root depends on girls' age, their exposure to these ideas, and their experiences in the family. It is nearly impossible (and undesirable) to monitor all information your daughter receives and control its presence at home and school. It is helpful to know what matters most so that you can minimize negative impacts on her developing body image.

What do we know about cultural effects on 3- and 4-year-old girls' body image? What do we need to watch out for the most at this age? Researchers have looked at various influences—exposure to television, movies, and toys—to address these broad questions. You may be surprised to learn that, overall, children's television and movie programming are not directly associated with negative body image or positive stereotypes about thinness for children at this age. For example, in a study with 3- to 6-year-old girls (Hayes & Tantleff-Dunn, 2010), researchers reported that watching appearance-focused movies (such as *Beauty and the Beast*) as compared to non–appearance-focused movies (such as *Lilo and Stitch*) was unrelated to differences in choice of toys or play behavior immediately afterward, and the girls spent only a small amount of time on appearance-focused play (e.g., vanity toys vs. Legos). Further, when asked, most girls reported that they could become princesses and that they were satisfied with their physical appearance. That said, other research has found that 3-year-olds who watched more television and DVDs than their peers also showed higher preference for positive stereotypes about thinness at 4 years of age (Rodgers et al., 2017). So, we hesitate to conclude that these exposures have no negative long-term impacts.

Is Princess Culture Really a Problem? What About Barbie?

Any discussion of cultural effects on girls' body image in the United States must include their involvement in "princess culture:" dressing up as princesses, watching movies that involve princesses, and playing with princess dolls. As you may know—perhaps you have a store's worth of tiaras and tutus scattered around your own home—princess culture is incredibly popular with young girls. In fact, Disney princesses and their associated movies are so influential that researchers have studied their impact on girls (Coyne et al., 2021). Disney has drawn a good deal of criticism in the past for portraying unrealistic ideals, failing to show diversity in racial and ethnic characteristics of their characters, and emphasizing traditional gender roles, but the tides have started to turn. Disney princesses now have many different characteristics: They range from sporty to highly feminine, they are racially diverse, and many take on less gender-stereotyped roles than they have in previous decades.

So, what is the impact of princess culture on body image for girls at this age? In a study by Coyne and colleagues (2021), researchers reported a small positive effect of princess culture participation on girls' body esteem over a 5-year time span, and this effect was especially strong for girls from low socioeconomic status backgrounds. This finding was a welcome surprise, and the researchers concluded that it may reflect a sense of empowerment that comes from seeing princesses who are relatable to girls. Furthermore, participation in princess culture was not associated with the promotion of traditional gender stereotypes later in development. Specifically, a girl's involvement in this kind of play was unrelated to her beliefs about the kinds of behaviors and characteristics that are appropriate for girls as compared to boys.

In addition, there is no doubt that Barbie is a major cultural influence on girls. Although other types of dolls have become increasingly popular over the years, statistics show that most 3- to 12-year-old girls in the United States own at least one Barbie (Dittmar et al., 2006). The *Barbie* movie (Gerwig, 2023), which provided a scathing critique of societal emphasis on physical appearance, resonated with millions of viewers and enjoyed strong commercial success. The developmental effects of this perspective remain to be determined.

Earlier, we mentioned that young girls associate thin dolls with positive characteristics. In a recent study (Harriger et al., 2019), researchers showed 3- to 10-year-olds variations of the Barbie doll—an original version, a curvy version, a petite version, and a tall version. Girls assigned the most positive characteristics to the original doll and reported that they did not want to play with the curvy doll, specifically mentioning that she was chubby or fat. Interestingly, girls wanted to befriend the petite doll the most; the authors noted that this choice may have been due to her relatability but also that she was very thin.

How to Navigate These Cultural Influences

What should we make of this information? This information may be confusing because these kinds of sociocultural effects are not uniform; they can be neutral, positive, or negative depending on the age of the child, the type of influence, and the amount of exposure to that influence. For example, toys may be more influential for younger children, but movies may have a greater effect on older children, and repeated exposure to both toys and movies may increase their impact. It is also the case that no single influence will determine the developmental outcome for our daughters; it is the combination of factors over time that matters.

Although some of these findings give us reasons to relax—such as the neutral impact of television or video and the positive impact of "modern" princesses—it is a good idea to be cautious in your decision making about appropriate types and amounts of exposure for your daughter. Most of these studies were conducted in the short term, so we do not know the long-term effects of constant exposure to unrealistic or idealized images. And even though children are generally positive about themselves at this age, some girls already report disliking their physical features when asked directly how they feel about their bodies (Tatangelo et al., 2016).

Healthy Body Image Building Tool

 Although the short-term impact of media exposure on body image is limited at this age, it is good practice to limit the number of hours that your daughter watches television, social media, and movies. Although the long-term effects on body image are unclear, these sedentary habits are related to overweight in childhood, and the more strongly they are established early on, the harder they are to break. Although we certainly do not endorse making conclusions about health status based on weight alone, we want to ensure that our daughters are healthy and encourage them to move their bodies. Lastly, there is no reason to forbid your daughter from engaging in princess or doll play, but it is good practice to include a variety of diverse types of toys as options to encourage her to expand her boundaries.

A FINAL NOTE ON COMMUNICATING WITH YOUR 3- TO 4-YEAR-OLD

Our suggestions in this chapter consider the amount and type of information that most children can manage at this age. You have probably noticed that you need to repeat many of the things that you say to your daughter before she fully understands and remembers them. For example, you might need to give multiple explanations for why we go to the dentist or to repeat the "no running in the house" rule before it sticks. This can be utterly exhausting, and it goes with this developmental territory. At this age, children have trouble acting on information even when they understand perfectly well what we have said and can repeat it right back to us (Zelazo et al., 2003). You may feel as though your words sometimes seem to go in one ear and out the other, and you are in good company!

Young children are also limited in terms of how long they can pay attention (approximately 5 to 10 minutes at a time) and how much information they can hold in mind at once (one to two pieces of information). Therefore, a good deal of patience is in order when discussing body image with your daughter. Keep discussions brief, frequent, and repetitive to help your daughter remember the dialogue that you have about body image. Rest assured; even though it may feel like it, you will not be wasting your efforts. Your daughter will take in your words at her own pace over time.

One of the greatest strengths of young children's minds is their sensitivity to feelings, both their own and those of other people (Thompson & Lagattuta, 2006). And we know from science that parents who discuss emotions with their children, especially negative emotions, help their children to better process information about themselves and others. Importantly, we are not talking about venting or about judging emotions harshly but rather about trying to help children understand what they feel and to aim to make sense of it together. We highlight this point to encourage you to allow for questions and discussions about awkward, unfamiliar, or even negative comments that your daughter may generate or hear about the topic of bodies and body image. For example, if your daughter witnesses or has the unfortunate experience of an incident of body shaming, you have an opportunity to validate her feelings, consider the feelings and perspectives of others involved, and discuss why these kinds of comments are inappropriate and misguided.

PUTTING IT ALL TOGETHER: ENGAGING YOUR DAUGHTER IN ACTIVITIES AND DISCUSSION

Throughout the chapter, we have provided developmentally appropriate tips for building a healthy body image beginning in early childhood. The following list summarizes some key takeaways:

- Your daughter is already paying attention to what you do and say, including whether you're dieting or making negative remarks about your body. Focus on health behaviors, not body weight or size. Getting an early start on this approach enables you to develop it as a habit.
- It's okay to compliment appearance, but aim to focus mainly on your daughter's attitude, skills, and actions (e.g., "I like how you shared your stuffie with those girls," "What great colors you used in your drawing!").

- Introduce a variety of toys while accepting your daughter's preferences. Refrain from describing certain toys or activities as more or less suitable for girls versus boys.
- Avoid using absolute terms like "good" or "bad" to describe eating behavior, bodies, or people in general.
- Make movement fun for children at this age! Hopscotch, skipping, and other unstructured activities are best. Talk about how great it feels to move your bodies.
- Media exposure is fine if it is age appropriate. Aim to fill most of her time with other activities, such as creative play, that she will look forward to and choose on her own.
- Repeating messages about healthy body image will help your daughter remember them and build a healthy body image schema. Discuss the topic often and openly as opportunities arise.

In the Appendix, we provide companion activities that support the application of the healthy body image building tips in each chapter. Your daughter may be responsive to some of these activities but less so to others, which is fine. All the activities that we present in this book are meant to be enjoyable and conversational, not to be treated as "work." Activities tied to the concepts in this chapter include

- Activity 4: Walk and Talk With Mother Nature—Healthy thoughts and feelings
- Activity 5: Toy Test Lab—Self-concept building
- Activity 6: Read and Share: *Shapesville* Storybook—Healthy thoughts and feelings
- Activity 7: Fun-Filled Foods—Food literacy
- Activity 8: My Miraculous Moving Body—Physical literacy
- Activity 9: Celebration Station—Body respect

Recommended Resources

These resources are for moms who are dealing with picky eating or who want to learn more about the topic:

- The American Academy of Pediatrics has a YouTube channel that offers advice for responding to picky eating: https://youtu.be/s1KvNv4Jxqw
- *Feeding Littles*, which offers advice from a dietitian and an occupational therapist: https://feedinglittles.com/
- *Good Inside*, which is a general podcast hosted by a clinical psychologist. It offers some discussion on picky eating, alongside other parenting topics, and is available on Apple Podcasts.

CHAPTER 5

YOUR DAUGHTER'S BODY IMAGE IN MIDDLE CHILDHOOD: AGES 5 THROUGH 7 YEARS

Before we know it, our preschoolers become elementary school girls who keep us on our toes with their already hectic schedules. Consider Laila and her 6-year-old daughter, Kiana, who is starting kindergarten in a couple of weeks. Sitting at the kitchen table while nursing a cup of coffee, Laila starts filling in the large family wall planner that she purchased the other day. She feels a sense of wonderment as she enters Kiana's various activities and upcoming events: gymnastics on Monday nights, soccer practice on Tuesday nights with games on Saturday afternoons, a playdate at current bestie Erin's house after the first day of school, and field trips with her class to the local zoo and fire station in the coming months. "What a difference from last year," she thinks to herself.

Kiana's world has expanded from a small social circle—mostly her family and a few playmates—to a much larger network of peers and adults that comes with the start of elementary school. Kiana's microsystem, the immediate surroundings that influence her development, has expanded considerably. And with more time spent outside the home, the influence of the macrosystem, or culture, will also become greater. Kiana's life has changed in ways that will influence how she thinks, feels, and behaves; she will also experience ongoing and new influences on her developing body image.

This chapter focuses on what is known about development and body image in middle childhood, specifically, in 5- to 7-year-old girls. We follow a structure similar to that in Chapter 4, first covering the major milestones of development that describe girls in this age group and then turning our focus to girls' body image at this age, the main influences on their body image, and your role in the body image development process. Along the way, we provide actionable tips and end with suggested activities to promote healthy body image development.

COGNITIVE, SOCIAL, AND EMOTIONAL DEVELOPMENT IN MIDDLE CHILDHOOD

Children experience many changes between 5 and 7 years of age. Below, we discuss some key areas of development that are relevant to girls' emerging body image.

Self-Concept: "I See Myself in You"

As girls' social circle expands, so do their ideas about who they are and what they are like as people. Improvements in both language and the understanding of others' thoughts, emotions, and behaviors contribute to advancements in self-concept. Girls begin to use more specific descriptions that capture both social roles and internal qualities, such as basic personality traits, rather than only physical appearance (Boseovski & Lee, 2006). They may describe themselves with sentences such as "I am a first grader. I am shy. I am funny" (Livesley & Bromley, 1973; Marsh et al., 2002). By 5 years of age, children incorporate social categories, such as race, into their self-concepts and they use their social relationships to help define themselves (e.g., their role as the daughter in their family). In other words, girls see their family members as reference points that help them determine who they are, and they assume that many characteristics that they see are shared among family members, a phenomenon that some scientists call *self–other overlap* (Collyer et al., 2018).

Most girls continue to have a fairly positive self-concept in middle childhood and a high sense of self-esteem or self-worth. It might be tempting to take this positive self-view for granted, but it does not necessarily occur naturally, and research shows that, unfortunately, it decreases with age as children become more realistic about their skills and attributes (Marsh et al., 2002).

As her mother, you play a key role in your daughter's self-concept development in two ways. First, because you are the main attachment figure in her life, your daughter is now using you as a reference point. So, it is especially important to consider how you talk about yourself around her. She is likely to assign many characteristics that she hears you talk about—whether real or imagined—to herself. For example, if you criticize your personality or a make a disparaging comment about your thighs, she may integrate this information into her own self-concept. Although you see the distinction between your body and your daughter's body clearly, she may not yet. And even if you make these comments jokingly or in a self-deprecating way, your daughter is not at an age at which she is likely to understand that you are doing so. Second, it is important to consider how you talk to your daughter about herself, both in general and particularly when weight is concerned. At this age, some children become or begin to show signs of being overweight. Although it may seem appropriate to make comments about your daughter's weight (e.g., if you have concerns about her health), these comments can have long-term effects and are especially problematic for girls who are overweight.

In one study, researchers wanted to understand if parents' comments were associated with a low self-concept in 5- to 7-year-old girls who were characterized as overweight (Davison & Birch, 2002).

Researchers evaluated the amount of parent-related weight criticism by asking the parents of each girl to report on the other parent's views about their daughter's weight (i.e., husbands rated wives and vice versa). The researchers noted whether each parent expressed concerns about how much their daughter ate and how much she weighed. Although negative parental comments about weight were not yet impactful in the 5-year-olds in this study, higher criticism was associated with lower body esteem and lower feelings of cognitive ability in the 7-year-old girls. So, we want to be particularly mindful about the comments that we make to girls at this developmental time point. And, although a higher body mass index (BMI) alone contributed to girls' lower self-concept, parents' criticism of girls' weight also contributed to a lower self-concept, including body esteem or worth. The take-home message is that it is unhelpful at best, and harmful at worst, to convey concerns to your daughter about her weight.

Indeed, decades of research by psychologist Rebecca Puhl and her colleagues has established that weight-based stigma from parents, peers, and educators is associated with a host of negative psychosocial and health-related outcomes (e.g., Puhl & Latner, 2007; Puhl & Lessard, 2020; Schwartz & Puhl, 2003). At this early age, girls' bodies are changing and growing rapidly, so it is important to avoid making premature conclusions about our daughters' health based on a single indicator at a single point in her life. As noted elsewhere in the book, BMI is a crude indicator of health that must be considered in the context of other factors that affect one's health status.

Healthy Body Image Building Tool

 Continue to emphasize your daughter's non–appearance-based qualities and point out positive characteristics that you share. Your daughter's cognitive and language abilities at this age open a whole new world of descriptors—such as personality traits—to which you can refer. If you have concerns about your daughter's weight or health, talk to a health care practitioner who can help you focus on positive behavior and lifestyle choices rather than food restriction. Refrain from weight-based comments or labels. Highlight your own strengths and talents in the presence of your daughter and aim to reduce or eliminate body-based criticism. To apply some of these ideas, see Activity 10, **Lunch Box Love Notes**, and Activity 11, **Literary Genius**, in the Appendix. Additionally, Activity 12, *Your Name Is a Song*, is a read-and-share activity centered on ethnic and cultural pride.

Gender Identity: Girls Are "Better," but Must They Be "Delicate?"

In Chapter 4, we discussed the development of gender identity and children's knowledge about the gender roles associated with boys and girls. By middle childhood, most girls have adopted a preference for their own gender, known as a *gender ingroup bias* (McLoughlin & Over, 2017). Girls say more positive things about their own gender, and they prefer to be around and to play with other girls. To a large degree, this ingroup bias is normative and perfectly healthy; it enables girls to create friendship bonds with other girls based on belongingness to the same social category, and this is a good thing. This bias will mostly fade later in childhood as social circles again expand and contact between boys and girls increases.

As discussed in Chapter 4, young children tend to believe in *gender essentialism*—the idea that people are born with qualities beyond anatomical characteristics that explain differences between girls and boys, and this tendency is especially strong between 5 and 7 years of age. For example, in one study, children predicted that a baby girl who grew up surrounded only by boys and men would have behaviors similar to other girls rather than to boys (Taylor, 1996; Taylor et al., 2009). Although biology is certainly important, children did not recognize the importance of any social influences, such as parents and peers, on personality and behavior.

Other research shows that during this age period, essentialist thinking is connected with interest in gender-stereotyped activities (i.e., activities that are designated as "appropriate" for females, such as playing with dolls, polishing nails, child care, and housework; Meyer & Gelman, 2016). Further, these kinds of ideas can be transmitted intergenerationally: Parents who themselves hold essentialist beliefs about gender are more likely to have children who show these gender-stereotyped preferences, which peak between 5 and 7 years of age.

Why does gender essentialism matter, and how does it relate to body image? Many gender-stereotyped activities associated with girls focus on physical appearance. Others focus on the idea that girls and women possess characteristics that are supposedly gender specific, such as being graceful, emotionally and physically fragile, and agreeable toward others. Although there is nothing wrong with many of these characteristics, we want to be certain to expose our daughters to the full range of possibilities for their lives. We do not want our girls to grow up believing that they are meant to achieve an impossible physical standard. Nor do we want them to miss all the amazing things that they can do and accomplish because they are worrying about their physical appearance or acting in a way that society has deemed as right for girls and women or because they fear being judged negatively.

Healthy Body Image Building Tool

 Encourage your daughter to participate in a variety of activities. If your daughter does not currently have any mixed-gender peer contact, it is a great idea to expose her to activities in which both girls and boys participate. For example, most kids enjoy a game of hide and seek! There may be social benefits when children identify with their own gender but also feel that they share similarities with the other gender (Martin et al., 2017; Perry et al., 2019). This kind of flexibility promotes breaking away from solely feminine-stereotyped activities, which encourage collaboration but discourage qualities such as assertiveness and mastery (Leaper, 2015). Building on the theme from Chapter 4, this kind of exposure can encourage your daughter to see that there can be just as many behavioral similarities between boys and girls as there are among girls.

In Chapter 4, we discussed displaying diverse roles in the home. Consider also what kind of exposure your daughter has to diverse roles for girls and women outside of the home. Research shows that girls who are given experiences that defy stereotypical career expectations (e.g., showing skills at science and technology) have increased self-efficacy and interest in those careers (Master et al., 2017). That said, it is fine to let your daughter take the lead here; there is nothing at all wrong with participating in gender-typed activities if she prefers, nor should you feel that you need to push gender role conformity or nonconformity. It is the exposure and openness to opportunities that is important.

Moral Development: The Vulnerability of Shame and Embarrassment

When children are around 5 years of age, parents often notice a considerable increase in their understanding of other people. Three- and 4-year-olds tend to think that other people share their views on just about everything, a phenomenon known as **childhood egocentrism** (Flavell et al., 1981). In contrast, 5-year-olds begin to have greater appreciation for others' points of view. This 3- to 5-year-old transition has been described as a key turning point or watershed for **theory of mind** development because children's thinking becomes much more sophisticated in a brief time span (Astington, 1993). Broadly, theory of mind refers to the ability to appreciate the inner workings of the mind (such as thoughts and emotions) and how they connect to behavior. For example, your daughter may suddenly be much more aware that other people may not feel or think the same way that she does about a variety of things: Her brother may prefer a different type of ice cream, and her friend may think that *Frozen* is a better movie than her beloved *The Lion King*.

> **Childhood egocentrism:** the cognitive inability to take the perspectives of other people. This focus on the self is not the same as "selfish" or self-absorbed behavior that is sometimes seen in adults. Young children often assume that other people see, think, and feel the same way that they do.
>
> **Theory of mind:** the understanding of other people's mental states—desires, emotions, knowledge, and beliefs—and the appreciation that mental states can differ among people and that mental states may or may not be consistent with reality (Astington, 1993).

At this age, children report experiencing emotions such as shame and embarrassment. The recognition and experience of these emotions increases throughout childhood, particularly between 6 and 8 years of age (Chobhthaigh & Wilson, 2015). Together with the advances in understanding others' point of view, these intense emotions may leave your daughter vulnerable to comments from others about her physical appearance and body, among other characteristics. It is important to recognize that family members are often singled out as the most common source of body shaming (Pont et al., 2017).

Body shaming does not promote positive health behavior, and it has a serious negative impact on children that can last over the long term (Knopf, 2018). Even when comments are well intended—such as when family members aim to protect their loved one from being shamed by others—they are inappropriate and perpetuate the idea that weight can be easily changed, which is simply not the case for some people. It is therefore important that we take action to protect our girls from this experience to the extent that we can do so. Realistically, we cannot shield them from every comment that they might hear, so we also want to foster resilience and arm them with tools that they can use on their own when confronted with this kind of inappropriate behavior from others.

Healthy Body Image Building Tool

 Your daughter may not be able to speak up for herself when adults make comments about her body, so we offer two approaches that can ward off potentially problematic encounters. First, you can request that other adults kindly refrain from talking about your daughter's body in her presence, with a gentle explanation that you have learned that this kind of talk can be damaging (and perhaps the observation that there are far more interesting things to talk about!). Second, you can talk with your daughter about how to manage unwanted body comments from others, particularly when weight is concerned. These inappropriate comments offer a terrific opportunity to discuss societal overvaluation of thin bodies, observe that bodies naturally come in different shapes and sizes, and reaffirm that there are no good or bad bodies. It is also a time to explain that what matters is how she feels about her body, not how other people feel about her body. For example, you might encourage her to say, "I am in charge of my body, and I like it just fine!" or "My body is my business." This second approach is important because it is self-determined and because you cannot always be there to help her manage outside influences.

Thoughts and Feelings About Food: "I'll Have What They're Having!"

As they approach middle childhood, children start to develop consistent eating patterns, and their food knowledge becomes more sophisticated. Building on their initial understanding, children as young as 5 years of age can classify food into many categories, including sweets, fruit, vegetables, dairy, and meats and fish, among others. Their emphasis shifts from the appearance of the food (such as its color) to its functional attributes (such as its importance for physical growth; Zeinstra et al., 2007) that increases over time. Five-year-olds understand that we need food for growth; by 6 years of age, children further understand that food gives us power and energy (Inagaki & Hatano, 2006). Children develop a better awareness of food rules imposed by their parents (e.g., "No candy until you finish your vegetables"), but they may not fully understand the basis for these rules until late childhood. This lack of understanding can persist despite repeated explanations that vegetables are good for us. And the increased knowledge about food does not necessarily translate into behavior: As you may have noticed, most children consider vegetables to be the least desirable food category!

By age 5, children are becoming aware that the quantity and quality of eating can result in a bigger body (Peretz-Lange & Kibbe, 2024) and in some cases discuss these associations in a negative way. For example, children may claim that an individual became fat by eating too much. A small proportion of children also believe that a bigger body results from a lack of activity. The relations among food intake, exercise, and body weight are far more complex—people come in smaller or larger bodies for a variety of reasons that often include a transaction between genetic, biological, psychological, and cultural influences. And although boys' and girls' ideas generally do not differ at this early age, it is important to notice these beliefs specifically in girls because they are thought to relate to body image issues as girls develop. For example, if a girl believes she is fat, she may impose unhealthy restrictions on her eating or engage in excessive amounts of physical activity to control her body size.

So much of children's learning about food during this time comes from watching what other people do and say, and eating behavior is no different. Eating is a highly social activity, especially for children at this age given that most of them do not yet prepare their meals independently and typically eat in the presence of or with other people. If you spend a good deal of structured time with your child at meals or snacks, your child is likely receiving a lot of information about your relationship with food—your feelings about what and how much you are eating, how food makes you feel, and its effect on your appearance. Increases in children's attention and information processing also translate to better memory for discussions about food and ways of eating. It may be unsurprising, then, that parents' knowledge about food predicts children's knowledge about food. Specifically, parents' understanding of genetically modified organisms, organic foods, and gluten influences their children's knowledge of what these labels mean, and this knowledge increases with age (Shtulman et al., 2020). We discuss more about parental influences on eating behavior later in this chapter.

In addition to parents, peers continue to have a strong influence on children's impressions of food at this age. Five- and 6-year-olds are more likely to eat a particular food if they think another child likes it and if they are told the food is popular with other kids but not adults (DeJesus, Shutts, & Kinzler, 2018). One study demonstrated that 5- to 7-year-olds were willing to eat an unfamiliar blue-colored food after exposure to positive peer modeling of that food (Greenhalgh et al., 2009). Interestingly, at this age children also display a *naturalism bias*, preferring food in its natural form. For example, children express preference for an apple that was grown on a farm over an apple that they were told was created in a laboratory (Wilks & Bloom, 2022).

Despite the increased knowledge about food during this period, there is, of course, a lot that children have not yet learned. Five-year-olds can categorize foods, but they do not understand the major nutritional components of food (e.g., protein, carbohydrates, fat; Michela & Contento, 1984). They can name some healthy foods, but they cannot explain why the foods are healthy (Slaughter & Ting, 2010). They do not seem to understand the difference between meals and snacks. Further, at this age, children do not seem very responsive to messages about the importance of healthy food and, in fact, these messages sometimes backfire. That said, children show some avoidance of food labeled as unhealthy (DeJesus, Kinzler, et al., 2018). Many children also continue to show a strong preference for familiar food, and they can be sensitive to the way the food is presented (e.g., visual appeal; Jansen et al., 2010).

Healthy Body Image Building Tool

 Because consistent eating patterns start to emerge at about 6 years of age, this time is ideal to teach children about the qualities of different foods. Drawing on what professionals call *food parenting practices* (Norton et al., 2023), aim to prepare balanced meals, create a positive atmosphere around the dinner table, and emphasize eating for body health and feeling good in your bodies rather than body weight. Model a varied diet and follow your daughter's cues when it comes to eating rather than dictating precisely how much she should eat or what she should eat. A neutral approach to food and eating is best. If you find that she is overly focused on a food that is less nutritious, you can offer that food as an option less frequently and substitute other items for it sometimes; also consider avoiding the term "healthy" as a motivator to get her to eat something. Although sometimes difficult with children at this age, try to involve your daughter in meal planning and food selection, using the opportunity to gain information about what she enjoys and to discuss how to put together healthy, tasty, and fun meals. Now that you may be spending more time at the dinner table together, think about how you discuss food. Are you often moralizing food or criticizing yourself for how much or what you are eating? Aim to reduce this dialogue, for your sake and hers.

Thoughts and Feelings About the Body: Learning the Basis for Health and Wellness Behaviors

Children's knowledge about the human body increases between 4 and 8 years of age. For example, children become better at identifying the location and functions of different body organs (Jaakkola & Slaughter, 2002). Beginning at about 6 years of age, children are thought to have a **naïve theory of biology**, a knowledge system that they use for making sense of biological phenomena such as how the body works (Hatano & Inagaki, 1994). Six-year-olds understand that many body organs are essential for life. They also appreciate that they cannot see some body structures and processes that are important for biological functioning.

> **Naïve theory of biology:** children's understanding and reasoning about biological phenomena, including bodily processes, reproduction, inheritance and properties of living as compared to nonliving things (Hatano & Inagaki, 1994).

Researchers have pointed out that these improvements in biological awareness are significant not just intellectually but also because biological understanding is an important motivator of health and wellness behaviors. For example, children understand that food provides energy that can help us to live longer or to recover from illness (Inagaki & Hatano, 2006). By 6 years of age, children understand that health behaviors (such as a poor diet) can affect whether a person is susceptible to a cold but that morally relevant behaviors (such as lying) cannot.

In contrast to their knowledge about food, children's health-related fitness knowledge is somewhat slow to emerge; additionally, scientists have reported that fewer than 25% of children between 6 and 17 years of age achieve the recommended physical activity standards (Centers for Disease Control and Prevention, 2022c). Because physical fitness is associated with so many health benefits, it is sensible to think about ways to encourage it so that it becomes an enjoyable habit at an early age. In fact, experts in physical education have pointed to the concept of physical literacy. Just as with food, parents are considered gatekeepers for managing their children's activity level; both your direct participation in activities and your support of your daughter's participation in activities are important to encourage her to adopt an active lifestyle.

> Physical literacy: an individual's knowledge, ability, and motivation for participating in physical activities over the lifespan (Gu et al., 2019).

Many children begin to participate in organized sports at this age—dance, soccer, gymnastics, horse riding, and others. These activities are excellent and enjoyable ways to encourage physical activity, and they provide opportunities to build friendships and personal qualities such as leadership, cooperativity, and self-efficacy. That said, participation in athletics can be positive or negative when it comes to the development of a healthy body image. The scientific literature is mixed, with some reports suggesting that athletic participation is beneficial and other reports suggesting that it can be harmful over the long term. The conflicting reports may be due, in part, to differences in activity type and context. For example, some researchers have found that aesthetic sports, which tend to be appearance oriented or leanness oriented (e.g., gymnastics, dance), can be problematic for girls' developing body image, and aesthetic sports participation can be considered a risk factor for eating disorder development. In one study (Lombardo et al., 2012), 6- to 12-year-old girls who participated in aesthetic sports had more negative body images than those who participated in nonaesthetic sports (e.g., karate, horse riding). Girls in aesthetic sports reported a desire to be much thinner than they were, even though they tended to be objectively thinner than the girls who participated in nonaesthetic sports. In contrast, this desire was uncommon in girls who participated in nonaesthetic sports. Researchers have noted that girls can desire thinness for different reasons: Some girls may be motivated by cultural ideals of thinness, and other girls may be motivated by ideas related to performance (e.g., that better dancers are thinner).

What should mothers make of these findings? Do they mean that we should ban our daughters from participating in aesthetic sports altogether? We are not suggesting that you do so; rather, your knowledge that this type of sport participation can be a risk factor can help you to choose appropriate programs for your daughter and to pay special attention to comments related to body image that may arise from her participation in these activities.

Healthy Body Image Building Tool

 Recognize your daughter's developing appreciation of how biology ties into health and well-being. Make connections between body functioning and behavior (e.g., "This hike is making our legs so strong!") and make it fun. Children enjoy physical activity when it is playful, when they feel competent at it, and when they have friends also engaging in it, so it is a great idea to enroll your daughter in activities with her friends or to invite her friends along on family activities. Concerning participation in aesthetic sports, we encourage you to seek information directly from the relevant coaches, instructors, or directors of these activities about their philosophy of training for young girls and their awareness of issues related to body image. Talk with other families about their experiences as well. In short, individuals who direct these programs should not comment on the body shape, size, or weight of your daughter or discuss her food intake or physical appearance in an evaluative way. To apply some of these ideas, see Activity 13, **Picture Perfect Memories**, and Activity 14, **My Amazing Hands and Feet**, as well as the read-and-share Activity 15, *Your Body Is Awesome*, all of which are in the Appendix.

Body Image

Unfortunately, research shows that children at this age are more likely than preschoolers to think negatively about people with larger bodies (Bensley et al., 2023; see also Cramer & Steinwert, 1998; Spiel et al., 2012). When given the option, children choose a thin figure as ideal and consider larger sizes to be less acceptable (Tiggemann & Lowes, 2002). At 5 years of age, children are more likely to assume that a fat story character is mean than they are to assume a thin story character is mean, and although many children do not verbalize the reason for this assumption, a small proportion mention body size outright, clearly endorsing negative stereotypes about people with larger bodies (Cramer & Steinwert, 1998; Spiel et al., 2012). Five-year-olds are also less willing than 3-year-olds to want to befriend a child who is fat (Harriger, 2015). Even in a study in which children did not have to choose among thin, typical, and chubby hypothetical friendships, they were still reluctant to befriend chubby children (Musher-Eizenman et al., 2004).

Although these views are unfortunate, the good news is that scientific knowledge can help us to reduce them. Specifically, these biases can be tempered when children hear about the reasons that people may be overweight. For example, Carvalho et al. (2021) found that children who heard biological explanations for a character's weight showed fewer weight-related biases than children who heard behavioral explanations. If you hear comments or see behaviors that reflect a fat bias, take the opportunity to talk with your daughter directly about the importance of not judging people by their body size.

What about girls' impressions of their own bodies? Children show an increase in general appearance concerns between 4 and 7 years of age (Tiggemann & Slater, 2014), and girls who have a higher BMI are more likely to report greater body dissatisfaction than those with lower BMI (Tatangelo et al., 2016). At this age, girls are more aware of the thin ideal and the purported ways to achieve it (e.g., by dieting; Dohnt & Tiggemann, 2005). Alarmingly, in one study (Damiano et al., 2015), 34% of 5-year-old girls reported engaging in some dietary restraint, and 50% showed thin ideal internalization. In another study (Pine, 2001), about 30% of 5- and 7-year-old girls said that they would hypothetically go on a diet, and it is noteworthy that most of the 7-year-olds reported being aware that someone else was on a diet. So, unlike 3-year-old Emily from the vignette in Chapter 4, by middle childhood children understand the meaning of "diet."

Some researchers have suggested that children gain a realistic sense of their own body size at around 5 years of age, but others have reported that this understanding emerges later (Smolak, 2004). Regardless, many children in this age range experience body dissatisfaction, with the numbers varying from 20% to 70% depending on how it is measured (Tatangelo et al., 2016). One study showed a large jump in the desire to be thin between 4 and 6 years of age (León et al., 2021), although the percentage of girls reporting this desire was modest. Some additional research suggests that girls show a greater tendency than boys to feel dissatisfied with their weight and to want to be thinner than their current size (León et al., 2021; Pine, 2001). Given these disturbing findings, it is unsurprising that some researchers have suggested we are seeing in these young girls something akin to normative discontent in women (Cuesta-Zamora & Navas, 2017; see also Chapter 1, this volume).

It is important to understand why children report the desire to be thinner. In one study (León et al., 2021), interviews with 4- to 6-year-olds clearly showed that children have a variety of ideas and preferences for thinness, with some preferences associated with nutrition or the desire to grow up (e.g., ideas about what adult bodies look like). So, we do not necessarily need to worry about all comments related to thinness. In other cases, however, children's preferences reflected desires related to the thin ideal, other specific beauty ideals, or comments that children heard from their mothers concerning their body size.

As with women, young girls' body image perceptions are complex even at this early age, and they cannot be described with a single measurement—see, for example, the variety of questionnaires for women presented in Chapter 1. One study (Perez et al., 2018) captured this complexity in girls by measuring self-objectification, internalization of the thin ideal, and body dissatisfaction in 5- to 7-year-old girls via an interview and a mirror activity in which girls were asked if they liked or disliked various parts of their bodies (e.g., stomach, hips, buttocks). Self-objectification was measured by having the girls talk about reasons that they liked or disliked their bodies and noting whether they focused on appearance rather than function, which would indicate seeing their body parts as objects to be evaluated. Internalization of the thin ideal was assessed with a figure-selection task in which girls chose their ideal body from a set of seven figures ranging from very thin to very obese. The findings of this study showed that self-objectification was higher for the 6- and 7-year-olds than for the 5-year-olds, although it wasn't particularly high in either case, consistent with other research findings on self-objectification in girls (Daniels et al., 2020). Interestingly, internalization of the thin ideal showed a reverse pattern: It was higher for 5-year-old girls than for 7-year-old girls. In the mirror activity, girls expressed both body satisfaction and dissatisfaction, but it is notable that more than half named at least one area that caused dissatisfaction. High body dissatisfaction was also related to the tendency to engage in self-objectification.

It is important to note that the research discussed in this chapter, along with the research reported in Chapter 4, focused primarily on White girls and their families. For this reason, we hesitate to draw the general conclusion that all children from ages 5 to 7 years exhibit these patterns concerning body image. As discussed in Chapter 1, children from different cultural backgrounds may have quite different opinions about body ideals, and body image problems may be more prominent in some groups than others. A limited body of research has exposed some cultural differences among children in this age group. For example, in a small research study (Davis et al., 2009), a greater number of African American 6-year-olds than White 6-year-olds wanted to be larger rather than smaller in size, although these groups did not differ in body dissatisfaction. That said, researchers have noted that some differences among groups have likely decreased because of the globalization of the thin ideal (Dittmar et al., 2006).

Of course, body image pressures go well beyond weight; they can involve all aspects of physical appearance, such as skin color, hair color and texture, body shape, facial features, and many other factors. We cannot speak to many of these characteristics in young children, as the research is not available, but the general advice given in this book will be useful for girls from a variety of backgrounds as you tailor it to address your unique family characteristics and context. These factors are addressed in Chapter 1, and we refer you to Activity 12 in the Appendix, *Your Name Is a Song*, which focuses on fostering pride in ethnic and racial identity.

MANAGING MAJOR INFLUENCES ON YOUR DAUGHTER'S BODY IMAGE IN MIDDLE CHILDHOOD

We next turn our attention to maternal influences, peer influences, and sociocultural factors that influence body image development in middle childhood. The focus on peers is highlighted, as researchers have documented that peer influence on emerging body image tends to develop in children at this age.

Parenting: You Daughter's Concerns Reflect Your Concerns

In Chapter 4, we discussed that moms' own feelings about fat, including fear of fat and antifat attitudes toward adults and children, predict young children's negative stereotypes about fat people (Holub et al., 2011). Similarly, mothers' concerns about their own body weight are associated with similar concerns in their 5-year-old daughters (Musher-Eizenman et al., 2003). In the Perez et al. (2018) study discussed previously, mothers and daughters also completed a joint mirror activity in which mothers were either told to state positive thoughts about their own bodies or not told what to say about their own bodies as they were in front of a mirror while in the presence of their daughters. The goal of this exercise was to determine whether mothers' comments about their bodies influenced their daughters' body image. Importantly, mothers' dislikes predicted daughters' dislikes; similarly, more likes by mothers predicted more likes by their daughters. In this study, mothers' body dissatisfaction and self-objectification were also positively associated with daughters' internalization of the thin ideal.

Earlier in the chapter, we discussed potential risks associated with girls' participation in aesthetic sports. In part, some of the concern may be rooted in the behaviors of mothers with daughters who participate in aesthetic sports. Lombardo et al.'s (2012) study showed that the mothers of girls who participated in aesthetic sports desired to be thinner than the mothers whose daughters participated in nonaesthetic sports and were more likely to restrict their own eating. These mothers also reported being more critical of their daughters. Mothers' desire to be thin was related to daughters' desire to be thin; similarly, a mother's body dissatisfaction was related to her daughter's body dissatisfaction. Although it is unclear why this association exists, it bears some consideration if it is relevant to you (that is, if your daughter participates in aesthetic sports). It is a good idea to think about whether this choice of activity may have been affected by, or may be impacting, your body image. If you feel that your daughter's participation affects you negatively, consider discussing alternative activities with her; myriad options may be psychologically healthier for both of you.

As children approach middle childhood, the effects of mothers' self-surveillance (their tendency to think about how their bodies look) become stronger (Slater & Tiggemann, 2014). Mothers' interests in material things also have an effect on daughters' appearance concerns and interests in grown-up or teen culture behaviors, including paying attention to clothes, wearing makeup, and wearing shoes with heels. Interestingly, reading and craft activities were not associated with these appearance concerns in girls, suggesting that activity choices matter. Although the impacts are relatively small overall, it is a good idea to consider how they might play out for you and your daughter.

It is not just your feelings about your own body and weight that have an impact on your daughter; the messages that you convey to her about her own weight, whether directly or indirectly, also have an impact. As previously discussed, parent criticism of girls' weight has a negative impact on girls' self-concept. But did you know that your feelings about your daughter's weight might also predict her future dieting behavior and weight?

It might seem reasonable to assume that special attention to children's weight is associated with weight loss, but research shows that it can instead result in weight gain. In one study that tracked children for several years (Robinson & Sutin, 2017), researchers first obtained information from parents of 4- and 5-year-olds concerning their views about their child's weight. When the children were 12 or 13 years old, they were interviewed regarding their own views about their weight and whether they had engaged in dieting behaviors. The researchers found that between childhood and 14 or 15 years of age, children whose parents viewed them as overweight as preschoolers gained significantly more weight than children whose parents reported them as "normal" weight. The authors suggested that this finding was due in part to children's own views that they were overweight, which were associated with dieting behaviors. Neither children's weight at baseline nor their waist circumference explained the results. The authors concluded that the stigma associated with being labeled "overweight" is associated with potential psychological distress and weight gain. Similarly, a review of the studies on parental weight criticism of children resulted in lower well-being and a greater likelihood of unhealthy eating behaviors (Gillison et al., 2016).

This research on parental influence does not suggest that parents are causing their children to become overweight. Rather, we need to be mindful of the effects of this label on children's feelings about themselves and their subsequent eating behaviors. The take-home message is that even if we are rightfully concerned about our daughters' body weight in relation to her health, we need to be careful about the ways that we approach it. Although little research has focused on the effects of parent–child discussions about weight, a review of the available information suggests that talking about health behavior without reference to weight can be beneficial for well-being in adolescence (Gillison et al., 2016).

As discussed earlier in this chapter, girls' knowledge about food increases as they approach middle childhood, but they do not have a solid sense of what it means to eat a balanced meal. So, you might be wondering how much monitoring of what our girls eat is appropriate. After all, how can we promote respect for the body and the development of health behaviors if we do not control our daughters' food intake? Research shows that here, too, mothers' body image influences their feeding practices. In one study (Damiano et al., 2016), moms who placed high emphasis on body weight and shape were more likely to engage in food restriction (i.e., controlling the consumption of foods) and weight restriction or monitoring of girls' weight. But not all moms veered in the direction of restriction. Valuing an athletic ideal was associated with the quality of food and eating more nutritious foods, and the authors suggest this finding reflects concerns about maintenance of a healthy weight.

Consistent with parenting research in general, it is ideal to set some rules while being responsive to your daughter's needs. In a study of Latina moms and their daughters, parental monitoring of eating (such as tracking general eating habits and praising them for eating healthy snacks) was related to healthy eating in daughters (Arredondo et al., 2006). However, excessive control over girls' eating (such as dictating how much they should eat or offering sweets only as a reward) was associated with unhealthy eating. It is also important to realize that your own food intake predicts how much your daughter will eat (DeJesus, Gelman, et al., 2018).

Healthy Body Image Building Tool

Avoid self-criticism about your weight in the presence of your daughter. If your daughter expresses concern about her weight, validate her concerns rather than minimizing them. Try to find the origin of these concerns so that you can address them. For example, if the concerns have arisen from an insensitive comment from another person, you can acknowledge the comment as inappropriate. If the origin of the concern is her personal discomfort with her body, you can talk about how bodies vary in shapes and sizes and that there are no bad bodies, including fat bodies. You can emphasize all the great things her body can do and plan activities that highlight body functionality and appreciation, including those in the Appendix. If your daughter is interested in aesthetic sports and embraces teen culture, we are not suggesting that you ban her from participating outright; these activities may be fine for her! But be attentive for any signs of distress. Avoid commenting on your daughter's weight; instead, focus on promoting health behaviors in fun, accessible ways. Similarly, monitor eating while allowing for leeway. Structured eating—such as family mealtime—is ideal for teaching children about balanced meals. Note that restriction of foods to encourage balanced eating can be indirect; you need not forbid her from eating certain foods. For example, you can limit the availability of foods that are nutritionally poor and the occasions on which they are served.

Peers: Establishing Healthy Relationships, Openness, and Boundaries

At the beginning of the chapter, we discussed Kiana's expanding world (microsystem), which includes a network of peers. In fact, by middle childhood, many children spend almost one third of their time with peers. Making positive age-appropriate friendships is a critical aspect of well-being, and it contributes to children's developing cognitive skills and academic success. Peer relationships are distinct from relationships with parents in that peers can offer additional or alternate sources of emotional support and help buffer stress (Gifford-Smith & Brownell, 2003).

What does healthy friendship look like for children ages 5 through 7 years? In general, peer contact is initially centered on play behaviors and ultimately transitions to friendships based on shared preferences and similarities. It is likely that you will know your child's closest friends well, and it is important to pay attention to these relationships as peers begin to play increasingly important roles in the development of your child's self-concept. Middle childhood is also the age at which teasing and bullying behaviors often begin. You may remember being teased by others or, worse yet, being bullied as a child. Bullying is not the same as teasing. Bullying is intended to be hostile, occurs repeatedly, is upsetting to the recipient, and involves a power differential in which the bully has more power in the peer group. Teasing tends not to be consistent, and it can be positively or negatively motivated; for this reason, it also needs to be monitored. These experiences can be very painful, and their effects are often long-lasting.

Bullying and teasing are often centered on physical appearance, which is why they are particularly relevant to body image. What does research about peer influences on body image show for children at this age? In one study, children reported that the greatest source of weight-related teasing (whether about being underweight or overweight) came from their friends (Kostanski & Gullone, 2007). In another study, researchers assessed the effect of peer teasing on girls' self-concept (Davison & Birch, 2002). Girls reported whether they had been teased about specific body parts (e.g., their waist or bottom) by a brother, sister, friend, or another child. At both 5 and 7 years of age, children who were teased more also showed lower levels of body esteem. Because teasing affects not only body esteem but also general well-being, it is important to pay attention to what is happening at school and in your daughter's peer networks.

What about body talk? How much do girls talk about their bodies at this age, and do peers influence how girls feel about their bodies? Relatively little research has examined how much girls spontaneously talk about their bodies with their peers, but some evidence suggests that peers have an indirect influence on girls' body image. In one study of 5- to 8-year-olds (Dohnt & Tiggemann, 2006), girls were asked how much they discuss appearance-related issues with their friends, how they felt about their own bodies, and their impressions of how their friends felt about their bodies. Overall, girls reported that they did not spend much time talking about appearance-related themes and generally reported high self-esteem and body satisfaction, but their perceptions of their bodies were influenced by what they believed their friends felt about their own bodies. Girls who thought that their friends wanted to be thinner also wanted to be thinner and showed a greater awareness of dieting. The researchers argued that shared peer norms or expectations can begin to promote the thin ideal. It is striking that these norms do not even need to be stated directly to affect girls' beliefs about the most desirable bodies.

Another study revealed that conversations with peers about appearance were associated with internalization of the thin ideal (Damiano et al., 2015) The very nature of how girls "do" friendship—the intimacy of it—lends itself to a great deal of peer influence on thoughts and behaviors. These ideas about the ideal body may also be motivated by the onset of social comparison, which can start to increase during middle childhood although it is more common in older children (Dittmar et al., 2006).

In Chapter 1, we noted that family compositions differ. If your daughter has a sibling, it is important to take the same approach as you would with her peers concerning teasing or negative body talk from her brothers or sisters. Establish house rules that center on health behaviors, and emphasize that each person's body is their own business.

Healthy Body Image Building Tool

Pay attention to your daughter's relationships with her siblings and peers. You may not be aware if she is being bullied or teased by her peers—these behaviors may take place only at school. Watch for indicators that she is being subjected to this behavior. For example, children who are teased or bullied often lose interest in going to school, are suddenly fearful or extra clingy to parents, and may report vague symptoms of physical illness, such as stomach aches. If you see these behaviors, talk with your daughter and check with the teachers and school administrators to see if there is cause for concern. If you know that she is being bullied, report the behavior to school authorities so that it can be dealt with swiftly. A zero-tolerance policy, not lenience, is the best approach to stop bullying behavior.

Sociocultural Effects: Teen Culture, Kidfluencers, and Dolls

As noted earlier, overinvolvement in teen culture behaviors such as attention to beauty products, personal grooming, and clothing—is associated with appearance concerns, which increase with age. Television and video viewing are popular activities for children in middle childhood, but even age-appropriate children's media promotes social norms about body weight, appearance, and skin and facial characteristics. One analysis revealed a great deal of emphasis on physical appearance in children's videos, although somewhat less in books (Herbozo et al., 2004). It is worth thinking about how much your daughter is exposed to these behaviors via various forms of media and play behavior. Just as greater time spent on these activities is associated with positive views thinness in 3- and 4-year-olds, the same relationship is seen at 5 years of age. Another study found that higher media use at age 4 was linked with higher dietary restraint (e.g., watching one's diet to avoid getting fat) in 5-year-olds, although the impact was relatively small (Rodgers et al., 2017). Additionally, that study suggested that the

5-year-olds with more exposure to television and DVD viewing had lower self-esteem, as reported by the girls' parents.

If you allow your daughter to watch YouTube, you are likely aware that you can set parental controls for appropriate content. Still, it is important to monitor what she is watching, as these controls are not fail-safe. There is also no avoiding the advertising marketed toward children, whether for food or for products such as toys. In middle childhood, children have a limited understanding of the intention behind advertising, and they do not yet have a grasp of the manipulative tactics of advertisers. Finally, children are exposed to *kidfluencers,* child stars who are often sponsored by advertisers and who have considerable influence over their followers. Although you do not need to forbid your daughter from using YouTube as an entertainment source, but rather you should set limits and observe how your daughter is affected by the content itself.

What about toys? In Chapter 4, we discussed mixed findings concerning doll use by preschool girls—they can be a positive or negative influence. Although many brands of dolls are available— Bratz, Monster High, Barbie, and others—most of the research has addressed the Barbie doll, which has long been popular with this age group and is likely even more popular today as a result of the movie *Barbie* (Gerwig, 2023). In one study, 6- to 8-year-old girls were shown images of either Barbie or another doll, Emme (intended to represent a more realistic body ideal), in the context of stories about everyday behavior (Dittmar et al., 2006). For example, the dolls were shown getting ready for a birthday party. A third group of girls was shown images of scenes that did not contain any dolls. Girls were then asked to respond to different statements, such as "I'm pretty happy about the way I look," and to indicate what they perceived their current body size and ideal body sizes to be. Body satisfaction and body esteem were both lower in the girls who viewed Barbie than in the girls who viewed the other images, whereas there was no difference in these outcomes between the girls who viewed Emme or neutral photos without dolls in them. What is particularly interesting about this finding, and especially relevant to this chapter, is that these effects were strongest in the 5.5- to 7.5-year-olds. So, girls in this age group appear to be especially vulnerable to these influences.

These findings were paralleled in a more recent study (Jellinek et al., 2016), in which 6- to 8-year-old girls played with Barbie or Tracy, a doll who depicted a fuller figure, and the dolls were either in modest clothing or in swimsuits. Regardless of the clothing worn by the dolls, the girls who played with Barbie had lower body esteem than those who played with Tracy. Further, girls who played with Tracy showed a decrease in body dissatisfaction over time, as defined by the difference between their actual and ideal bodies. In contrast, girls who played with Barbie showed an increase in body dissatisfaction. A follow-up study using unfamiliar dolls revealed the same general pattern, although girls who played with modestly dressed dolls had higher body esteem than those who played with dolls in swimsuits. The authors noted that these effects were obtained with relatively little play time with the dolls—only 3 minutes!

However, not all studies show negative effects of playing with dolls. For example, in one study, 6- to 10-year-old girls played with Emme, Barbie, Tyler (a thin doll included to equate for height differences between Emme and Barbie), or Lego toys (Anschutz & Engels, 2010). The findings showed no differences in body esteem or body dissatisfaction as measured by actual–ideal body difference, but girls did differ in how much they ate afterward when given access to M&Ms candy and asked to evaluate the taste. Girls who played with the Emme doll ate significantly more candy than those who played with the thinner dolls.

In another study, 5- to 8-year-old girls were exposed to Barbie in one of three different formats (print observation/photos, physical observation/watching scenarios, and physical engagement/acting out scenarios) or were in a control group exposed to a My Little Pony doll (Rice et al., 2016). Girls exposed to Barbie in all formats had higher thin ideal internalization than girls exposed to the My Little Pony doll, but body dissatisfaction and body esteem did not differ across conditions. There were no differences based on the type of interaction with Barbie, and these effects did not differ by age.

It is unclear why some studies show negative effects of exposure to Barbie and others do not. Some authors have suggested that the modality in which these toys are experienced can matter—whether they are used to enact play scenarios, for example, or whether they are used in a more appearance-focused way, such as for dress-up. Additionally, the amount of exposure might matter: The amount of play time was longer in some of the studies that obtained negative effects of exposure than it was in studies that did not show these effects. How these studies were conducted is also a consideration. Because many studies do not assess body dissatisfaction before girls are exposed to Barbie, we do not know if the outcomes that we see in girls are due specifically to Barbie or if the girls already felt body dissatisfaction before this exposure. We also do not know the long-term effects of this exposure, since the studies are typically conducted at one point in time. Finally, the effects might depend on each girl's personal characteristics and cultural expectations and values. Most of this research has been conducted with White, upper middle-class girls, so these results do not represent all girls and all families.

Overall, our impression of the research on Barbie and other such dolls is that the negative effects, if any, are relatively minor. Most girls were not distressed by the exposure to Barbie in these studies, although some expressed wanting to be thinner. We do not think that is a reason to explicitly ban Barbie or other dolls from your daughter's play repertoire if she enjoys these dolls.

Healthy Body Image Building Tool

 Cultural influences are everywhere, and it may be overwhelming to think about how to work with your daughter to navigate them successfully. In general, limiting the amount of exposure to media is a good idea not only to protect body image but also because greater use of media comes with health risks such as obesity (e.g., Rodgers et al., 2017; Tiberio et al., 2014). To be clear, we are advocating for the regulation of your daughter's media consumption behavior rather than her weight or BMI. Children who move their bodies, as all children should be doing, will naturally vary in body size. Decide what sources of media to prioritize or avoid depending on both your daughter's interests and the effects that you see on her: Does she become excessively preoccupied with or upset about what she sees or plays with? Does she compare herself to people or characters that she watches or interacts with in the media? Is she interested in activities that are on par with her developmental level, or is she delving into teen territory too early? These decisions are best made individually and based on open discussion with your daughter.

A FINAL NOTE ON COMMUNICATING WITH YOUR 5- TO 7-YEAR-OLD

Children show tremendous increases in physical, cognitive, and social development in middle childhood. You have probably noticed that, in contrast to the preschool years, your daughter is better able to pay attention, follow rules, engage in problem solving, and control her emotions and behavior (Marcovitch et al., 2010). Researchers have referred to the period between 5 and 7 years of age as the onset of the *age of reason*. These developments make it easier for you to have more meaningful and extensive dialogue with her. However, your daughter has not suddenly become a miniature adult, as you have also likely noticed.

As we discussed previously, parenting styles are personal and there is no single way to "do" parenting correctly. Generally speaking, research strongly supports a parenting approach that is warm and responsive but also appropriately structured and rule based (e.g., Balantekin et al., 2020). As your daughter's skills continue to develop, consider ways to provide opportunities for her to develop independence, with guidance. For example, you might discuss what kind of summer camp she would like to attend while gently steering her toward options that you feel best fit with her temperament and interests (and your schedule!).

One of the most challenging transitions that children can face is entry to school. Although it is exciting, formal schooling brings a new set of rules and expectations that may differ from those at home and requires navigating the peer landscape. This transition is even more pronounced for children who were not previously in day care or preschool settings. Academic expectations also increase during middle childhood. All of these changes are not just challenging for your daughter but possibly for you as well, and they require quite a bit of communication. Talk with your daughter regularly about her experiences at school, both academically and with her peers, so that you can keep open lines of communication if you have concerns about her adjustment.

Given the amount of time that your daughter will likely spend at school and among her peers, it is important to know how she manages this new microsystem. You may find that she is increasingly emotional or sensitive about her academic performance or her social interactions with her peers—this increase in emotionality is natural given her developing theory of mind abilities, in particular perspective taking. Because at this age she is able to think about how others see her, she may be increasingly influenced by the things that her peers do, say, and wear, some of which may not be agreeable to you as her parent. In this case, it is important, when possible, to use induction (i.e., explain your decisions) rather than to engage in power assertion ("Because I say so!"), recognizing that you cannot expect to use induction all the time and that overall consistency matters most. Explanations are particularly important for children at this age given their developing reasoning skills (and they want answers!), but they are also prone to sulking when they do not get their own way. Aim to be firm but responsive to your daughter's point of view.

Finally, during these few years, you may start to see changes in how your daughter views herself or her self-concept. Advances in *autobiographical memory*—memory for personally relevant events—will shape how she sees herself. Not only does the self-concept continue to develop during this time, but research suggests individual differences in children's optimism about themselves and others. For example, if you notice that your daughter tends to be pessimistic about her abilities, direct her toward a **learning and mastery approach** rather than focusing excessively on performance.

> **Learning and mastery approach:** a focus on the process of developing new knowledge rather than a specific performance outcome, such as a particular grade (see Dweck, 2017).

Building your daughter's self-efficacy will encourage her to move away from self-evaluation and toward a problem-solving approach, whether for academic or for social challenges. You may also start to see evidence of stable personality characteristics that can be relevant to body image development; one that is particularly relevant is perfectionism. As discussed in Chapter 2, perfectionism is associated with body dissatisfaction and the risk of eating disorders. Mothers who are perfectionistic tend to have daughters with these same tendencies. If this characteristic describes you, aim to be attentive in monitoring these tendencies in front of your daughter. Note that being perfectionistic does not in any way mean that your daughter is "doomed" in terms of body image. Rather, you might need to be a bit more vigilant when looking for signs of body image distress and to consider carefully monitoring the external influences that could contribute to it. If you see signs of perfectionism in your daughter, consider discussing the importance of self-compassion with her, perhaps applying the activities aligned with Chapters 1 and 2.

PUTTING IT ALL TOGETHER: ENGAGING YOUR DAUGHTER IN ACTIVITIES AND DISCUSSION

Some key takeaways from this chapter:

- Because children at this age are developing their understanding of personality, highlight your daughter's stable, positive attributes. Watch for perfectionistic thinking so that you can help her practice self-compassion, reframing, and a process-oriented learning approach.
- Encourage some exposure to mixed-gender play, and take advantage of opportunities outside of the house to show the diversity of roles and characteristics of girls and women, such as by observing female scientists at a local science center or university.
- Consider enrolling your daughter in a sport or other movement-related activity. If she pursues an aesthetic sport, talk with the instructors to ensure that they emphasize a body-healthy environment that does not focus on physical appearance, weight, or BMI.
- Start teaching your daughter informally that it's important to eat in a balanced way to support body functioning, and do your best to model this behavior consistently. Aim for a structured, positive environment when she is eating, and praise healthy eating behavior but refrain from controlling her intake excessively.

- Be watchful of your daughter's peer group, as teasing and bullying can begin at this age for some children, often centered on physical appearance. Enforce a zero-tolerance policy for bullying.
- Set parental controls on media and filter inappropriate content. Have discussions with your daughter about what she is watching, and explain that she should approach you if she sees something unusual or upsetting.
- Because shame emerges at this age and can be fueled by appearance or weight-related comments from others, prepare your daughter by explaining that her body is nobody's business but her own and reminding her that there are no good or bad bodies.

The Appendix contains optional activities that further support the healthy body image development goals at this age:

- Activity 10: Lunch Box Love Notes—Healthy thoughts and feelings
- Activity 11: Literary Genius—Healthy thoughts and feelings
- Activity 12: Read and Share: *Your Name Is a Song*—Healthy thoughts and feelings
- Activity 13: Picture Perfect Memories—Body respect
- Activity 14: My Amazing Hands and Feet—Body respect
- Activity 15: Read and Share: *Your Body Is Awesome*—Body respect

CHAPTER 6

YOUR DAUGHTER'S BODY IMAGE IN LATE CHILDHOOD: AGES 8 THROUGH 10 YEARS

Rebecca and her 10-year-old daughter, Lucy, are strolling through the local outdoor mall on a balmy Saturday morning. Their plan is to do some shopping—Lucy has grown quite a bit this year and she needs new summer clothes—and have lunch at their favorite cafe. As they approach the window display of a favorite store that carries lifestyle clothing for girls and women, Lucy pauses to look at a pair of fitted capris on the junior girl mannequin. "Do you want to go in and check them out?" asks Rebecca. Lucy sighs and says, "Cameron has these." Rebecca has been hearing a lot about Lucy's friend Cameron these days, including that she has beautiful long hair and a collection of cool sneakers and is the prettiest girl in the class. "Well, you can get them, too, if you want them," counters Rebecca. Lucy pauses for a moment and then says, "I don't know. They'll look better on her—she's thin." Rebecca is saddened to hear her daughter compare herself to another girl, but she understands her daughter's feelings all too well, having compared herself to other women in this way. "You know what?" Rebecca says. "It doesn't matter how these look on Cameron or anyone else. What matters is if *you* like them and how they make *you* feel. C'mon, let's just have a look and you can decide!" They enter the store together.

As girls transition into late childhood (i.e., ages 8 through 10 years), the way they view and judge themselves shows a major change: the budding tendency to compare oneself to others, especially in relation to physical appearance. In Chapter 1, we discussed this tendency, known as *upward social comparison*, among adult women. In late childhood, as in Lucy's case, peer comparisons among girls are centered on their physical appearance. In contrast, for boys these comparisons are centered on functional aspects of bodies, such as sports performance. Lucy's statement also highlights the importance of peers in children's lives at this age: Girls begin to pay attention to what their friends say, do, and wear. The share of the microsystem devoted to friends has expanded considerably, and although expected, this change can have consequences for girls' body image development.

This chapter covers development and body image in late childhood, specifically for 8- to 10-year-old girls. The structure is generally similar to Chapters 4 and 5, with information about developmental milestones, girls' feelings about their bodies, and major influences on body image at this age, including maternal and peer influences. Because this chapter addresses preadolescence—and therefore covers a range of challenges from biological to physical to social—it may feel overwhelming to think about whether or how you can guide your daughter through it successfully. Rest assured! Armed with scientific knowledge and a good dose of compassion, you can do this. And you need not be perfect—there is no such thing as perfect parenting. Remember that it is never too late to take steps in a positive direction, even if you are getting started in late childhood; you are already well ahead of the game given that many parents do not address body image until adolescence, or at all. As in the previous chapters, this chapter includes actionable tips and ends with suggested activities that promote healthy body image development.

COGNITIVE, EMOTIONAL, AND SOCIAL DEVELOPMENT IN LATE CHILDHOOD

Changes in self-concept, gender flexibility, and emotions, among other aspects of development, continue to impact body image development in 8- to 10-year-olds. The next sections describe these changes in more detail for children in this age range.

Self-Concept: The Removal of Rose-Colored Glasses

No two children are the same, but in general, children's self-concept becomes less positive and more negative over time (Harter, 2006; Onetti et al., 2019). This increase in negativity is somewhat disheartening, but if we understand why it occurs, we can help to soften the blow. The change is partly due to increases in social comparison (Lapan & Boseovski, 2017) and because children start to realize that they simply are not good at everything they do. Based on feedback in the academic and social arenas, children begin to identify their strengths and weaknesses more realistically. Increases in cognitive skills also mean that children can engage in some self-evaluation without needing others' feedback (Demo, 1992).

The decrease in self-concept positivity is especially meaningful for girls and their body image because the positive nature of the appearance component of girls' self-concept declines in later childhood. This pattern is the opposite of what is seen in younger children—in the short term, younger girls often report a higher self-concept than younger boys do. In girls, self-esteem and body image both decline during the elementary school years (Leaper, 2015). It is unclear whether these decreases are related to current body weight, changes in body weight (Onetti et al., 2019), or actual appearance as compared to perceived appearance. As discussed later in the chapter, changes in girls' cognitive development, more intense interactions with peers, and increased exposure to media also influence girls' self-concept in later childhood.

Healthy Body Image Building Tool

 You can help your daughter work on developing her self-concept by redirecting any tendencies to compare herself to others or to adopt their behaviors, especially if they are not necessarily right for her or, importantly, if her peers are starting to embrace diet culture and fat talk. Avoid excessive discussion about physical appearance about yourself, her, and other women. Talk about aspects of herself that she admires and that she would like to develop further, including personal characteristics, behaviors, and skills. For example, you might focus on enhancing her physical competence in a new sport or an activity that she would like to try. This focus on physical skill development is associated with a stronger physical self-concept and an interest in physical activity. Come up with a plan if you like, and let her take the lead so that she has a strong sense of self-efficacy about what she can accomplish. See Activity 16 in the Appendix, **Our Amazing Adventures**, for ways to apply this idea.

Gender Identity: Feminine and Masculine Activity Choices

During later childhood, you may notice that your daughter's interest in specific activities waxes and wanes, and this variability is common. Girls' interest in "feminine" activities (e.g., dancing, gardening) as compared to "masculine" activities (e.g., competitive sports, fishing) often changes over the course of late childhood and early adolescence (McHale et al., 2004). It is important to note, however, that there is nothing naturally masculine or feminine about activities; activities are designated as feminine or masculine based on children's own classifications or liking ratings (i.e., more girls than boys report liking the activities labeled as feminine, whereas more boys than girls report liking the activities labeled as masculine). Overall, researchers have found a specific pattern: Between 8 and 9 years of age, girls' interest in feminine activities increases, but this trend reverses when the girls are between 9 and 10 years of age and begin to show more interest in masculine activities. During later childhood, girls' involvement in feminine activities generally declines, but this pattern changes again in early adolescence: When girls are 11 to 13 years of age, they tend to become more interested in feminine activities. Finally, interest in feminine activities again declines when girls are 15 to 17 years old.

What explains these patterns? During some periods, girls experience social pressures from peers to conform to gender expectations, regardless of their own interests or how they think about these activities. This tendency toward conformity likely coincides with girls' increased attention to physical appearance. At the same time, advances in moral reasoning (in general, the ability to distinguish right from wrong) and **gender flexibility** are associated with better understanding of issues related to gender discrimination and different treatment of girls and boys. So, girls' preferences for activities do not reflect their cognitive limitations but are instead related to social demands. As with many tendencies, girls' activity choices reflect individual differences that are also influenced by parenting.

> **Gender flexibility:** the ability to recognize that characteristics (such as personality traits) and preferences (such as toy or activity choices) can apply to all people, regardless of sex (see Leaper, 2015).

Storm and Stress? Emotional Roller Coaster? Navigating the Entry Into Puberty

You may have just done a double take, or you may be completely unsurprised, to see a reference to emerging puberty in a chapter about girls from ages 8 to 10. Depending on how the data are compiled,

Healthy Body Image Building Tool

 It is healthy for children to experiment with a range of activities and behaviors. That said, for girls in later childhood, we suggest that you pay attention to whether these activities may translate to beliefs about the self. For example, dressing up for fun is different than associating the way one dresses with personal characteristics (e.g., that a girl must look pretty) or morality (that a girl "ought" to dress a particular way). Continue to expose your daughter to a variety of activities that move beyond gender-typed boundaries. For example, cultural messages encourage girls to take on nurturing roles in play and interactions with others, engage in activities oriented toward physical appearance, and avoid activities like competitive sports. You can present other options for your daughter's consideration, such as playing with gadgets or monster trucks, working on a stimulating science kit, or joining a child trivia group or sports team. As discussed in Chapter 5, the types of activities that children choose or are given play a role in shaping their skills. The societal myth that girls are more vulnerable than boys can discourage the development of important skills. For example, if girls do not have the chance to practice standing up for themselves or serving as leaders, they may be less likely to be able to do so later in life.

and for reasons that are still unclear to scientists, puberty begins earlier than it used to in previous decades. In girls, the typical onset of puberty occurs between 8 and 13 years of age. This age range is wide, and girls of the same age can look very different. You may have noticed differences in your daughter's peer group. You may see your daughter as an early bloomer or a late bloomer relative to her friends, and this timing is likely to have consequences for her body image, especially given the social comparison tendencies common among girls at this age. Girls who develop early may feel self-conscious and may experience unwanted attention and teasing about the changes in their bodies. Girls who develop late may be envious of peers who develop early, although research shows that later pubertal timing is protective for health (e.g., early-maturing girls are more likely than later-maturing girls to engage in risky behavior; Skoog & Stattin, 2014). The differences between your daughter and her friends can also affect her feelings about puberty.

Because addressing puberty is beyond the scope of this book, we have provided suggested resources at the end of the chapter. In this chapter, we focus primarily on changes in girls' emotional experience to provide a useful context for understanding challenges with body image and enacting strategies for helping the girls to navigate them.

Adolescence is a period during which both the body and the brain mature physically (Casey et al., 2010). You may have heard that adolescence is associated with raging hormones, intense emotions, and reckless behavior, but research has shown that this characterization is overstated (Arnett, 1999). Adolescent children are not walking around in a constant state of emotional turmoil, nor are they completely illogical or unable to control their behavior. That said, there are some changes in how children experience emotions, and these changes happen earlier in girls than they do in boys because girls generally enter puberty before boys do. When we think about and remember our own experiences with puberty, we recognize that so many changes take place all at once. Some rapid changes in biological development are not readily visible (e.g., the brain, hormones), while others are highly visible (e.g., wider hips, breast development) and require adjusting to a "new" body. The nature of parent–child relationships also changes, with most children desiring increased independence and becoming increasingly concerned with their peer relationships and the onset of romantic crushes. Advances in cognitive skills allow for more self-evaluation and a better understanding of the self and others. These changes are a lot to deal with all at one time, so it is unsurprising that girls may seem less content than they were previously.

In one study (Griffith et al., 2021), researchers followed boys and girls over time and mapped changes in the negative and positive emotions (referred to as *affect*) they experienced between 9 and 17 years of age. Every 18 months, participants reported the frequency and type of positive affect (e.g., cheerful, delighted, calm) and negative affect (e.g., frightened, ashamed, upset) that they experienced. Negative affect decreased between 9 and 11.5 years of age but increased starting at 12 years of age. Positive affect was relatively high at 9 years of age but decreased steadily over time, and this pattern did not differ based on the child's race or parental education. Other studies have also reported increases in negative affect between 10 and 14 years of age (Larson et al., 2002).

It is important to recognize that these studies describe general trends—some girls find this prepubertal transition relatively easy, and others find it highly challenging. And in some cases, it might not be obvious to you that your daughter is struggling, which is why establishing open and nonjudgmental lines of communication is so important. In those moments when your daughter experiences unpredictable ups and downs—and when everything you say and do is wrong and annoying to her—do your best to show compassion and empathy for the changes that she is experiencing (or just leave the room and take a breather if things get heated!).

Healthy Body Image Building Tool

 Many schools include some programming about puberty fairly early, such as in the fourth or fifth grade. This kind of preparation is important so that the changes do not come as a shock to girls. Researchers have shown that girls at the cusp of puberty can experience quite a bit of shame (Riboli et al., 2022), and the goal is to prevent or minimize this feeling. It is a great idea to raise the topic with your daughter, both to emphasize that there is nothing to be ashamed about and to show her that you would like to hear about her experience, if she wants to discuss it, and to support her through puberty when it happens.

Thoughts and Feelings About Food: Awareness of Nutrition or Introduction to Diet Culture?

By late childhood, children understand that food is a necessary energy source for the body rather than only being able to describe it as important for growth. For example, 9-year-olds are more likely than younger children to believe that healthy food makes us stronger. They are aware that a healthy and balanced diet includes fruits and vegetables and that these foods provide vitamins (Edwards & Hartwell, 2002). By 9 to 10 years of age, children also understand that what you put into the body affects both height and weight (Raman, 2014). Food classification skills are quite strong at this age, but children are better able to identify fruits than vegetables. Children also have a tendency to classify foods according to preference or taste rather than according to health value. Unsurprisingly, children report a preference for unhealthy over healthy foods, although liking healthy foods increases with age (DeJesus, Kinzler, & Shutts, 2018).

Some research suggests that girls are more knowledgeable than boys about food and nutrition. In one focus group with 7- to 11-year-olds, girls demonstrated greater knowledge about healthy foods than about unhealthy foods and greater knowledge than boys about the link between foods and nutrients (K. H. Hart et al., 2002). Girls also had more knowledge than boys about which foods are fattening, and they showed a stronger awareness of the importance of controlling food intake (Edwards & Hartwell, 2002). These findings suggest that girls either have more interest in learning about food or that they have greater or different messaging around food than boys do. A look at the research on parents' messages to their children about eating provides some insight. One notable research finding (K. H. Hart et al., 2002) is that boys report that parents talk about the importance of manners around the table and finishing their food, whereas girls are more likely to report that parents talk about food restriction (e.g., not allowing certain food) and make prescriptions or "deals" around food (e.g., a less desirable food must be eaten before a more desirable food). Somewhat concerning, girls may also associate healthy eating with dieting.

As discussed in Chapter 5, mothers' dieting behaviors are associated with girls' dieting behaviors, as are negative comments or teasing about girls' bodies, and these behaviors can convey negative attitudes about people who are overweight. Parental encouragement of dieting is associated with daughters' desire to be thinner (Thelen & Cormier, 1995) and predicts the emergence of dieting in preadolescence (Balantekin et al., 2014). These effects are not just temporary; they can continue to have an impact on girls' and women's body image for many years.

To some degree, peer influence begins to overtake the influence of parents on children's eating and ideas about food. Children in late childhood spend more time with their peers than they did when they were younger, and they are influenced by their peers' attitudes and behaviors. In fact, and rather disturbingly, girls' dieting behaviors can be predicted based on their friends' dieting behaviors. Whereas younger girls might have mimicked peer eating behavior just to be like their friends, in later childhood the girls have a different purpose, such as the goal of weight loss or weight maintenance.

In one study (Hutchinson & Rapee, 2007), researchers conducted a social network analysis with 10- to 14-year-old girls. "Social network analysis" is a fancy way of describing a study of thoughts and behaviors of closely connected groups of friends, known as *cliques*. The researchers wanted to know if behavioral similarities within a clique were greater than similarities between cliques, which would suggest that girls in close circles of friends have a meaningful impact on each other. The findings showed exactly this: Cliques of friends participated in the same kinds of eating behaviors, such as dietary restraint or extreme weight loss behaviors. This result held even when the researchers considered girls' body mass index (BMI), self-esteem, and negative affect.

As with 5- to 7-year-olds, in late childhood girls' impressions that their peers care about dieting and weight loss, whether true or not, are associated with dieting behavior. Research indicates that 8- to 11-year-olds' dietary restraint is similar to their friends' dietary restraint, and that for children with higher anxiety, this behavior is associated with greater external eating (i.e., eating based on others' eating behavior rather than attending to one's own hunger cues; Farrow et al., 2011). As we noted in Chapter 1, siblings as well as peers can influence girls' eating, but little research on this topic has been conducted with this age group. The same guidelines apply in terms of paying attention to sibling interactions as for the peer group.

Healthy Body Image Building Tool

 Late childhood can be a tricky time to navigate messages about food: You may see weight gain in your daughter (which is natural), she may panic about the weight gain, and she may be around peers who are dieting or engaging in disordered eating. This period is high risk for the development of eating disorders, so it is a good idea to pay attention to what is happening in your daughter's closest circle of friends and talk to her directly about her beliefs around eating, particularly if you start to see changes in her eating behaviors (e.g., rejecting certain foods that she typically enjoys, making excessive comments that certain foods are fattening). You should not abandon attempts to promote eating balanced meals to support health and well-being, but it is important both to explain and to model the difference between eating for health and energy and dieting to become smaller. Remember that you are still a key role model! Having structured eating times with gentle guidance about what is best for our bodies at various times is a great way to convey the responsibilities and benefits of eating well without connecting it to dieting behaviors. See Activity 17 in the Appendix, **Happy, Healthy Balance**, for a way to apply some of these ideas.

Thoughts and Feelings About the Body: Getting Holistic for Health

Knowledge about food and knowledge about how the body uses food to function become a lot more sophisticated between 8 and 10 years of age (Schultz & Danford, 2016). And because children in this age group are more verbally capable than their younger counterparts, we can learn a lot about them by conducting interview studies. One such study (Slaughter & Ting, 2010) revealed key changes in how children think about the purpose of food in late childhood, which are related to children's biological reasoning abilities in late childhood. In particular, children develop a better understanding of the connection between food and physiology, they refer more to internal organs and nutrients in relation to eating, and they come to understand the negative effects of an unbalanced diet (e.g., eating only one food or eating only sugary foods). By about 10 years of age, children show an adultlike understanding of digestion. For example, rather than simply thinking about the stomach as the location where food is stored, they are aware that food changes in form when it is digested so that it can be used by the body.

Physical literacy also continues to increase, in part because children often receive some formal education about the importance of physical activity for well-being. Also, with the advent of the Title IX education amendment in 1972, girls' participation in sports increased dramatically through the decades (Kaestner & Xu, 2006). If it were only a matter of education and exposure, we might see girls embrace physical activity, but quite the opposite is true for many girls. Why do so many girls become less interested in or uncomfortable with the idea of moving their bodies? At this age, physical activity takes on a complex role in girls' lives because it is tied to body image and ideas about gender and gender roles (Spencer et al., 2015). Further, both girls' bodies and peer relations (e.g., interest in romantic relationships) are changing because of puberty.

Girls are very much aware of gender stereotypes and expectations about activity. Some girls report pressure to look feminine; others have a heightened awareness of their bodies in gym class and feel uncomfortable with required attire, which is sometimes more revealing for girls than it is for boys. But it goes beyond this: Girls also report pressure to meet feminine ideals, which can limit their desire to participate in sports seen as competitive or aggressive or that make them red-faced or sweaty (see Spencer et al., 2015). The goals for physical activity often differ for boys and girls: Boys talk about wanting to build strength with physical activity participation, while girls tend to focus on minimizing body size (McCabe & Ricciardelli, 2003). In Chapter 5, we discussed participation in aesthetic sports as a risk factor for girls, and this concern carries over for this age group too, particularly as girls start to gain weight and see body shape changes with the onset of puberty. Such changes are natural and expected and should not be taken as a sign to put your daughter on a diet.

Healthy Body Image Building Tool

 During late childhood, we can take advantage of girls' increasing knowledge of biological processes, physical health, and nutrition by helping them to develop a holistic view of health (Warburton et al., 2022). This view incorporates physical, social, emotional, and intellectual well-being. By helping our girls to see the connection between these aspects of health, we can remove the emphasis on physical appearance. If your daughter is physically active, whether in aesthetic or nonaesthetic sports (noting the higher risk associated with the former), discuss with her the connections among eating in a balanced way, having the energy to move her body, and feeling good about moving her body. Encourage her to get involved in food preparation and to make choices for herself. One way to frame these choices is in terms of the value or quality that they add to our lives and emphasize that being thoughtful about how we eat applies to all of us, not just girls.

See Activity 18, **Relaxation Station,** in the Appendix to apply some ideas about holistic health while also bonding with your daughter.

Body Image

Despite the many positive qualities that emerge in children at this age, such as enhanced perspective taking, many children show weight-based biases throughout late childhood, and some research suggests that the stigmatization of overweight people quickly becomes adult-like, including judgments about overweight people that range from lazy to sloppy, less smart, and less athletic than people who are not overweight. Children are also less likely to want to be friends with overweight children than with thin or average children, and overweight children sometimes show discrimination against other overweight children (Rex-Lear et al., 2019). These kinds of attitudes are adopted from societal messages, whether individual comments directed at children or comments about other people. As we discussed earlier, they are associated with internalization or application of these messages to the self (e.g., children start to see themselves as meeting these negative stereotypes; Rancaño et al., 2021). That said, some interview research with children suggests that they acknowledge that some people are fat and show considerable empathy for "naturally" fat children (Dixey et al., 2001, p. 206).

What about girls' feelings about their own bodies? Concerns that arise earlier in childhood (see Chapters 4 and 5) begin to escalate. Girls are aware of, and buy into, body ideals. In general, the ideal figure is considerably thinner than girls' current body sizes, even for girls at a healthy weight. Girls who have tendencies toward perfectionism may strive unrealistically toward achieving these ideals. Body objectification is fairly low among fifth graders but increases through ninth grade (Daniels et al., 2020). Between 8 and 10 years of age, there are increases in gender differences in body dissatisfaction, with girls expressing greater dissatisfaction than boys in many studies (Hutchinson & Rapee, 2007; Ricciardelli & McCabe, 2001). In some studies, both boys and girls express body dissatisfaction, but more girls express wanting to become thinner, whereas more boys want to become larger (Ricciardelli et al., 2003), and a greater percentage of girls openly express body dissatisfaction, although the precise numbers vary.

BMI is also influential: As with younger children, in late childhood a higher BMI is associated with more body dissatisfaction and the tendency to diet and/or produce other strategies to change body shape (Ricciardelli et al., 2003). In contrast, some evidence suggests that a low BMI is associated with attempts to gain weight, so poor body image does not always reflect a desire for thinness. This association between BMI and body dissatisfaction is thought to be partly due to societal influence, but it may also reflect girls' own discomfort with their body size or shape. In late childhood, girls show greater concern about weight and about becoming overweight, and for some girls, weight becomes a preoccupation. Some research suggests that girls, but not boys, believe that being thin increases their likeability (Dohnt & Tiggemann, 2005; K. K. Oliver & Thelen, 1996), which can serve as motivation for weight management behaviors. These facts are worrisome on their own, but even more so with the timing of puberty, when it is natural for girls to gain weight and experience changes in body shape.

MANAGING MAJOR INFLUENCES ON YOUR DAUGHTER'S BODY IMAGE IN LATE CHILDHOOD

Parents, peers, and the media continue to influence body image development between 8 to 10 years of age. The relative contributions of these influences change as peers and media use become more prominent in girls' lives.

Parenting: Continuing to Monitor Your Body Image to Protect Her Body Image

In Chapter 5, we noted that mothers' dissatisfaction with their bodies predicts daughters' dissatisfaction with their own bodies, and this remains the case for children in late childhood. In addition, as your daughter's body starts to change, you may be reminded of your own experience with puberty, or you may be thinking more about your own body image, which may raise a new uneasiness for you and may affect the way that you talk to your daughter about her body. This is natural, and being aware of it can be a very positive preventive step, so you may want to revisit Chapters 1 and 2 and reflect on how some of these issues affect your communication about this topic.

Despite the shift from parent to peer influences for girls in late childhood, you are still a key influence on your daughter's body image. Research shows that girls' interest in dieting and losing weight is associated with mothers' and, to a lesser extent, fathers' concerns about their weight and placing a high importance on weight (Phares et al., 2004). Body image concerns are also associated with depressive symptoms. In one study that tracked 7- and 8-year-olds for a 1-year period (Rodgers et al., 2020), mothers' comments about girls' weight, shape, and eating behavior—such as criticizing their clothing or suggesting that they stay away from certain foods because they are fattening—were associated with girls' disordered eating at both 7 and 8 years of age. Mothers who had more body concerns of their own reported making more of these comments, which is again why it is important to reflect on whether your own body image influences what you are thinking about and saying to your daughter.

One study with 8- to 12-year-olds (Handford et al., 2018) provides particularly powerful evidence that the types of comments that mothers make matter. In the presence of their daughters, the researchers asked mothers to view thin-ideal images and make either negative comments about their weight and appearance (e.g., stating that they needed to lose weight) or no comments about weight or appearance (e.g., making general comments about clothing). The researchers measured girls' body esteem before and after these events with their mothers as well as girls' body satisfaction, eating attitudes, and actual eating behaviors. The findings showed that girls whose mothers made negative comments had lower body esteem, greater body dissatisfaction and more disturbed eating attitudes, and they showed more restrained eating.

What about direct comments about your daughter's weight? These comments tend to be both unwanted and unhelpful, and they can be particularly problematic when they come from family members rather than from other sources (Hunger & Tomiyama, 2014). For example, being labeled as "too fat" at 10 years of age predicted obesity 10 years later even after adjusting for factors such as BMI, socioeconomic status, parent education, and race. Researchers believe that this weight gain may be due to increased stress and coping behaviors such as overeating. Notably, this outcome also depends on other factors, such as a girls' BMI. In general, children do not like parents to talk about their weight unless they bring it up first, even when the comments are positive. This finding applies to children who are both overweight and underweight (Puhl et al., 2022).

Girls' impression that others want them to lose weight also influences their body image, whether or not the impression is accurate, but this perception again depends to some degree on their BMI. In a study with 8- to 11-year-olds (Ricciardelli et al., 2003), girls who felt high pressure to lose weight more likely to engage in weight loss strategies, regardless of their BMI. Of the girls who felt low pressure to lose weight, only the heavier girls were likely to attempt weight loss strategies. For girls with a higher BMI, messages about increasing their muscularity also predicted the desire to lose weight. So, your daughter may be more or less vulnerable, depending on her

BMI. A key point is that even if we are not pressuring our girls to lose weight, they may have a desire to lose weight. And if our messages do not refer to weight directly but rather to other aspects of physical appearance enhancement, they may be potentially harmful.

If you find it difficult to refrain from these type of comments, some personal exploration might be in order. Why is your daughter's weight or physical appearance so important to you? Your daughter is, of course, an extension of you in the biological sense, but she is also her own developing person, and sometimes it can be hard to separate yourself from her given the intimate nature of the mother–daughter relationship. Consider whether your concern is based on thin-ideal values that you have learned or whether it reflects tendencies such as perfectionism in yourself, or perhaps the fear of judgment that might occur if your child is or were to become overweight, which is a very real concern. If any of this rings true, you should not feel guilty or bad about it. As we discussed previously, many women have been conditioned to feel this way without even realizing it. Being aware of these feelings is important so that you can recognize the difference between an appearance-based approach to body image and one that is centered on constructing a health-based body image.

Peer Influence: Keeping an Eye on Her Friendship Circles

Girls' friendships become more intense and involved during late childhood. Girls talk to their friends a lot, and they also talk about their friends a lot. As with Rebecca in the vignette at the beginning of the chapter, when your daughter is in this age range, chances are that you will hear a whole lot about what your daughter's friends are doing. These friendships can take the form of pairs or peer groups that hang out together, and it is likely that a girl will be a part of several such groups (e.g., school friends, church friends, extracurricular activity friends). Friendships are increasingly important to girls' self-worth,

Healthy Body Image Building Tool

Much of the information presented in this section seems to be sending messages about what not to do in your parenting behaviors regarding body image: Do not make comments about appearance; refrain from commenting about weight. If you are taking a health-centered approach to your daughter's health, aim to work on behaviors that center on the family, such as taking family walks together, preparing a variety of meals together, and practicing balanced approaches to eating. You can provide a good deal of structure for the experiences that your daughter will have, consistent with the authoritative parenting approach discussed in Chapter 2. In a study with 8- to 12-year-olds and their mothers (Lopez et al., 2018), researchers measured parenting style and food-related parenting practices, such as modeling healthy eating and structured eating times. They also assessed the quality of girls' diets, including fruit and vegetable consumption and sugar intake. Structured but warm parenting (i.e., authoritative parenting) was associated with a more healthful diet, as measured by a healthy eating index measure. And part of this positive outcome seems to be a result of structured mealtime practices. We also do not want to suggest that all comments toward your daughter are off limits or that you should teach her to fear the mirror or never comment on her appearance—appearance is a part of who people are. Instead, we suggest an approach that steers clear of weight-based discussion and that is diverse in focus. See Activity 19 in the Appendix, **Reflecting High Regard**, which emphasizes that the mirror can be used in ways that focus on non–appearance-based qualities.

and it is meaningful for girls to feel reciprocity with and to identify with their peers (Maunder & Monks, 2019). At this age, your daughter may show an increased tendency to want to do all the same things as her friends, or what we call *conformity*, and this is a natural way of trying to fit into the group. Conformity is often presented as undesirable in adulthood (at least in Western culture), but keep in mind that at this point in development, your daughter is taking in a lot of information and learning how to interact appropriately with her peers. There is plenty of time to stand out on her own and assert herself when she is ready.

Our advice to refrain from commenting on your daughter's weight may have given you the impression that you should also stay silent about her relationships with her friends, but given the intensity and influence of friendship at this age, we have quite the opposite advice. We suggest that you take a more active, informed role than you might have when she was younger: Know who her friends are, what they are like, what they generally talk about, and the kinds of activities that they engage in together. This knowledge about her friendships is critical because her friends will shape her values and play a large part in who she will become.

We already talked about peers' influences on diet: Girls are more likely to diet if they believe that their peer group values this kind of behavior, and girls in the same peer group tend to engage in the same dietary behaviors, although they do not necessarily share the same body image concerns. Physical appearance also matters in children's relationship with their peers. Unfortunately, like adults, children tend to judge other children by physical appearance, and they tend to like others who are physically attractive (Hartup, 1984) and to trust them more than they trust people who are less attractive (Bascandziev & Harris, 2014). Because of this focus on physical appearance, peer relations can become fraught in late childhood.

As is the case with younger girls, quite a bit of teasing occurs at this age, and children who are underweight or overweight are the most common targets. Children tend to engage in teasing that is centered on saying mean things to others and calling them unpleasant names. Children on the receiving end of this criticism often believe that these statements about them are factually true, which is why it is important to know about them and to deal with them directly. In a study with 7- to 10-year-olds (Kostanski & Gullone, 2007), children reported that their friends were the biggest source of teasing in their lives. Girls who were overweight were teased more than those who were normal weight or underweight. For children outside of normal weight, both BMI and teasing predicted body dissatisfaction, but only their BMI predicted dieting behavior. Other research has shown, however, that teasing predicts dieting in children older than those tested in this study. In a study with fifth and sixth graders (average age 10.7 years; Nelson et al., 2011), researchers examined the effects of weight-related criticism and non-weight-related criticism on body size perception, body dissatisfaction, and self-esteem. The researchers found that children whose weight was criticized saw themselves as larger than they were, regardless of whether it was true. Children who are larger also realize that they are larger.

As reflected in the example at the beginning of this chapter, peer groups are a major source of social comparison in girls' lives in late childhood, and these comparisons often focus on physical attractiveness (Tatangelo & Ricciardelli, 2017). In addition to engaging in social comparison more frequently than boys do, girls are much more critical of their appearance when making these comparisons. Girls also report that they compare themselves directly to other girls in the same age group. So, if a girl feels that she falls short in some way, her body image and her actual behavior may both be affected (e.g., she may begin dieting or exercising to change her appearance).

Sociocultural Influences: Unpacking the Media Together

Not only do social circles expand as girls get older, but girls also spend more time engaging with various forms of media, including the internet, television, and movies. For this reason, we focus on media influences in this section. Children as young as 8 years of age use social media and may spend several hours per week watching television and movies. One study of children between 8 and 11 years

Healthy Body Image Building Tool

 When it comes to understanding your daughter and her relationship with her friends, aim to listen more than you talk, and you will find that you can learn a lot without being overly intrusive. Listen for openings in which she reveals information, and ask her to elaborate. Ask her about her closest friends, but also ask her about new friends who are unfamiliar to you. Talk to her about the importance of being comfortable with her own choices as an independent young woman while respecting that her friends' choices may be different. As with younger children, it is important to be watchful for any evidence of excessive teasing, bullying, or cyberbullying. Although cyberbullying can occur during late childhood, it is more common in adolescence. The guidelines apply at both ages: Be watchful of her relationships and online interactions, talk with her directly about her activities, and watch for signs of distress (e.g., emotional withdrawal, sadness, reluctance to go to school or to share information about happenings at school, physical symptoms such as stomachaches or headaches). If your daughter is having social difficulties with a particular friend or group of friends, remind her about other social circles in which she is accepted, and encourage her to engage with them more frequently. If your daughter is being called fat by peers, it is important to tell her that this behavior from her peers is not her fault and that it is inappropriate. Also, it is important to emphasize that "fat" is not a bad word, that her body shape has nothing to do with her value as a person, and that those who are worth knowing do not judge us by our physical appearance. By all means, do not suggest that she should lose weight to deal with the issue, even if she is overweight. Encourage her to associate with peers who value and support her and to engage in activities she enjoys to build self-efficacy in areas that have nothing to do with her physical appearance. If social difficulties or teasing escalate to the point of bullying, as mentioned previously, deal with the issue at a higher level (e.g., report it to school authorities). Activity 18 in the Appendix, **Relaxation Station**, is a great way to bond with your daughter and to learn more about how she experiences her social world.

of age found that most children use the internet for game playing and entertainment purposes rather than to socialize directly with others (Slater et al., 2017). According to some reports, the percentage of "tweens" (i.e., 8- to 12-year-olds) who use social media has increased dramatically over the past years, likely due in part to the COVID-19 pandemic, and some research has shown that media internalization predicts body surveillance in adolescence (Rousseau & Eggermont, 2018).

It is well established that much of the media and advertising directed toward girls is highly gender stereotyped, appearance focused, and sometimes sexualized. Even if your daughter does not engage with the internet or social media yet, or very much, she will ultimately be exposed to it given the society in which we now live. For this reason, preparing your daughter to digest this information is important.

It is also important not to unnecessarily rule out participation in these activities. Social media, in particular, has become a hot-button topic. Research reveals many benefits to social media participation, but that participation can be helpful or harmful depending on who is using it. For example, girls with a mental illness such as depression are more likely to suffer negative consequences from social media participation than are other girls (Heffer et al., 2019).

As discussed previously, no single factor is responsible for body image problems. The key point about media exposure at this particular age is that it intersects with several developmental challenges—puberty, the emergence of social comparison, and lower self-esteem for many girls. Some researchers have described the combination of these factors as a "perfect storm" for increased body image concerns (Choukas-Bradley et al., 2022, p. 681). At this time in childhood, girls' focus on the appearance of both self and others increases, so we need to be mindful about both the type of exposure that girls are getting and the ways we can assist them to interpret what they see and hear.

So, how do girls experience the effects of media? The good news is that among 8- to 10-year-olds, girls show some awareness that fame culture is far removed from their regular lives and that comparison to celebrities is unrealistic (Tatangelo & Ricciardelli, 2017). But girls are not immune to the effects of celebrities, models, internet personalities, musicians, and television stars. Indeed, girls report that comparisons to celebrities are likely to elicit negative feelings, such as sadness and jealousy, whereas boys are more likely to see them as inspiring or to respond to them neutrally.

The emphasis on thinness and beauty in media is highly pervasive even when it is not transmitted directly. In a study with 10- to 13-year-olds (Blowers et al., 2003), researchers found that perceived pressure to be thin from the media, rather than from family and friends, was associated with thin ideal internalization at this age, which in turn was associated with body dissatisfaction. Girls who internalized the thin body ideal were also more likely to engage in social comparison with others. Importantly, in this study, only girls who subscribed to the thin ideal experienced body dissatisfaction with exposure to media. And as with other studies, higher BMI was associated with body dissatisfaction. So, individual differences determine the effect of media use on body image; one size does not fit all.

Young girls also engage in appearance management as early as 9 years of age (e.g., applying makeup, styling their hair), and this tendency increases over time. This behavior appears to be related to the viewing of tween television shows (Trekels & Eggermont, 2017). Another concern about girls' media consumption is the increased exposure to sexualized images and clothing in magazines and on television. In a study with 6- to 9-year-old girls (Slater & Tiggemann, 2016), exposure to this type of material was related to a preference for sexy clothing and higher body dissatisfaction, prompting the authors to conclude that parents should attempt to limit their daughters' access to sexualized media.

As mentioned previously, video games are popular at this age, and they vary drastically in the extent to which they are appearance focused. In particular, the female characters in many of these games tend to have unrealistic body shapes, and they are highly physically attractive. In one study (Slater et al., 2017), 8- to 9-year-olds played either an appearance-focused video game in which a female character works on enhancing her appearance to be attractive to a male ("Dream Date Dress Up") or a non–appearance-focused game that documented a penguin's work as a waiter and did not have any human figures in it ("Penguin Diner"). The findings revealed that girls who played the appearance-based game reported wanting a thinner figure and also reported a greater interest in traditionally feminine careers, but the two groups did not differ on measures of self-objectification in this study. The researchers noted that video games may be especially potent influences on body image because they often prompt players to assume the identities of the characters. That said, it is important to emphasize that this effect was short-term and that the focus was on one specific game, so we certainly should not conclude that all such games are harmful to girls. The researchers, too, advised monitoring the amount of exposure to games that emphasize appearance rather than ruling them out entirely.

As noted, no single factor causes body image problems in girls, and some researchers have turned their attention to the transaction of multiple potential risk factors. In one such study with 9- to 12-year-olds (L. Clark & Tiggemann, 2006), the researchers observed that the dual influence of peers and the media can be problematic. Engaging in appearance culture is related to conversations among friends about appearance, which in turn relates to thin-ideal internalization and body dissatisfaction. Because so many factors are at play, we must take a multifaceted approach to building healthy body image over the course of several years.

Healthy Body Image Building Tool

 There is an increasing emphasis on teaching our children to be critical consumers of media and also to use media in moderation. The American Psychological Association offers excellent science-based tips for navigating social media successfully (American Psychological Association, 2023). It is crucial to monitor the content your daughter is viewing across platforms. It is also a good idea to talk with her about what she has seen and to discuss together what it means and why it might be problematic. For example, you can raise awareness that images of models and celebrities are heavily filtered and note that these individuals also have very different lives than those led by the rest of us, with a high appearance investment in which their careers hinge on physical attractiveness. You can also discuss the selfie culture, which can be misleading in that it encourages girls to take numerous photos of themselves to find the most flattering one and to add filters that enhance their appearance. These activities can breed insecurity and encourage social comparison. One suggestion is to engage in Activity 13, **Picture Perfect Memories**, with your daughter at this age.

Discussing the purpose of media content with your daughter is good prevention for avoiding self-sexualization. The American Psychological Association (2007) offers a resource on how to deal with the problem of media sexualization of girls. You can talk about advertisers' intent to use images of girls and women to sell products and to play on our insecurities to compel us to buy their products. Finally, in the interest of continuing to expand self-concept development, you can generate lists of desirable things to do that do not involve engagement in social media and reliance on others' feedback (such as "likes") but instead serve as their own reward. See Activity 20 in the Appendix, **The Media and Me**, for ways to implement some of these tips.

A FINAL NOTE ON COMMUNICATING WITH YOUR 8- TO 10-YEAR-OLD

Children are very insightful at this age; their reasoning skills increase and reveal a much better understanding of the world. Children can draw logical conclusions based on what they observe around them, in part because they have better memories and more knowledge about the world in general, and they can hold more information in mind from moment to moment (see Goswami, 2010). Classification skills also improve. Children know that people can be categorized in many ways, for example according to gender, race, age, or type of job. They are also better able to appreciate multiple causes of people's behavior, along with increased perspective-taking skills (see Devine & Lecce, 2021). Behavioral control is much stronger; children can follow sets of rules and are far less distracted by irrelevant information when they are working toward goals (Zelazo et al., 2004). Children also become more skeptical at this age, in the sense that they understand that some of what they hear is untrue and people may be motivated to lie or misrepresent themselves for various reasons (Mills & Keil, 2008). This skill continues to develop in later years.

Emotionally, children in late childhood can understand that people might feel differently about the same situation based on experience, knowledge, or biases. They can think about their own thinking and understand mixed emotions, and they show increases in the ability to cope with emotions by reframing situations or distracting themselves (Lagattuta & Kramer, 2021). At this age, they also begin to share their feelings and emotions with friends rather than with parents, and they are increasingly motivated by rewarding social situations.

As discussed in this chapter, advanced thinking skills can come with a high emotional cost, including decreases in self-concept positivity and increases in social comparison. The positivity bias that children show toward themselves and others starts to decrease in late childhood as children begin to see things more realistically (Boseovski, 2010). Children also become more concerned about academic performance as they learn to manage constructive feedback from teachers.

This reality check is a normal developmental progression, so we need not fret about it, and there are approaches that we can take to help our girls navigate it successfully. Aim to show warmth and sensitivity to your daughter's concerns, even if they may, at times, seem trivial to you from the seasoned adult perspective. Emphasize that it is okay not to be the best at everything, whether academic, athletic, or otherwise. Instead, she can aim to be her best at the things that she values. Aim to problem solve *with* her rather than *for* her so that she can continue to develop self-efficacy. Realize that you cannot always make it all better, but you can always show your daughter that she is valued and loved. In fact, your daughter will experience substantial emotional development through late adolescence, so rest assured that your support is critical, even if it feels like you are dealing with someone who seems, or thinks that she is, very adultlike. Activity 21 in the Appendix, **Dear Diary**, may be used to encourage your daughter to express her thoughts and emotions via journaling.

PUTTING IT ALL TOGETHER: ENGAGING YOUR DAUGHTER IN ACTIVITIES AND DISCUSSION

The key takeaways from this chapter are as follows:

- Self-concept becomes less positive, and it can be fueled by social comparison with peers. Discourage this tendency and partner with your daughter to make a plan aimed at building skills and capabilities that she values and that are not appearance oriented.

- If your daughter loses interest in gym or other movement opportunities, talk to her directly about gender stereotypes, such as "Women don't sweat," and show her counterexamples, such as women athletes. The same approach can be applied to other situations (e.g., leadership opportunities, involvement in science).
- Have open discussions about puberty before it happens, emphasizing that this process is normal, nothing to be ashamed of, and comes with body changes including weight gain.
- Peers are a critical influence. Emphasize to your daughter that her friends' choices—should they involve dieting or excessive appearance-focused activities such as following celebrity culture—do not have to be her choices.
- Be careful with your dialogue and actions around food and eating. You are still a key role model! Discourage dieting and focus on holistic health—the connection between physical and emotional well-being—and emphasize our responsibility to take care of our bodies.
- Social media participation tends to start or increase in girls at this age, and it can have benefits and drawbacks. Determine how your daughter uses and responds to it when deciding to set limits.

Themed companion activities designed for this age group are available in the Appendix:

- Activity 16: Our Amazing Adventures—Healthy thoughts and feelings
- Activity 17: Happy, Healthy Balance—Body respect
- Activity 18: Relaxation Station—Healthy thoughts and feelings
- Activity 19: Reflecting High Regard—Body respect

- Activity 20: The Media and Me—Healthy thoughts and feelings
- Activity 21: Dear Diary—Healthy thoughts and feelings

Recommended Resources

Holmes, M., Hutchison, T., & Lowe, K. (2022). *You-ology: A puberty guide for every body.* American Academy of Pediatrics. https://doi.org/10.1542/9781610025720 (directed toward children)

Kowal-Connelly, S. (2018). *Parenting through puberty: Mood swings, acne, and growing pains.* American Academy of Pediatrics. https://doi.org/10.1542/9781610022132 (directed toward parents)

THE POWER OF THE MOTHER–DAUGHTER PARTNERSHIP

After reading this book, our hope is that you feel a sense of calm capability around the topic of building healthy body image with your daughter. This process will be ongoing, of course, but your investment here has equipped you to deal with it, and we hope that you can pat yourself on the back for doing this work. Given how busy mothers are with so many issues related to parenting, work, and other commitments, body image development may seem less pressing than many other issues. However, as we have discussed throughout this book, body image is a serious issue deserving attention. Negative messages about body image are damaging, pervasive, and unending; culture consistently fuels girls' and women's insecurities in attempts to sell something. As science has shown, your proactive approach to healthy body image development—buffering your daughter from negative influences and exposing her to positive ones—is a very worthwhile undertaking. Let's review some essential implements that you now have in your body image toolbox.

You have agency; use the tools according to your needs. As we have emphasized throughout the book, there are similarities that women share with other women and that girls share with other girls, but there are also differences. Our intention for the book is to offer concrete guidance but not a precise prescription for how to approach body image. Although we have identified the essentials when it comes to having a healthy body image, each woman and her daughter can feel a sense of self-determination or independence to make the choices that are right for them. After all, you have done a lot of work reading this book to better understand your strengths, challenges, and needs. Some women and girls will ultimately choose to spend more time attending to physical appearance or on social media than others, for example, and will feel simply fine about this decision. Others may decide it is best to de-emphasize physical appearance or distance themselves from social media, and that is fine too. What we want is for women, and girls growing up, to think critically about their choices and behaviors and to feel that they oversee them. You do not have to "merely" react to external influences and demands that consistently tell you that you are not good enough.

You have provided your daughter with her own starter toolbox. We have talked about building healthy body image as a collaboration and co-construction between mother and daughter, and much of what she learns from you will come from your role modeling, your behavior, and the many conversations and activities that you have done together that navigate body image development—whether about food, body movement, or difficult emotions about physical appearance. But your daughter is also her own person, growing up in a different time, and with her own unique strengths and challenges. She will begin to make her own decisions about the tools she might use less frequently and will add new ones to her personal toolbox. Rest assured, the open lines of communication that you have built are highly valuable; she will likely be comfortable talking with you about her own experiences as she navigates them, and you will continue to be a trusted and important influence in her life.

You and your daughter are building a sturdy self-concept that is not centered on physical appearance. One of the main premises of this book concerns the importance of developing a complex or multifaceted self-concept, one that is defined by the roles, attributes, and skills that girls and women have, many of which have nothing to do with physical appearance. Although we see the merit in the body positivity and body neutrality approaches, we have advocated for spending less time thinking about your bodies in general, and we have provided several suggestions for how to do so. This strategy is protective because by choosing to develop other aspects of yourselves, you can spend less of your time and energy on how you look and limit your attention to outside influences that attempt to preoccupy you with your supposed physical appearance "flaws." Developing this strategy together with your daughter is exciting for other reasons; you will both see the ways that her self-concept develops with age—the person that she becomes—and you will play an important part in shaping it. We do not mean that physical appearance is not part of the self-concept, but rather, we are giving it the limited amount of attention that it deserves when we consider the overall self-concept.

You and your daughter have adopted body-healthy behaviors as a key aspect of healthy body image. Having a healthy body image does not just involve monitoring and working on your thoughts and beliefs, or managing outside influences on your body image, but also mindfully engaging in health behavior. In other words, it requires a commitment for us as women to be responsible for our bodies and to respect and take care of them. We have talked about the importance of establishing healthy behaviors early in life, modeling them for your daughter, and participating in them together with your daughter. This approach involves moving the body, eating a varied diet that incorporates both necessary nutrients and fun treats without moralizing food as "good" or "bad," and treating data such as body mass index (BMI), body weight, and body fat as individual pieces of information that need not be avoided but rather need to be considered in the context of other health indicators that you can discuss with your health care practitioner.

We also know that engaging in behavior that promotes body functionality (such as exercising our bodies so that we can readily perform the activities of daily living) is associated with a healthy body image. Early adoption of these behaviors can promote their incorporation into your daughter's self-concept; she will be able to see herself as a person who shows care and responsibility for her body in a way that is independent of her physical appearance. This is not to say that these behaviors cannot support physical appearance goals that you can ultimately choose for yourselves. But we have intentionally separated such goals from the body responsibility approach that we have taken here.

Moving forward, these tools provide a strong foundation for the ongoing development of healthy body image. But having a good foundation does not mean that you will be spared from challenges or uncertainties in parenting your daughter or in managing your own body image concerns in the future. It is important to recognize that you have done your part—including the reflection, discussion, and activities presented in this book—but you will not be able to control many external influences that you or your daughter are likely to face in the future. And that's okay. There will be times when you feel that you haven't applied the tools correctly, or often enough, or that you've said the wrong thing to your daughter yet again (cue the eye rolling or deep freeze!). And that's okay, too. As we have said throughout the preceding chapters, perfection isn't the goal; it isn't necessary or even possible. Your awareness of the complexity of body image, your ongoing communication with your daughter, and your use of these tools—even some of the time—is a major accomplishment.

Congratulations, Mom. We want to acknowledge all the thought and effort you have put into your and your daughter's body perspectives. In doing so, you have already contributed to the healthier body image community that girls need and deserve.

APPENDIX

COMPANION ACTIVITIES

Janet Boseovski, Ashleigh Gallagher, and Julianne Peebles

CHAPTERS 1–3: ACTIVITIES FOR MOTHERS

The following activities are designed for mothers to complete independently after reading Chapters 1, 2, and 3 of this book. These activities encourage mothers to engage in self-reflection and serve as a guide for implementing select strategies for bringing awareness and intention to the thoughts, feelings, and behaviors that research has shown can influence both mothers' and daughters' body image, as discussed in the relevant chapters.

Activity 1. Who Am I Now? Exploring Past, Present, and Future Selves

In this activity, you will reflect on who you were 10 years ago compared to who you are today and identify the parts of your values, beliefs, and personal characteristics that have evolved or remained stable across time.

The goals of this activity are to

- Appreciate your unique journey of personal growth and evolution.

- View yourself as capable of transformation in both the present and the future.
- Foster joy for the versions of yourself that are yet to be.

Supplies

1) Journal or notebook
2) Pen or pencil

Directions

1) Find somewhere in your home where it is quiet and where you can be alone. If you have a young child at home, you might do this during their naptime or after they've gone to bed.
2) Watch Dan Gilbert's TED Talk, *The Psychology of Your Future Self*, which can be found by searching for the title at https://www.TED.com or https://www.YouTube.com.
3) Think about who you were 10 years ago and the values, beliefs, and behaviors that defined your sense of self at that time. In your journal, write down these core aspects of your former self. When journaling, avoid listing characteristics that relate to your physical appearance alone.
4) Next, take some time to reflect on who you are today and the core values and beliefs that currently drive your behaviors, goals, and interactions with others. List these characteristics next to or below those of yourself from 10 years ago.
5) Notice the personal characteristics of yours that have persisted over the past decade, ones that have naturally subsided, and ones you may have actively transformed.
6) Finally, consider the aspects of yourself that you continue to see change in, and imagine the many possibilities of who you might become in the future. Next to or below your first two

lists, create a third list for the personal characteristics, values, and beliefs that you aspire to or anticipate will define yourself 10 years from today.

Guidance & Reflection Questions to Consider

1) Prior to viewing Dan Gilbert's TED Talk, did you see your self as stable and finished, or did you see your self as continuously flexible and changing?

2) Prior to completing this exercise, do you think that you under-estimated or overestimated the degree to which you have grown and changed over time? Does the amount of change that you see represented in your journal surprise you?

3) In what ways have your values (e.g., about pleasure, success, confidence, relationships) changed in the past 10 years? In what ways have they remained the same?

4) What might you tell a longtime friend, loved one, or your daughter about the ways they have changed over the years? Would you show them compassion, gentleness, or support?
   a. In the same way that you carry love and hope for your daughter and who she might become in the future, extend warmth to yourself for your own ability to evolve.

5) Which aspects of your former and current selves do you admire? Which characteristics do you hope to still have 10 years from now?

6) Examine your list of current values, beliefs, and behaviors. Do these align with or support your current goals and aspirations?

7) Use your imagination, think big, and challenge yourself to pic-ture your future self 10 years from now. What positive changes might she have made?

8) In what ways do you have hope or excitement for your future self? What wishes might you have for her?

Activity 2. Perspective Taking & Taking Charge: Exploring the Unfamiliar

In this activity, you will practice distancing yourself from your own thought or behavioral patterns and will imagine how another individual might think or behave in the same situation.

The goals of this activity are to

• Practice examining situations from a variety of perspectives.
• Develop strategies to challenge negative thoughts, feelings, or outside messages.
• Work toward positive growth on a specific characteristic, thinking style, or behavioral pattern that you would like to change.

Supplies

1) Journal or notebook
2) Pen or pencil

Directions

1) In your journal, identify one characteristic of yours in which you would like to see a positive change. This could be a thought, behavioral, or emotional pattern. Some examples include worrying about your body and appearance, interrupting others, or getting quick to anger.
2) Common thought distortions you might also consider include
   a. Black-and-white or all-or-nothing thinking (e.g., either good or bad; either success or failure)
   b. Jumping to conclusions
   c. Catastrophizing (i.e., focusing on the worst-case scenario)

   d. Filtering (e.g., emphasizing the negatives and disregarding the positives)
   e. Overgeneralizing (e.g., thinking in terms of "never," "always," "everything," "nothing")
   f. Personalizing (i.e., taking blame or responsibility for events outside your control)
   g. Should-ing (i.e., self-critical language)
   h. Comparing yourself to others
   i. Labeling and mislabeling (e.g., defining yourself globally based on a single or temporary event)
3) After identifying the thought, behavior, or emotional characteristic that you would like to improve, think about the types of circumstances or environments that seem to exacerbate or worsen it. When can you picture yourself engaging in this pattern, and why? For instance, perhaps you interrupt others when you are excited or enthusiastic about something, or perhaps you frustrate easily when you are under high levels of stress at work.
4) Think of a specific situation that you were in recently; you will use this situation for the rest of this activity. What happened in this situation, and what did you think, feel, do, or say as a result?
5) Next, take time to step into an unfamiliar perspective. Imagine yourself as another person, characterized by thoughts, behaviors, and emotions different from your own. For instance, how might someone who has less neuroticism respond in this same situation? How might someone who has less perfectionism, more conscientiousness, more confidence, or less authoritarianism respond?
6) Consider whether the reactions and perspectives of this imaginary person may be successful or beneficial to you in the given circumstance. How might adopting some of these approaches

look or feel? What are viable ways in which you might put these strategies into practice? What challenges might you face in implementing them?

7) An alternative approach that may help you to take a step back from your own immediate thoughts, feelings, and behaviors and begin to think more objectively about a situation is to speak to yourself in the third person and practice thinking about yourself in the same way that you would think about someone else. How does referring to yourself by name or using "she" pronouns change the way that you consider a problem, as opposed to using "I" or "me" pronouns? For more information on this mental strategy, refer to Dr. Ethan Kross's (2021) book, *Chatter: The Voice in Our Head, Why It Matters, and How To Harness It.*

Guidance & Reflection Questions to Consider

1) How might considering alternate points of view help you to combat negative thoughts or feelings about yourself?
   a. Consider how this strategy may be applied to your own internal thoughts and feelings, including those related to your body image, self-esteem, or self-efficacy.
   b. Consider how this strategy might be applied to different domains of your life, such as at work or home, or to different roles that you occupy, such as mother, spouse, or supervisor.

2) Do you find it easier to evaluate your own habits and characteristics after taking on someone else's perspective? Why or why not?

3) Do you find it easier to consider the bigger picture of a situation when thinking about yourself as if you were a different person?

4) How might creating distance from your immediate thoughts, feelings, or responses to a situation affect your decision making in the moment? How might construing a situation differently have an impact on your choices?
   a. Consider your levels of self-control and objectivity.

Activity 3. Who Will She Become? Wishes for Your Daughter's Future

In this activity, you will consider the hopes and wishes that you have for your daughter's future by writing a legacy statement for her.

The goals of this activity are to

- Appreciate who your daughter is today and imagine the ways in which she will grow and change over the years.
- Reflect on the values and characteristics you hope to pass on to her and those of her own that you hope she nurtures.
- Foster love and hope for your daughter's future.

Supplies

1) Journal or notebook
2) Pen or pencil

Directions

1) Complete Activity 1, Who Am I Now? After you have completed it, get situated in a comfortable spot in your home.
2) In your journal, reflect on who your daughter is and the interests, values, and beliefs she holds. What seems to define her or drive her behaviors? List these characteristics.

3) Examine this list of your daughter's personal qualities and strengths. How have they changed or remained stable over the years? Which do you hope she continues to nurture and strengthen throughout her life, and how do you hope they will benefit or bring joy to her?

4) Next, review the three lists from Activity 1, in which you reflected on your own past, present, and potential future values, beliefs, and behaviors. Which of these personal characteristics do you hope to pass on to your daughter, and why? What value or benefit do you hope these characteristics will bring to her life? In what ways do you hope she will differ from you?

5) Finally, write a letter to your daughter in which you imagine the many possibilities for whom she might become in the future, with honor, love, and respect. Outline how you imagine she will move through the world, what impact she might leave on it, and your desires and dreams for the life she will live.

Guidance & Reflection Questions to Consider

1) What values pertaining to pleasure, success, and honesty do you hope that your daughter develops? Do you hope they will be different from or the same as your own?

2) Which aspects of your daughter do you admire? Which characteristics of hers might you be able to learn from?

3) Consider your daughter's current goals and aspirations. Do her values, beliefs, and behaviors align with or support them? If not, how might you be able to encourage ones that do?

4) Use your imagination, think big, and challenge yourself to picture your daughter 10 years from now. What positive growth do you hope she will have made?

5) In what ways do you have excitement for your daughter's future? Is it similar to the excitement that you have for your own future?

CHAPTER 4: ACTIVITIES FOR 3- TO 4-YEAR-OLDS

The following activities are designed for mothers to complete together with their daughter(s) in early childhood, between the ages of 3 and 5, after mothers have read Chapter 4 of this book. These activities serve as a guide for mothers to help their daughters develop broad self-concepts, encourage physical activity and appreciation for the body and its abilities, promote a balanced and neutral approach to food, and de-emphasize physical appearance. These research-based activities support the healthy development of young girls' body image while being developmentally appropriate for the early childhood period and its associated features, milestones, and influences, as discussed in Chapter 4.

Activity 4. Walk and Talk With Mother Nature

Activity Type: Healthy Thoughts and Feelings
    In this activity, you and your daughter(s) will walk through a local park, arboretum, or nature trail and will take pictures of the plants, animals, and natural features that you each see beauty in.

The goals of this activity are to

- Demonstrate the purpose of photography for capturing fun activities and loving memories.
- Emphasize that beauty can be found anywhere, not only in one's physical appearance.
- Spend time outside while encouraging an active lifestyle.

Supplies

1) Phone or camera

Directions

1) Go for a stroll together at a local greenway, park, or nature trail. Some footpaths and hiking trails are designed for educational purposes and have marked stations and informational signs, but you can do this activity in any safe location outside.
2) Use this opportunity to take a break from the hustle and bustle of your daily life. Spend time looking at the plants around you, listening to the birds, or watching the clouds pass by. Take a deep breath in and smell the fresh air. You might also incorporate other sensory experiences on your walk, such as feeling how rough or smooth the bark of a tree is, how prickly a pinecone is, or how smooth a pebble is.
3) Stop to admire and take pictures of things that you find particularly beautiful, interesting, or fun. Aim to get a wide array of pictures, such as vibrant flowers, interesting rock formations, chatty birds, or funny-looking clouds. Make sure to give your daughter a turn being the photographer, and try to both remain behind the camera instead of being in the photographs.
4) After you return home, take a moment together to look through the pictures and remember all the sights, sounds, smells, and textures that you experienced.

Possible Discussion Starters to Engage Your Daughter After This Activity

1) "What was your favorite part of our walk today? What did you like most about being outside?"

a. Emphasize that being in connection with nature is one way to take care of our bodies and brains. Brainstorm ways to include more outdoor movement in your lives and ways to incorporate the aspects of today's walk that your daughter particularly enjoyed.

2) "What did you find beautiful on our walk?"

a. Share with your daughter what you found beautiful and discuss that everyone has their own personal opinions and preferences about what they find pleasing to the eye.

b. Point out that we can find beauty even in small parts of our days and that bringing attention to the dazzling things around us helps us live joyful and happy lives.

3) "Did you see anything in your favorite color?"

4) "Did you hear any interesting sounds in nature?"

5) "Did you touch anything on our walk that was soft? Bumpy? Prickly?"

a. If you took a hands-on, sensory approach to your nature walk, refer to the photos that you took together and ask your daughter what each item felt like.

6) "Next time, do you want to be in charge of taking pictures when we go on a walk together?"

a. By encouraging your daughter to be behind the camera rather than in front of it, you are challenging society's high valuation of physical appearance and encouraging your daughter to develop a self-concept that relies on her interests and achievements rather than her body.

Activity 5. Toy Test Lab

Activity Type: Healthy Thoughts and Feelings

In this activity, you and your daughter(s) will take a field trip to a local toy store or public library to pick out new and different toys.

The goals of this activity are to

- Broaden your daughter's interests by introducing her to toys that she wouldn't normally play with.
- Demonstrate that she can engage with any type of play that she is interested in, regardless of gender.
- Emphasize that it is okay if she has different interests and hobbies than her peers.

Supplies

1) Transportation
2) A selection of new toys, for example from a toy store, library, or friend's house

Directions

1) Drive or take public transportation to a local toy store. Alternatively, some public libraries have toy lending or toy rental programs that allow you to check out toys from their collection for free, as you would with other library materials. You might also consider doing a toy swap with one of your daughter's siblings or friends, in which you exchange toys so that the children have access to toys they don't own themselves.
2) Peruse the toy selection together. Rather than exploring toys that your daughter would normally play with and would pick out for herself, try to look at toys that are new and different. If you are in a physical store, you might venture to a new aisle instead of walking past it as you might usually do or spending time looking at traditionally masculine or gender-neutral toys.

3) Try to find characteristics of the new toys that your daughter might enjoy or think of ways that your daughter could incorporate them into her own play. Be imaginative and creative. For instance, if your daughter enjoys make-believe play with Barbie dolls, could you get her an airplane toy for her Barbie to fly?
4) After selecting an unfamiliar toy, take some time to play with the toy. Take it for a test run as if you were members of a product test lab, trying to figure out what might be fun about the toy.

Possible Discussion Starters to Engage Your Daughter During This Activity

1) "This toy might not look like your other toys, but did you still enjoy playing with it? Is there anything special about this toy?"
   a. During this activity, try to avoid using phrases like "boy toys" or "girl toys." Emphasize that girls and boys can play with any toy that they're interested in, regardless of their gender, and that your daughter is not limited to feminine toys just because she is a girl.
2) "We tried something very new today, and I'm proud of you. How did it feel to play with a different kind of toy?"
   a. Was it exciting? Scary? Boring? Whatever your daughter felt about the experience is okay, even if she did not particularly like the new toy. What matters instead is that she knows she's able to play with different or masculine toys.
3) "Are there other new toys or games that you would like to try?"
   a. Continuing to explore a wide variety of activities enables your daughter to expand her interests and find what she is passionate about. This exposure to a range of activities, including but in no way limited to traditionally feminine activities, opens opportunities for her in play, hobbies, and her other interests.

4) "Are there some activities that your friends enjoy but you don't? What are some activities that you enjoy but your friends don't?"

   a. Highlight that individual differences are okay and that your daughter does not have to be interested in the same toys or hobbies as her friends or siblings. Encourage her to cultivate her own interests and passions regardless of what her peers, siblings, or other girls may be interested in.

   b. Similarly, acknowledge that your daughter does not have to enjoy traditionally feminine toys or activities simply because she is a girl and that exploring other possibilities is also okay. Some girls like feminine activities and others don't, some boys like masculine activities and others don't, and all these interests are possible and acceptable.

Activity 6. Read and Share: *Shapesville*

Activity Type: Healthy Thoughts and Feelings

In this activity, you and your daughter(s) will appreciate how bodies come in all shapes and sizes as you read the book *Shapesville* together.

The goals of this activity are to

- Increase appreciation for your personal attributes beyond physical appearance.
- Broaden how you think about beauty.
- Decrease the desire to compare yourselves to others.

Supplies

1) A copy of the book *Shapesville*, available for purchase online, to rent through your local library, or as a read-aloud video on online platforms such as YouTube.

Bibliographic information:
Title: *Shapesville*
Authors: Andy Mills, Becky Osborn
Illustrator: Erica Neitz
Publisher: Gurze Books, 2003
ISBN: 9780936077444, 9780936077475, 9780936077734
Length: 32 pages

Directions

1) Read the book *Shapesville* with your daughter and use the discussion questions at the back of the book, also included here, to guide your conversation about important topics from the story. Make sure to share your answers with your daughter and to appreciate how your perspectives are similar or different from one another.

Possible Discussion Starters to Engage Your Daughter After This Activity

1) "Which character do you like best? Why?"
2) "What are the most important qualities that you look for in a friend?"
3) "Are your friends different sizes, shapes, and colors?"
4) "Do you think it's okay for kids to be different sizes, shapes, and colors?"
5) "Do you think it's okay that kids tease each other about being different sizes, shapes, and colors?"
6) "What special talents do you have that make you a star?"
7) "What famous people are different sizes, shapes, and colors?"
8) "What activities make you feel good about your body?"

Activity 7. Fun-Filled Foods

Activity Type: Body Respect

In this activity, you and your daughter(s) will work toward healthy attitudes about food by creating a fun and balanced snack to enjoy together.

The goals of this activity are to

- Demonstrate that eating can be for both nutrition and pleasure.
- Practice talking about food in a neutral way, without assigning it moral values of "good" or "bad."
- Promote a well-balanced diet in which foods with less nutritional value are not forbidden but are some of many options available.

Supplies

1) Two rice cakes
2) Spread of choice (e.g., Nutella, peanut butter, jam/jelly, honey)
3) One banana
4) Berries or small fruit of choice (e.g., blueberries, strawberries, raisins)
5) Additional nonfruit toppings (e.g., chocolate chips, Cheerios, nuts)
6) Child-safe knives or other utensils for spreading

Directions

1) Give yourself and your daughter one rice cake each.
2) While you prepare your snack throughout this activity, let your daughter be responsible for preparing her own, including choosing her own ingredients, applying the spread, and

arranging the toppings. Feel free to give her small pointers or suggestions, but try to let her do the hands-on work herself.

3) Select each of your ingredients, such as spreads, fruit, and other toppings. Acknowledge that healthy foods and "fun" foods can coexist and that neither is a wrong choice when balanced.

4) Cover the rice cakes in your preferred spreads. While doing so, name reasons why you might choose one option over another, such as choosing peanut butter for the long-lasting energy that it will give you or choosing Nutella or honey because its taste will make you happy.

5) Slice the banana and other fruit to your liking.

6) Arrange your fruit and other toppings on the rice cakes, such as by designing an animal or a silly face.

7) Enjoy your snacks together!

Possible Discussion Starters to Engage Your Daughter During This Activity

1) "What part of this snack do you like best? Why?"
   a. Your daughter may answer this question with a healthier ingredient like bananas, or a "fun" ingredient like Nutella. When describing these food items, avoid labeling either as "good" or "bad." Instead, describe them based on whether they improve the health of our bodies and brains or that of our emotions.

2) "Do you think it's okay to eat only one type of food, or do you think it's better to eat lots of different kinds of foods? Do you think it's okay to eat junk food sometimes if we also take care of our bodies with healthy food, too?"
   a. Strive toward an everything-in-moderation approach to food in which junk food items are balanced with healthier

choices, rather than an all-or-nothing approach to food where junk-food items are forbidden or seen as wrong.

3) "How does your body feel when you eat snacks like this? How does your heart (e.g., emotions) feel?"

   a. Talk with your daughter about the benefits that different types of food give us, such as physical energy, mental focus, or happiness. Try to develop attitudes toward food that include both healthy foods and foods with less nutritional value as acceptable choices while recognizing that they may serve different purposes and may be best suited to different situations.

4) "Would you like to try more snacks like this? What could we have next time?"

   a. Allowing your daughter to be involved with the food selection and preparation processes can get her excited to try new fun and healthy snacks and give her a feeling of involvement and responsibility.

Activity 8. My Miraculous Moving Body

Activity Type: Body Respect

In this activity, you and your daughter(s) will spend quality time together while encouraging healthy play and movement habits. You might go for a walk or bike ride outside, play together on a playground, or select and follow along with one of the short, guided movement videos listed in Table A.1.

The goals of this activity are to

- Encourage physical activity in a fun and engaging way by connecting it to your daughter's hobbies and interests.
- Provide movement activities that are developmentally appropriate.
- Introduce your daughter to new types of movement or play.

TABLE A. I. Short, Guided Movement Video Channels

YouTube channels	Type(s) of videos
Children's Healthcare of Atlanta Strong4Life	Dance, exercise, stretching
Cosmic Kids Yoga	Yoga
Danny Go!	Dance, games
GoNoodle | Get Moving	Dance, exercise, meditation
GO WITH YOYO – Fitness Fun For Kids	Dance, exercise, games
Jack Hartmann Kids Music Channel	Dance, exercise, games, stretching
KIDZ BOP	Dance, exercise
Koo Koo	Dance, exercise
Miss Linky – Educational Videos for Kids	Exercise
THE MOVERVERSE – Dance and Movement	Dance
Patty Shukla Kids TV – Children's songs	Dance, exercise, stretching, yoga
The Kiboomers – Kids Music Channel	Dance
TheLearningStation – Kids Songs and Nursery Rhymes	Dance, games, yoga

OPTION 1: OUTDOOR PLAY

Supplies

1) Bike, jump rope, sidewalk chalk, sports balls (optional)

Directions

1) Choose an activity that you and your daughter can do together outside. Some options include going for a walk around your neighborhood or a bike ride in a nearby park, playing hopscotch or jump rope, spending time at a playground, or kicking a ball in your backyard.
2) Enjoy the sunshine and fresh air while helping your daughter develop important gross motor skills.

OPTION 2: HOME-BASED PLAY

Supplies

1) Electronic device (e.g., phone, tablet, computer, television)
2) Internet access (e.g., to watch YouTube)

Directions

1) On your electronic device, open a web browser and navigate to https://www.youtube.com or open the YouTube app, available for free on Google Play or the Apple App Store.
2) Use the search bar to explore some channels and movement videos with keywords from Table A.1 (e.g., "Jack Hartmann exercise").

3) Select a video based on your daughter's interests. Many of the recommended channels have themed movement videos, including princess yoga, superhero workouts, and dance-alongs to popular songs or children's movie soundtracks.

4) Complete the video together and cheer your daughter on!

Possible Discussion Starters to Engage Your Daughter After This Activity

1) "Do you think it is important to move our bodies like this every day?"
   a. Share with your daughter that movement keeps our bodies and minds strong and healthy and it's important to be active throughout the day.

2) "What was your favorite part of today's activity?"
   a. Try to find other options for physical activity that include your daughter's interests. By making physical activity fun, engaging, and relatable, you encourage your daughter to want to engage in similar movement activities in the future. Note that what is fun and engaging for you may not be for your daughter, and tailor the activities to her interests.

3) "You really enjoy _____ (e.g., jumping, playing outside, dancing). Do you think we can find other activities that are fun like this, too?"

4) "How does your body feel after this activity?"
   a. You can focus the conversation on the physical or emotional effects that movement has, such as getting sweaty or out of breath, and talk about the ways in which your bodies are getting stronger or your mood and energy levels are improving.

Activity 9. Celebration Station

Activity Type: Body Respect

In this activity, you and your daughter(s) will explore how your bodies bring joy to your lives by helping you perform meaningful tasks and activities.

The goals of this activity are to

- Celebrate the tasks that your strong and capable bodies can achieve.
- Increase appreciation for your bodies and how they help you live, move, and play.
- Emphasize how the body functions rather than how the body looks.

Supplies

1) Hypoallergenic or skin-safe stickers

Directions

1) Take inventory of your body parts first by naming them.
2) Then, take turns with your daughter identifying tasks and abilities that those body parts help you perform. Try to think of activities that your daughter finds fun, exciting, or interesting and not just activities that are helpful or practical but that she may have less interest in (e.g., household chores).
3) Phrase these bodily functions within "I love," "I respect," "I celebrate," or "I appreciate" statements. For example, you might say, "I love my legs because they help me run and jump," or "I appreciate my ears because they let me listen to my favorite music."

4) Place a sticker on or near each body part that you acknowledge. Try to cover multiple areas of the body, making a game to see how many body parts you can "adorn" with your admiration for them.

5) After you've placed several stickers, ask your daughter to notice how sparkly or colorful her body is with all her love and celebration for it. You may also take this opportunity to remind her that her body is always strong, capable, powerful, and appreciated, even without the stickers.

Possible Discussion Starters to Engage Your Daughter During This Activity

1) "Our bodies are made for movement. What is your favorite way to move?"
   a. Notice the body parts involved in the movement that your daughter identifies. If she lists a movement that has not yet been celebrated, give her a sticker for the corresponding body part(s).
2) "What can your body do that makes you proud?"
   a. If your daughter has a hard time answering this question herself, offer something for which you were proud of her recently and discuss how her body helped her during that task.
   b. Model positive self-talk by sharing with your daughter some functions that your body performs that make you proud of yourself as well and give yourself a corresponding sticker.
3) "Our bodies help us perform fun and important tasks. What does your body help you do throughout the day?"
4) "What activities make you feel strong and powerful?"

CHAPTER 5: ACTIVITIES FOR 5- TO 7-YEAR-OLDS

The following activities are designed for mothers to complete together with their daughter(s) in middle childhood, between the ages of 5 and 7, after mothers have read Chapter 5 of this book. These activities serve as a guide for mothers to help their daughters develop broad self-concepts, encourage appreciation and respect for the body and its abilities, and de-emphasize physical appearance. These research-based activities support the healthy development of young girls' body image and are developmentally appropriate for the middle childhood period and its associated features, milestones, and influences.

Activity 10. Lunch Box Love Notes

Activity Type: Healthy Thoughts and Feelings
    In this activity, you and your daughter(s) will write each other "love notes" to keep in your purse, backpack, or lunch box, which you can both take with you throughout your days.

The goals of this activity are to

- Help build a strong, positive self-concept that does not depend on your daughter's physical appearance.
- Highlight and encourage pride in your daughter's strengths and unique characteristics.
- Contribute to a warm and supportive mother–daughter relationship.

Supplies

1) Paper (e.g., construction paper, sticky notes, napkins, paint swatches)
2) Writing utensils (e.g., pens, markers)

Directions

1) Together, select your paper of choice. You may choose something you already have around the house, such as loose construction paper, sticky notes, or napkins, or you might take a trip to a local home improvement store to pick out complementary paint swatches of your favorite colors.
2) On your individual papers, write notes to put in each other's day bags. For instance, you might leave a note in your daughter's lunch box or backpack while she leaves her note for you in your purse or work bag.
3) When writing this note, you can choose to leave her compliments or encouraging messages, or you may inspire her to say or do something nice for a peer. If leaving a compliment for your daughter, emphasize her personality characteristics rather than physical appearance characteristics.
4) Let your daughter write her own note for you, whether it is a written message or a drawing.
5) Place the notes in each other's bags for a special surprise later in the day.
6) The following day, write similar notes to gift to other people in your lives, such as a sibling, friend, bus driver, teacher, or coworker. Again, focus any compliments on personal strengths and nonphysical characteristics (e.g., confidence, creativity, loyalty, intelligence).

Possible Discussion Starters to Engage Your Daughter After This Activity

1) "How do you feel when you see these notes? Do they make you happy? Proud? Confident?"
   a. Give your daughter an opportunity to share any emotions that may start to surface around this age and help her to process them.

b. If your daughter does not feel proud of or confident in herself, take this opportunity to share why you are proud of her. You might give her examples of what makes you feel confident in yourself, as well.

2) "In today's love note, I complimented your [nonphysical characteristic]. Do you see this in yourself? What other traits do you have that you appreciate?"

   a. Prompting your daughter to name positive characteristics about herself allows her to practice positive self-talk while exploring her roles, strengths, and interests.

3) "What do you and I have in common? And how are we different from each other? Do you think it's okay that we have some differences, too?"

   a. Discussing similarities and differences between you and your daughter from a perspective of love and acceptance helps demonstrate that everyone is worthy of love, no matter their individual strengths, personalities, and differences.

   b. An understanding of others' thoughts, emotions, and behaviors helps your daughter develop her sense of self and additionally gives her an opportunity to get to know you outside of being "mom."

4) "Is there anyone else in your life who you'd like to leave a kind note for?"

Activity 11. Literary Genius

Activity Type: Healthy Thoughts and Feelings

In this activity, you and your daughter(s) will practice self-love, appreciation, and positive comments by creating acrostic poems using personal characteristics that begin with the letters in your names.

The goals of this activity are to

- Bring appreciation to characteristics outside of your appearance.
- Help develop confidence in your personality traits, skills, and interests.
- Instill value and worth in all aspects of your identity.

Supplies

1) Two pieces of paper
2) Markers, crayons, or colored pencils

Directions

1) Write your daughter's name or nickname vertically on a piece of paper, with the letters of her name arranged from top to bottom in descending order. Do the same for your own name, or for "mom" if you prefer. For example, for the name "Alice," write

   A

   L

   I

   C

   E

2) Together, take a minute or two to color, decorate, or draw around the letters of your names, leaving room to the right of the letters for additional writing. This is where you will fill in your poems.

3) While doing so, discuss your daughter's personal characteristics, interests, hobbies, and achievements. Ask her about

her thoughts, feelings, and beliefs about herself, and with her input, write down a word or phrase beginning with each letter that describes her in an empowering and action-oriented way. Try to limit or avoid appearance-oriented adjectives. For example, for the name "Alice," you might write

A fearless adventurer

Loves to sing

Imaginative storyteller

Coloring master

Eager to try new things

4) Complete your own acrostic poem and discuss with her some of your personal characteristics that make you feel happy, confident, proud, or strong.

Possible Discussion Starters to Engage Your Daughter During This Activity

1) "What do you love about yourself?"
   a. Share some things that you love about your daughter and some things that you love about yourself.
2) "What are some activities that you like or that you're good at?"
3) "Do you think these things about you are beautiful?"
   a. Emphasize that beauty does not have to mean physical characteristics and that beauty can be found in our skills, talents, achievements, and personalities as well.
4) "I was proud of you recently when you __. Have you done anything recently that made you proud of yourself?"
   a. Refer to a difficult task that she completed, a new accomplishment of hers, a kind gesture she made to someone, or anything else that has made you proud of her.

Activity 12. Read and Share: *Your Name Is a Song*

Activity Type: Healthy Thoughts and Feelings

In this activity, you and your daughter(s) will foster pride in your ethnic and racial identities and appreciate those of others as you read the book *Your Name Is a Song* together.

The goals of this activity are to

- Foster admiration for your own and others' names and the origins and meanings that they carry.
- Encourage respect for your own and others' cultures.
- Celebrate the things that make you unique and see beauty in the individual differences between people.

Supplies

1) A copy of the book *Your Name Is a Song*, available for purchase online, to rent through your local library, or as a read-aloud video on online platforms such as YouTube. Bibliographic information:
   Title: *Your Name Is a Song*
   Author: Jamilah Thompkins-Bigelow
   Illustrator: Luisa Uribe
   Publisher: The Innovation Press, 2020
   ISBN: 1943147728, 9781943147724
   Length: 40 pages

Directions

1) Read the book *Your Name Is a Song* with your daughter and use the discussion questions shown here to guide your

conversation about important topics from the story. Make sure to share your answers with your daughter and appreciate how your perspectives are similar to or different from one another.

2) For additional children's books that feature diversity and multiculturalism, please visit the following resources. These websites include curated book lists and collections as well as a book search tool (Diverse BookFinder), which allows you to filter children's books by keyword or by categories including ethnicity, tribal affiliation/homelands, race/culture, immigration status, gender, and religion.

   a. https://www.diversebooks.org
   b. https://www.diversebookfinder.org
   c. https://www.theconsciouskid.org
   d. https://www.socialjusticebooks.org

Possible Discussion Points and Starters to Engage Your Daughter After This Activity

1) Discuss with your daughter why you chose to name her what you did and explain any meanings or stories behind her name. Look in the back of the book to see if her name is included in the glossary of names and meanings, or search online for the meaning and origin of her name as well as your own.

   a. You might additionally come up with your own meanings for your names based on personal qualities and attributes that you take pride in.

2) "Have people ever had trouble saying your name? How did that make you feel?"

   a. Encourage your daughter to take pride in her name and to be confident in teaching others how to say it correctly. Discuss the importance of speaking up for herself and for others.

3) "Do you like your name? Are you proud of it?"
   a. Share with your daughter what makes you proud of your unique names, identities, and cultural backgrounds.
4) "What is special about our family or community? How do we celebrate our culture?"
   a. Discuss how other families, communities, and cultures might differ from your own, such as by values, beliefs, or practices, and discuss how they celebrate. What similarities can you see?
   b. Emphasize that cultural differences are good, that each culture has value, and that no cultural identity is any better or worse than another.
5) "What kind of song do you think your name is?"
6) "Do any of your classmates have names that you've never heard of before? Where do you think they come from, and what do you think they mean?"
   a. Encourage curiosity about other people's cultural identities and experiences. Offer to look up friends' names in the back of the book or online to learn more about her classmates, as you did with your own names.

Activity 13. Picture Perfect Memories

Activity Type: Body Respect

In this activity, you and your daughter(s) will take turns taking pictures of each other completing different activities that you enjoy. You will then look back at the photographs and the memories you created together.

The goals of this activity are to

- Emphasize the body's functionality over its appearance.
- Encourage respect and love for your daughter's body and the tasks that it achieves.

- Demonstrate the purpose of photography for capturing and remembering fun activities and loving memories.

Supplies

1) Phone or camera

Directions

1) You and your daughter will take turns performing activities that you enjoy. Activities you might consider include jumping in a puddle if it has rained recently, swinging on the swings or crossing the monkey bars at a playground, or cooking a meal together. The possibilities are endless!

2) You might prompt your daughter with "exploration" questions such as "How big of a splash can you make in that puddle?" or "How high do you think you can climb on the rock wall?"

3) While your daughter is performing different tasks, use your phone or camera to take action shots of her. Take turns so that you capture images of both you and her. Alternatively, you can prop your phone or camera against something and set a timer for hands-free photography so that you are in the images together.

4) Afterward, sit down with your daughter and look at the pictures together. Emphasize her capability and adventurousness by pointing out how high she jumped, how far she climbed across the monkey bars, or how strong she was whisking ingredients together.

5) Have fun brainstorming some creative, action-oriented captions for your photographs!

Possible Discussion Starters to Engage Your Daughter After This Activity

1) "Did you feel [strong, courageous, powerful] when you did these activities?"
   a. Help your daughter to appreciate her body's capabilities and accomplishments, as well as to focus on how her body feels rather than how it looks.
   b. Point out that these images serve as reminders or memories of how much fun she had and how strong she was. Emphasize photography's use in commemorating positive experiences.
2) "Your muscles were working hard when you were [jumping, climbing, etc.]. How did that feel in your body?"
3) "Which of these activities was your favorite? Why?"
   a. Finding new ways to stay active in a fun and enjoyable way, even if small, encourages a healthy perspective on physical and emotional well-being.
   b. Make note of her responses. You might try to prioritize your daughter's activity preferences on days when she may not be feeling particularly active or adventurous.
4) "Do you think it matters how we look when we're doing activities, or do you think it matters more that we are having fun, staying healthy, and doing what we love?"
   a. Bring focus to how your bodies help you accomplish tasks and the positive experiences that you have while doing them.

Activity 14. My Amazing Hands and Feet

Activity Type: Body Respect

In this activity, you and your daughter(s) will celebrate your bodies' skills and abilities as you think about the amazing things your hands and feet can do.

The goals of this activity are to

- Foster admiration for the body's abilities.
- Emphasize how the body functions rather than how the body looks.
- Strive toward an overall body-healthy perspective.

Supplies

1) Two pieces of construction paper
2) Writing utensil (e.g., marker, pen, pencil)
3) Coloring supplies (e.g., crayons, colored pencils)

Directions

1) Place your daughter's hand flat on the first piece of construction paper, leaving enough space for your own hand to fit on the paper as well. Test the spacing to make sure that both your hand and her hand will fit on the same page.
2) Trace your daughter's hand to create an outline. Then, place your own hand on the paper next to her handprint, and let your daughter trace around your hand.
3) Talk with your daughter about the different things that your hands can do. As you come up with some examples, write them inside your respective handprints. Examples include baking, writing, cooking, drawing, playing piano, braiding hair, sewing, drawing, and painting.
4) Once you have several skills and abilities written inside each handprint, color in the rest of the hands using crayons or colored pencils.
5) Next, repeat Steps 1 through 4 with your feet. Place your daughter's foot flat on the second piece of construction paper

and trace it to create an outline, followed by your own foot directly beside hers, just as you did with each other's hands.

6) After you've traced both feet onto the paper, begin talking with your daughter about the different things your feet can do. As you come up with some examples, write them inside of your respective footprints. Examples include dancing, walking, running, riding a bicycle, skipping, skiing, and skating.

7) Finally, use your crayons or colored pencils to decorate the rest of the footprints.

Possible Discussion Starters to Engage Your Daughter During This Activity

1) "What are some things that your hands and feet can do that make you feel happy? Strong?"

2) "Do you use your hands or feet in any of your favorite activities? How?"

3) "Did we write any of the same things in our handprints or footprints? Do we share any favorite activities?"

4) "Which do you think helps you do the most things, your hands or your feet? Do you think this might be different for different people?"

5) "This craft helps us see all the cool ways that our hands and feet can make us feel happy and healthy. Our bodies are strong and capable of amazing things, and it has been so fun exploring with you what our hands and feet can do!"

Activity 15. Read and Share: *Your Body Is Awesome*

Activity Type: Body Respect

In this activity, you and your daughter(s) will appreciate the many amazing tasks that your bodies are capable of as you read the book *Your Body Is Awesome* together.

The goals of this activity are to

- Foster admiration for your bodies and how they help you live, move, and play.
- Emphasize how the body functions rather than how the body looks.
- Increase appreciation for your personal attributes beyond physical appearance.

Supplies

1) A copy of the book *Your Body Is Awesome*, available for purchase online, to rent through your local library, or as a read-aloud video on online platforms such as YouTube. Bibliographic information:

    Title: *Your Body Is Awesome: Body Respect for Children*
    Author: Sigrun Danielsdottir
    Illustrator: Bjork Bjarkadottir
    Edition: Second
    Publisher: Jessica Kingsley Publishers, 2023
    ISBN: 9781839975325, 1839975326
    Length: 40 pages

Directions

1) Read the book *Your Body Is Awesome* with your daughter and use the discussion questions provided here to guide your conversation about important topics from the story. Make sure to share your answers with your daughter and appreciate how your perspectives are similar to or different from one another.

Possible Discussion Starters to Engage Your Daughter After This Activity

1) "What is your favorite thing that your body lets you do? What makes that fun or exciting?"
2) "What sorts of things make your body feel good? What can you do that makes you feel good?"
3) "What does it mean to listen to your body? How do you do this?"
   a. Discuss body signals such as hunger and fullness cues, sleep and rest cues, and pain cues. Encourage your daughter to be aware of how her body feels and to take care of it by giving it what it needs (e.g., food, water, sleep, movement).
4) "Do you think it's okay that some people might move differently than you, or do things in a different way than you do?"
   a. Emphasize that all bodies are built differently and are unique, and because of that, not all bodies move or accomplish tasks in the same way. Additionally, some people's bodies might function differently than her body even if they look the same on the outside, and other people's bodies might look different from hers but move and function in the same way.
   b. This may be a good opportunity to discuss disability and illness with your daughter, noting that disabilities can be visible or not and that some people use assistive devices to help their bodies move or function (e.g., eyeglasses, hearing aids or cochlear implants, wheelchairs, prosthetics). Stress that the way that these people's bodies move and function is just one part of who they are.

CHAPTER 6: ACTIVITIES FOR 8- TO 10-YEAR-OLDS

The following activities are designed for mothers to complete together with their daughter(s) in late childhood, between the ages of 8 and 10, after mothers have read Chapter 6 of this book. These activities serve as a guide for mothers to help their daughters develop broad self-concepts, encourage appreciation and respect for the body and its abilities, promote a balanced and neutral approach to food, de-emphasize physical appearance, and encourage productive strategies for expressing and processing one's emotions. These research-based activities support the healthy development of young girls' body image and are developmentally appropriate for the late childhood period and its associated features, milestones, and influences.

Activity 16. Our Amazing Adventures

Activity Type: Healthy Thoughts and Feelings

In this activity, you and your daughter(s) will choose one day a month to have a mother–daughter adventure date in which you sample a variety of new activities.

The goals of this activity are to

- Frame new experiences as opportunities for discovery and excitement.
- Encourage your daughter to explore different activities or hobbies during a period in which her interests may be evolving.
- Help your daughter develop a strong self-concept while fostering respect for and confidence in her individuality.

Supplies

1) N/A

Directions

1) Devote one day per month (or as your schedule allows) to go on adventures together and to try an assortment of new and different activities.
2) Select activities that sound fun and exciting but are new. Some activities might be ones that your daughter wants to try but hasn't had the opportunity, and others might differ markedly from her main interests. Possible ideas include visiting a children's museum, going for a short hike, browsing through books at the library, or trying indoor roller skating.
3) Additionally, you might sit down together to browse classes and events offered in your area. Many community education centers offer exploratory children's classes in subjects such as sports and recreation, cooking and baking, the arts, and engineering and craftsmanship. Local arts council may also offer family-friendly events such as concert series, theatre performances, runway shows, or historical reenactments.
4) Afterward, reflect on your adventure date. Discuss whether it was more or less fun than you each expected and whether your daughter would like to try it again in the future. You and your daughter might turn this discussion into a game in which you rank each activity based on how interesting and exciting you found it. Notice any patterns or similarities between the most successful activities.

Possible Discussion Starters to Engage Your Daughter After This Activity

1) "Why do you think it's important for us to try new activities?"
    a. Explain that it is normal and expected for interests to change, narrow, or broaden over time, and that it is okay if hers do as well. Emphasize that exploring different

activities can help her to learn more about herself and her own interests, particularly during childhood.

2) "What interests do some of your friends have? What are some activities that you do together?"

3) "Do you ever feel like you need to have a certain hobby because your friends are interested in it, or because other girls are interested in it?"

   a. Discuss that her hobbies and interests are valid regardless of whether they are shared by her peers or socially prescribed by her gender, and stress that friendships are not contingent on liking the same activities.

   b. Encourage your daughter to pursue activities that she finds intrinsically rewarding and valuable and help her to foster love and respect for her individual interests.

4) "Which of our outings have you enjoyed the most so far? Which have you enjoyed the least?"

   a. Speak authentically about how you've both experienced these activities. Highlight in your conversation that finding out what types of activities you don't enjoy is equally as important as finding out what you do. Try to recognize what you got out of the activity, even if it was not your favorite.

   b. Emphasize that you are not expected to know or be good at everything. Give yourselves grace and allow yourselves to laugh when an activity does not go as planned.

5) "What activity, class, or event would you like to try on our next outing?"

Activity 17. Happy, Healthy Balance

Activity Type: Body Respect

In this activity, you and your daughter(s) will work toward healthy attitudes about food by preparing a "chunky monkey" smoothie to enjoy together.

The goals of this activity are to

- Demonstrate that eating can be for both nutrition and pleasure.
- Practice talking about food in a neutral way, without assigning it moral values of "good" or "bad."
- Promote a well-balanced diet in which foods with less nutritional value are not forbidden but are some of many options available.

Supplies

1) Blender or food processor
2) Two medium peeled, frozen bananas
3) One to two cups milk of choice (e.g., whole milk, almond milk)
4) Two tablespoons nut butter of choice (e.g., peanut butter, almond butter, sunflower butter)
5) Two tablespoons chocolate chips or cacao nibs
6) One handful of ice cubes (optional)

Directions

1) Add one cup of milk and the other ingredients, to taste, to a blender or food processor.
2) Blend the ingredients together, adding any remaining milk to thin the smoothie to your desired consistency.
3) Pour the smoothie into two glasses, one for you and one for your daughter. Enjoy your snacks together!
4) Take this opportunity to discuss food as a source of nutrition and the different types of energy that various foods provide. For instance, fruit and vegetables have important nutrients and vitamins that keep us healthy, whereas "junk food"

typically does not. Additionally, natural and refined sugars such as bananas and chocolate provide quick-acting, short-term energy, whereas starches and fibers such as grains or leafy greens provide long-lasting energy.

Possible Discussion Starters to Engage Your Daughter During This Activity

1) "We might want to eat different foods depending on what activities we're doing and what types of energy we need for them. When do you think it might make sense to eat foods that give us quick energy? When do you think it might be better to eat foods that give us long-lasting energy?"
   a. Explain that our food choices often depend on our activities and schedules and that both healthy and less nutritious food choices are reasonable in different circumstances. For instance, if you have a soccer practice after school, you may want to fuel your body with natural or unrefined foods that will give you energy over the course of several hours, such as vegetables and whole grains. Likewise, it also makes sense to eat "junk food" or highly processed foods such as ice cream or cake on special occasions and celebrations.
   b. Try to develop attitudes toward food that see both healthy and less nutritious foods as acceptable choices that have different purposes and may be best suited to different situations.
2) "This smoothie is a balanced snack because it includes healthy ingredients, like bananas and peanut butter, and chocolate for a 'fun' ingredient. Can you think of other ways that we practice eating in balance?"

a. Examples of practicing balanced food choices include enjoying a scoop of ice cream after eating a healthy dinner, enjoying an apple along with a serving of chips as an after-school snack, and enjoying a sliced banana with a drizzle of Nutella spread on top.
b. Emphasize that balanced food habits can be both fun and healthy.

Activity 18. Relaxation Station

Activity Type: Healthy Thoughts and Feelings

In this activity, you and your daughter(s) will practice self-compassion and self-care behaviors by taking an evening to relax, recuperate, and pamper yourselves.

The goals of this activity are to

- Demonstrate a healthy balance between activity and rest.
- Exemplify behaviors that foster self-respect and self-compassion.
- Check in with your daughter and give her an opportunity to discuss her feelings.

Supplies

1) Two plastic basins or "foot spa" soaking tubs
2) Water beads, Epsom salts, bath bombs, or essential oil
3) Manual massage tool (e.g., massage ball, massage stick; optional)
4) Hand or body lotion (optional)
5) Nail polish (optional)
6) Relaxing music or white noise nature tracks (optional)
7) Scented candles or an essential oil diffuser (optional)

Directions

1) Devote an evening to yourself and your daughter. Set up the activity materials in a comfortable room in your house such as your living room or family room.

2) Fill the plastic tubs with warm water at a comfortable temperature, typically between 95 and 105° Fahrenheit. Additions that will give your footbaths a spa-like feel include water beads, Epsom salts, small bath bombs, or a few drops of lavender essential oil.

3) Place a towel near each footbath so that you can dry off easily after soaking and can clean up any splashes or spills.

4) To create an atmosphere of relaxation and luxury, you might dim the light fixtures in the room, light candles, diffuse essential oils, and/or play soothing music or nature tracks.

5) While soaking your feet, you can give each other hand massages using hand or body lotion or at-home manicures with your favorite shades of nail polish. Alternatively, you might use tools such as a roller ball or massage stick to give yourselves at-home back or foot massages.

6) As you pamper yourselves, discuss the importance of taking time for yourself and allowing your body to recuperate after a long week. Use this opportunity to check in with you daughter about how she has been feeling lately, allowing her to take the lead on sharing information with you.

Possible Discussion Starters to Engage Your Daughter During This Activity

1) "How does it make you feel to take this time to relax? Do you think it's important for us to make time for rest?"

a. Address the tendency in society to be always on the go (i.e., "hustle culture"). Explain to your daughter that although you have many activities and responsibilities in life that keep you busy—such as school, sports and hobbies, and work—it is important to find equilibrium by allowing yourselves to slow down and unwind as well.

b. If you and your family struggle to carve out time for relaxation, you might ask your daughter if she would like to schedule activities such as this into your weekly or monthly routines.

2) "What do you think it means to take care of ourselves? What might caring for our health and well-being look like?"

a. Discuss that self-care behaviors include those that take care of your physical body (e.g., eating a balanced diet, staying physically active, getting enough sleep) as well as those that take care of your mental health and emotional well-being (e.g., talking with people that you trust about your thoughts and feelings, granting yourself permission to decompress).

b. Avoid discussing self-care as appearance-oriented behaviors, and bring the focus instead to holistic, multidimensional health behaviors.

3) "How has school been recently? How are your friends?"

a. Ask your daughter about her peers and her social circle. Notice any indicators of social comparison and self-esteem concerns, both of which often increase during late childhood, and redirect any negative comments.

b. Let your daughter lead this conversation. Avoid pushing for more information than she is willing to share and emphasize that you will be there to support and listen to her whenever she feels comfortable.

4) "Is there anything you want to talk about?"

Activity 19. Reflecting High Regard

Activity Type: Body Respect

In this activity, you and your daughter(s) will practice using mirrors to see the goodness, strength, and potential that you each possess and to associate your reflections with positive and empowering attributes about the self.

The goals of this activity are to

- Celebrate your unique, personal strengths and capabilities.
- Increase appreciation for your bodies and how they help you live, move, and play.
- Emphasize how the body functions rather than how the body looks.

Supplies

1) Dry-erase marker (recommended)

   OR

2) Sticky notes
3) Writing utensil (e.g., marker, pen, pencil)

Directions

1) Take inventory of the mirrors in your house and select one or several that your daughter passes by every day and that she is tall enough to see her reflection in, such as a bathroom vanity or a full-length mirror.
2) Put yourself at your daughter's eye level. Take a moment to gaze into the mirror together and see your daughter from her perspective.

3) With the dry-erase marker, write positive messages on the mirror (or place sticky notes) on top of or adjacent to where your daughter would see her own reflection, so that brain-related messages are at head height, torso-related messages are at midlevel, and so on. It may be helpful also to identify tasks that certain body parts help her perform, such as by writing "learning machine!" next to her head.

4) Individualize these messages to your daughter's strengths, abilities, hobbies, and interests. For instance, if she practices soccer, you might write "powerful kicks" next to her legs or "speed racer" next to her feet. Try to cover multiple areas of the body, making a game to see how many body parts you can "adorn" with your love and appreciation for them.

5) In addition to or instead of messages about body parts, you may leave your daughter general positive notes across the mirror using first-person language, such as "I am strong, capable, and determined," "I am smart and creative," or "I celebrate my body for all that it is and does." Together, practice saying these phrases out loud while looking in the mirror. It's okay to smile and laugh if this feels funny, but give it your best try anyway!

6) Finally, ask your daughter to notice how full the mirror is with notes of love and celebration for herself, and emphasize its role in reflecting her strength, competence, and power.

Possible Discussion Starters to Engage Your Daughter During This Activity

1) "What things about yourself make you feel powerful, confident, or proud?"
   a. Redirect the conversation away from her appearance and toward other characteristics such as her personal strengths or the functionality of her body.

b. Notice the body parts involved in the tasks or characteristics that your daughter references, and leave "love notes" in their corresponding locations on the mirror. For instance, if your daughter responds that she's good at math, you could either write "good at math" next to the reflection of her head or reinterpret that sentiment into a message such as "math whiz," "number ninja," or "multiplication genius!"

c. Model positive self-talk by sharing with your daughter some functions that your body performs that make you proud of yourself.

2) "How do you feel when you look in the mirror? What do you think about when you see your reflection?"

a. Address any insecurities or negative emotions that your daughter communicates, and try to reinterpret these insecurities as characteristics to take pride in.

b. Emphasize that mirrors can be used to foster love and appreciation for ourselves and our abilities. By intentionally practicing positive and empowering thinking when we view our reflections, we can begin to develop healthy thoughts and feelings about ourselves and our bodies.

c. Avoid discussing mirrors in reference to one's appearance alone. Interrupt the tendency to use mirrors to monitor and identify one's physical flaws and be aware of your own thought and behavioral patterns that may reflect this tendency.

3) "What do you admire about your best friend? Do you share any of these characteristics with her?"

Activity 20. The Media and Me

Activity Type: Healthy Thoughts and Feelings

In this activity, you and your daughter(s) will discuss images in the media, the types of people represented, and ways that these images might be filtered, retouched, or otherwise manipulated.

The goals of this activity are to

- Encourage using a critical eye when looking at images in magazines, advertisements, and social media.
- Acknowledge that television shows, movies, and other forms of media often do not represent the average, healthy woman.
- Decrease the desire to compare yourselves to others, and especially to celebrities, models, and social media influencers.

Supplies

1) Magazines (optional)
2) Movie or television show DVDs (optional)

Directions

1) Together with your daughter, look at the people featured in popular movies, TV shows, or magazines. To do so, you might flip through the pages of magazines in your house, peruse the DVD aisle of a local library, or search online for the cast of a specific TV show.
2) Ask your daughter to notice what types of people are featured in the pages of the magazines or on the covers of the DVD cases. What do they look like? What characteristics do they share with each other? How are they different from or similar to you?
3) Discuss with your daughter that, until recent years, popular media such as movies, television shows, advertisements, and magazines had little diversity. The individuals featured in such media were, and often continue to be today, White or light-skinned, thin, and conventionally attractive (by Hollywood standards). These actors, models, and celebrities do not represent people of the global majority and do not

represent healthy, attainable beauty standards or body ideals. Emphasize that the reason your daughter may not see herself reflected in the media is that it does not accurately reflect the real world that we live in and should not be used as a tool for comparison.

4) Finally, explain how many images in the media—such as the pictures in magazines or the videos in TV advertisements—are filtered and retouched. Women's faces and bodies are often edited, reshaped, and recolored to make them look thinner, more or less muscular, or more made-up. The "raw" images of models and celebrities are digitally changed and altered so that what we see online, on TV, and in magazines does not reflect the actual person.

Possible Discussion Starters to Engage Your Daughter After This Activity

1) "Do you and I look, sound, or act like the people in [the media]? In what ways?"

   a. Consider physical attributes such as skin tone, facial features, and hair texture as well as individuals' names, spoken languages, and cultural attributes such as clothing, food, music, religion, or celebrations.

   b. Emphasize that the beauty standards that we see in the media are not realistic for or representative of the average human and that they do not reflect naturally attainable health or beauty. Encourage your daughter to find beauty in her body's abilities and in her personal strengths, attributes, and accomplishments instead of in her physical appearance.

2) "Who is your favorite character from a book, movie, or TV show? Do you think it's important to see individuals in movies and TV shows who look like us?"

a. It is important for children to see people of the same race or ethnicity in the media that they consume, as what they see in the media can affect their self-concept and identity development as well as their understandings of race, ethnicity, and culture. If your daughter does not currently see representative individuals in the media, consider exposing her to increasingly diverse and inclusive content with visibly diverse individuals as well as culturally authentic plots or themes.

3) "Do any of the characters in your favorite movies or TV shows look like you and me? Do they sound or act like you and me?"

4) "Is it easy or hard to think of characters in the media that are similar to you?"

5) "Think of some characters in movies or TV shows that look like us. Do you think they are treated differently than other characters?"

a. Children are often exposed to concepts related to race and ethnicity through the media, including themes of racial bias, prejudice, and violence. Examine how these themes may be present in the media that your daughter consumes and whether this media affirms or harms her racial, ethnic, or cultural identity.

Activity 21. Dear Diary

Activity Type: Healthy Thoughts and Feelings

In this activity, you and your daughter(s) will encourage emotional literacy skills by decorating and personalizing journals for future reflection and self-expression.

The goals of this activity are to

- Provide a safe, private space for your daughter to recognize and process her thoughts, emotions, and experiences.

- Promote healthy strategies for coping with stress and complex emotions.
- Highlight mental and emotional wellness as an important aspect of overall health.

Supplies

1) Notebook
2) Pen or pencil
3) Craft supplies (e.g., stickers, puffy paint, washi tape, googly eyes)
4) Coloring supplies (e.g., markers, colored pencils)

Directions

1) Take a trip to a local dollar store and allow your daughter to pick out a notebook and various craft supplies for decoration, such as fun stickers, puffy paint, colorful washi tape, or glitter glue. You might agree on a small budget together and challenge her to a game of picking out as many items as she can without going over that amount. You might also encourage her to pick out a special pen to go with her journal.

2) When you get home from the store, give your daughter some time to personalize the notebook by decorating the front cover or some of the inside pages as she pleases.

3) Then, work together to develop two or three personal mantras that promote positive body image, self-confidence, and self-efficacy. Examples include "I am kind and loving to my body and my mind" and "My body is beautiful and strong, and it takes care of me because I take care of it." Write these affirmations on the first blank page of the notebook.

4) On the second page of the notebook, write a handful of journal prompts that your daughter can refer to for guidance. Possible

prompts include "How was your day today? What happened?," "Did you experience anything fun? Frustrating? Surprising?," "Did anything make you feel happy, grateful, or excited?," and "Is there anything that you are sad, angry, or worried about?"

4) Emphasize that your daughter can use this journal however she sees fit. She may narrate and reflect on her day from beginning to end, write about her thoughts and emotions as they come to mind, respond to specific prompts that you add to the journal, or even express herself through drawings.

5) Establish with her that her journal is private, that you will never read it unless she directly asks you to, and that you will not push her to share what she writes in it. Establish that her journal is a safe space to explore topics that she might not be comfortable talking about with others and that you are always there to listen and support her if she wants to process these thoughts or feelings out loud.

6) Finally, offer your daughter a cup of tea or hot chocolate, encourage her to go someplace comfortable in the house, and give her some time alone to begin writing in her journal.

Possible Discussion Starters to Engage Your Daughter During This Activity

1) "Journaling can help us to recognize, understand, and detangle our thoughts and feelings when they start to feel overwhelming. Would you like to try journaling for a couple of minutes each day this week to see if it's something that you like?"

   a. During this period in your daughter's life, she is beginning to navigate complicated emotions and is developing her capacity to understand them. By fostering a family culture that recognizes and addresses emotions, you can encourage the development of adaptive coping mechanisms and emotional literacy skills.

   b. Traditional journaling may not work for everyone. If she does not enjoy processing her emotions this way, you can suggest she try drawing or creative writing instead. Allow her journal to be a flexible medium for self-expression.

   c. If you happen to journal yourself, share with your daughter your own journaling habits, such what types of things you write about or how you fit it into your day. Otherwise, you might explain that everyone journals in their own way and that it's okay if she experiments to find her own journaling style.

2) "It's okay to not feel happy or confident all the time. Talking or writing about the ways that you feel can help make difficult emotions feel less strong and powerful. Have you ever felt better after talking things out with someone? Did your negative emotions feel a little less sharp and jagged?"

   a. Emphasize that although we may not be able to change our emotions or make them go away, addressing and processing them can help to give them less control over our thoughts, words, and behaviors.

3) "Do you talk with your best friend about your thoughts and feelings? Do you tell them about your day? Do you share with them the things that you enjoy and the things that bother you?"

   a. Tell your daughter that keeping a journal can be much like talking with a trusted best friend. Encourage her to try writing in her journal about topics she would share with that friend.

REFERENCES

Adams, C. E., & Leary, M. R. (2007). Promoting self-compassionate attitudes toward eating among restrictive and guilty eaters. *Journal of Social and Clinical Psychology, 26*(10), 1120–1144. https://doi.org/10.1521/jscp.2007.26.10.1120

Ainsworth, M. S., & Bowlby, J. (1991). An ethological approach to personality development. *American Psychologist, 46*(4), 333–341. https://doi.org/10.1037/0003-066X.46.4.333

Alberga, A. S., Russell-Mayhew, S., von Ranson, K. M., & McLaren, L. (2016). Weight bias: A call to action. *Journal of Eating Disorders, 4*(1), Article 34. https://doi.org/10.1186/s40337-016-0112-4

Allen, M. S., & Robson, D. A. (2020). Personality and body dissatisfaction: An updated systematic review with meta-analysis. *Body Image, 33,* 77–89. https://doi.org/10.1016/j.bodyim.2020.02.001

Allen, M. S., & Walter, E. E. (2016). Personality and body image: A systematic review. *Body Image, 19,* 79–88. https://doi.org/10.1016/j.bodyim.2016.08.012

Alleva, J. M., & Tylka, T. L. (2021). Body functionality: A review of the literature. *Body Image, 36,* 149–171. https://doi.org/10.1016/j.bodyim.2020.11.006

Alleva, J. M., Tylka, T. L., & Kroon Van Diest, A. M. (2017). The Functionality Appreciation Scale (FAS): Development and psychometric evaluation in U.S. community women and men. *Body Image, 23,* 28–44. https://doi.org/10.1016/j.bodyim.2017.07.008

Altman, J. K., Linfield, K., Salmon, P. G., & Beacham, A. O. (2020). The Body Compassion Scale: Development and initial validation. *Journal of Health Psychology, 25*(4), 439–449. https://doi.org/10.1177/1359105317718924

Alvarez, J. M., Ruble, D. N., & Bolger, N. (2001). Trait understanding or evaluative reasoning? An analysis of children's behavioral predictions. *Child Development, 72*(5), 1409–1425. https://doi.org/10.1111/1467-8624.00356

Ambwani, S., Baumgardner, M., Guo, C., Simms, L., & Abromowitz, E. (2017). Challenging fat talk: An experimental investigation of reactions to body disparaging conversations. *Body Image, 23*, 85–92. https://doi.org/10.1016/j.bodyim.2017.08.007

American Psychological Association. (n.d.). *APA dictionary of psychology.* Retrieved April 17, 2024, from https://dictionary.apa.org/

American Psychological Association. (2007). *Report of the APA task force on the sexualization of girls: Executive summary.* https://www.apa.org/pi/women/programs/girls/report

American Psychological Association. (2010). *The impact of food advertising on childhood obesity.* https://www.apa.org/topics/obesity/food-advertising-children

American Psychological Association. (2023, May). *Health advisory on social media use in adolescence.* https://www.apa.org/topics/social-media-internet/health-advisory-adolescent-social-media-use

Anschutz, D. J., & Engels, R. C. M. E. (2010). The effects of playing with thin dolls on body image and food intake in young girls. *Sex Roles, 63*(9–10), 621–630. https://doi.org/10.1007/s11199-010-9871-6

Arnett, J. J. (1999). Adolescent storm and stress, reconsidered. *American Psychologist, 54*(5), 317–326. https://doi.org/10.1037/0003-066X.54.5.317

Aron, A., Norman, C. C., Aron, E. N., McKenna, C., & Heyman, R. E. (2000). Couples' shared participation in novel and arousing activities and experienced relationship quality. *Journal of Personality and Social Psychology, 78*(2), 273–284. https://doi.org/10.1037/0022-3514.78.2.273

Arredondo, E. M., Elder, J. P., Ayala, G. X., Campbell, N., Baquero, B., & Duerksen, S. (2006). Is parenting style related to children's healthy eating and physical activity in Latino families? *Health Education Research, 21*(6), 862–871. https://doi.org/10.1093/her/cyl110

Astington, J. W. (1993). *The child's discovery of the mind* (Vol. 31). Harvard University Press.

Baker, S., Maïano, C., Houle, S. A., Nadon, L., Aimé, A., & Morin, A. J. S. (2023). Profiles of body image concerns and their associations with disordered eating behaviors. *Appetite, 191*, Article 107082. https://doi.org/10.1016/j.appet.2023.107082

Bakhshi, S. (2011). Women's body image and the role of culture: A review of the literature. *Europe's Journal of Psychology, 7*(2), 374–394. https://doi.org/10.5964/ejop.v7i2.135

Balantekin, K. N., Anzman-Frasca, S., Francis, L. A., Ventura, A. K., Fisher, J. O., & Johnson, S. L. (2020). Positive parenting approaches and their association with child eating and weight: A narrative review from infancy to adolescence. *Pediatric Obesity, 15*(10), Article e12722. https://doi.org/10.1111/ijpo.12722

Balantekin, K. N., Savage, J. S. I., Marini, M. E., & Birch, L. L. (2014). Parental encouragement of dieting promotes daughters' early dieting. *Appetite, 80*, 190–196. https://doi.org/10.1016/j.appet.2014.05.016

Bandura, A. (1989). Human agency in social cognitive theory. *American Psychologist, 44*(9), 1175–1184. https://doi.org/10.1037/0003-066X.44.9.1175

Bandura, A. (1991). Social cognitive theory of self-regulation. *Organizational Behavior and Human Decision Processes, 50*(2), 248–287. https://doi.org/10.1016/0749-5978(91)90022-L

Bandura, A. (1997). *Self-efficacy: The exercise of control*. W. H. Freeman/Times Books/Henry Holt & Co.

Bandura, A., & Schunk, D. H. (1981). Cultivating competence, self-efficacy, and intrinsic interest through proximal self-motivation. *Journal of Personality and Social Psychology, 41*(3), 586–598. https://doi.org/10.1037/0022-3514.41.3.586

Bascandziev, I., & Harris, P. L. (2014). In beauty we trust: Children prefer information from more attractive informants. *British Journal of Developmental Psychology, 32*(1), 94–99. https://doi.org/10.1111/bjdp.12022

Batres, C., & Shiramizu, V. (2023). Examining the "attractiveness halo effect" across cultures. *Current Psychology, 42*, 25515–25519. https://doi.org/10.1007/s12144-022-03575-0

Baumeister, R. F., & Leary, M. R. (1995). The need to belong: Desire for interpersonal attachments as a fundamental human motivation. *Psychological Bulletin, 117*(3), 497–529. https://doi.org/10.1037/0033-2909. 117.3.497

Beaver, K. M., Boccio, C., Smith, S., & Ferguson, C. J. (2019). Physical attractiveness and criminal justice processing: Results from a longitudinal sample of youth and young adults. *Psychiatry, Psychology, and Law, 26*(4), 669–681. https://doi.org/10.1080/13218719. 2019.1618750

Bensley, J., Riley, H. O., Bauer, K. W., & Miller, A. L. (2023). Weight bias among children and parents during very early childhood: A scoping review of the literature. *Appetite, 183,* 106461. https://doi.org/10.1016/ j.appet.2023.106461

Berggren, M., Akrami, N., Bergh, R., & Ekehammar, B. (2019). Motivated social cognition and authoritarianism: Is it all about closed-mindedness? *Journal of Individual Differences, 40*(4), 204–212. https:// doi.org/10.1027/1614-0001/a000293

Blowers, L. C., Loxton, N. J., Grady-Flesser, M., Occhipinti, S., & Dawe, S. (2003). The relationship between sociocultural pressure to be thin and body dissatisfaction in preadolescent girls. *Eating Behaviors, 4*(3), 229–244. https://doi.org/10.1016/S1471-0153(03)00018-7

Boone, L., & Soenens, B. (2015). In double trouble for eating pathology? An experimental study on the combined role of perfectionism and body dissatisfaction. *Journal of Behavior Therapy and Experimental Psychiatry, 47,* 77–83. https://doi.org/10.1016/j.jbtep.2014.11.005

Boseovski, J. J. (2010). Evidence for "rose-colored glasses": An examination of the positivity bias in young children's personality judgments. *Child Development Perspectives, 4*(3), 212–218. https://doi.org/10.1111/ j.1750-8606.2010.00149.x

Boseovski, J. J., & Lee, K. (2006). Children's use of frequency information for trait categorization and behavioral prediction. *Developmental Psychology, 42*(3), 500–513. https://doi.org/10.1037/0012-1649.42. 3.500

Boswell, R. G., & White, M. A. (2015). Gender differences in weight bias internalisation and eating pathology in overweight individuals. *Advances in Eating Disorders, 3*(3), 259–268. https://doi.org/10.1080/ 21662630.2015.1047881

Boyington, J., Johnson, A., & Carter-Edwards, L. (2007). Dissatisfaction with body size among low-income, postpartum black women. *Journal of Obstetric, Gynecologic, and Neonatal Nursing, 36*(2), 144–151. https://doi.org/10.1111/j.1552-6909.2007.00127.x

Brand, S., Colledge, F., Ludyga, S., Emmenegger, R., Kalak, N., Sadeghi Bahmani, D., Holsboer-Trachsler, E., Pühse, U., & Gerber, M. (2018). Acute bouts of exercising improved mood, rumination and social interaction in inpatients with mental disorders. *Frontiers in Psychology, 9,* Article 249. https://doi.org/10.3389/fpsyg.2018.00249

Brathwaite, K. N., & DeAndrea, D. C. (2022). BoPopriation: How self-promotion and corporate commodification can undermine the body positivity (BoPo) movement on Instagram. *Communication Monographs, 89*(1), 25–46. https://doi.org/10.1080/03637751.2021.1925939

Bronfenbrenner, U., & Morris, P. A. (2007). The bioecological model of human development. In W. Damon & R. M. Lerner (Eds.), *Handbook of child psychology: Vol. 1. Theoretical models of human development* (pp. 793–828). John Wiley & Sons. https://doi.org/10.1002/9780470147658.chpsy0114

Brown, Z., & Tiggemann, M. (2016). Attractive celebrity and peer images on Instagram: Effect on women's mood and body image. *Body Image, 19,* 37–43. https://doi.org/10.1016/j.bodyim.2016.08.007

Brummelman, E., Nelemans, S. A., Thomaes, S., & Orobio de Castro, B. (2017). When parents' praise inflates, children's self-esteem deflates. *Child Development, 88*(6), 1799–1809. https://doi.org/10.1111/cdev.12936

Burke, N. L., Schaefer, L. M., Karvay, Y. G., Bardone-Cone, A. M., Frederick, D. A., Schaumberg, K., Klump, K. L., Anderson, D. A., & Thompson, J. K. (2021). Does the tripartite influence model of body image and eating pathology function similarly across racial/ethnic groups of White, Black, Latina, and Asian women? *Eating Behaviors, 42,* Article 101519. https://doi.org/10.1016/j.eatbeh.2021.101519

Carter, A., Gilbert, P., & Kirby, J. N. (2021). Compassion-focused therapy for body weight shame: A mixed methods pilot trial. *Clinical Psychology & Psychotherapy, 28*(1), 93–108. https://doi.org/10.1002/cpp.2488

Carvalho, K., Peretz-Lange, R., & Muentener, P. (2021). Causal explanations for weight influence children's social preferences: Biological-essentialist explanations reduce, and behavioral explanations promote, preferences for thin friends. *Child Development*, *92*(2), 682–690. https://doi.org/10.1111/cdev.13519

Casey, B. J., Jones, R. M., Levita, L., Libby, V., Pattwell, S. S., Ruberry, E. J., Soliman, F., & Somerville, L. H. (2010). The storm and stress of adolescence: Insights from human imaging and mouse genetics. *Developmental Psychobiology*, *52*(3), 225–235. https://doi.org/10.1002/dev.20447

Cash, T. F. (2001). The treatment of body image disturbances. In J. K. Thompson (Ed.), *Body image, eating disorders, and obesity: An integrative guide for assessment and treatment* (pp. 83–107). American Psychological Association. https://doi.org/10.1037/10502-004

Cash, T. F. (2012). Cognitive-behavioral perspectives on body image. In T. F. Cash (Ed.), *Encyclopedia of body image and human appearance* (pp. 334–342). Academic Press.

Cash, T. F., & Fleming, E. C. (2002). The impact of body image experiences: Development of the body image quality of life inventory. *International Journal of Eating Disorders*, *31*(4), 455–460. https://doi.org/10.1002/eat.10033

Cash, T. F., Fleming, E. C., Alindogan, J., Steadman, L., & Whitehead, A. (2002). Beyond body image as a trait: The development and validation of the Body Image States Scale. *Eating Disorders*, *10*(2), 103–113. https://doi.org/10.1080/10640260290081678

Cash, T. F., & Labarge, A. S. (1996). Development of the Appearance Schemas Inventory: A new cognitive body-image assessment. *Cognitive Therapy and Research*, *20*(1), 37–50. https://doi.org/10.1007/BF02229242

Cash, T. F., Melnyk, S. E., & Hrabosky, J. I. (2004). The assessment of body image investment: An extensive revision of the appearance schemas inventory. *International Journal of Eating Disorders*, *35*(3), 305–316. https://doi.org/10.1002/eat.10264

Cash, T. F., Santos, M. T., & Williams, E. F. (2005). Coping with body-image threats and challenges: Validation of the Body Image Coping Strategies Inventory. *Journal of Psychosomatic Research*, *58*(2), 190–199. https://doi.org/10.1016/j.jpsychores.2004.07.008

Cash, T. F., & Szymanski, M. L. (1995). The development and validation of the body-image ideals questionnaire. *Journal of Personality Assessment*, *64*(3), 466–477. https://doi.org/10.1207/s15327752jpa6403_6

Cavico, F. J., Muffler, S. C., & Mujtaba, B. G. (2012). Appearance discrimination, "lookism" and "lookphobia" in the workplace. *Journal of Applied Business Research, 28*(5), 791–802. https://doi.org/10.19030/jabr.v28i5.7223

Centers for Disease Control and Prevention. (2022a, April 1). *Childhood overweight and obesity.* https://www.cdc.gov/obesity/childhood/index.html

Centers for Disease Control and Prevention. (2022b, May 17). *Adult obesity facts.* https://www.cdc.gov/obesity/data/adult.html

Centers for Disease Control and Prevention. (2022c, July 26). *Physical activity facts.* https://www.cdc.gov/healthyschools/physicalactivity/facts.htm

Chisuwa, N., & O'Dea, J. A. (2010). Body image and eating disorders amongst Japanese adolescents: A review of the literature. *Appetite, 54*(1), 5–15. https://doi.org/10.1016/j.appet.2009.11.008

Chobhthaigh, S. N., & Wilson, C. (2015). Children's understanding of embarrassment: Integrating mental time travel and mental state information. *British Journal of Developmental Psychology, 33*(3), 324–339. https://doi.org/10.1111/bjdp.12094

Choukas-Bradley, S., Roberts, S. R., Maheux, A. J., & Nesi, J. (2022). The perfect storm: A developmental-sociocultural framework for the role of social media in adolescent girls' body image concerns and mental health. *Clinical Child and Family Psychology Review, 25*(4), 681–701. https://doi.org/10.1007/s10567-022-00404-5

Clark, D. A., & Leahy, R. L. (2020). *The negative thoughts workbook: CBT skills to overcome the repetitive worry, shame, and rumination that drive anxiety and depression.* New Harbinger.

Clark, L., & Tiggemann, M. (2006). Appearance culture in nine- to 12-year-old girls: Media and peer influences on body dissatisfaction. *Social Development, 15*(4), 628–643. https://doi.org/10.1111/j.1467-9507.2006.00361.x

Clark, L., & Tiggemann, M. (2008). Sociocultural and individual psychological predictors of body image in young girls: A prospective study. *Developmental Psychology, 44*(4), 1124–1134. https://doi.org/10.1037/0012-1649.44.4.1124

Clarke, L. H. (2002). Older women's perceptions of ideal body weights: The tensions between health and appearance motivations for weight loss. *Ageing & Society, 22*(6), 751–773. https://doi.org/10.1017/S0144686X02008905

Cohen, R., Irwin, L., Newton-John, T., & Slater, A. (2019). #bodypositivity: A content analysis of body positive accounts on Instagram. *Body Image*, *29*, 47–57. https://doi.org/10.1016/j.bodyim.2019.02.007

Collyer, D. A., Boseovski, J. J., & Marcovitch, S. (2018). Reviewing the development of self-concept: Implications for an enhanced model. *Journal of Educational and Developmental Psychology*, *8*(1), 171–177. https://doi.org/10.5539/jedp.v8n1p171

Coomber, K., & King, R. M. (2008). The role of sisters in body image dissatisfaction and disordered eating. *Sex Roles*, *59*(1–2), 81–93. https://doi.org/10.1007/s11199-008-9413-7

Coyne, S. M., Linder, J. R., Booth, M., Keenan-Kroff, S., Shawcroft, J. E., & Yang, C. (2021). Princess power: Longitudinal associations between engagement with princess culture in preschool and gender stereotypical behavior, body esteem, and hegemonic masculinity in early adolescence. *Child Development*, *92*(6), 2413–2430. https://doi.org/10.1111/cdev.13633

Cramer, P., & Steinwert, T. (1998). Thin is good, fat is bad: How early does it begin? *Journal of Applied Developmental Psychology*, *19*(3), 429–451. https://doi.org/10.1016/S0193-3973(99)80049-5

Crandall, C., & Biernat, M. (1990). The ideology of anti-fat attitudes. *Journal of Applied Social Psychology*, *20*(3), 227–243. https://doi.org/10.1111/j.1559-1816.1990.tb00408.x

Crandall, C. S. (1994). Prejudice against fat people: Ideology and self-interest. *Journal of Personality and Social Psychology*, *66*(5), 882–894. https://doi.org/10.1037/0022-3514.66.5.882

Cuesta-Zamora, C., & Navas, L. (2017). A review of instruments for assessing body image in preschoolers. *Universal Journal of Educational Research*, *5*(10), 1667–1677. https://doi.org/10.13189/ujer.2017.051001

Damiano, S. R., Hart, L. M., & Paxton, S. J. (2016). Correlates of parental feeding practices with pre-schoolers: Parental body image and eating knowledge, attitudes, and behaviours. *Appetite*, *101*, 192–198. https://doi.org/10.1016/j.appet.2016.03.008

Damiano, S. R., Paxton, S. J., Wertheim, E. H., McLean, S. A., & Gregg, K. J. (2015). Dietary restraint of 5-year-old girls: Associations with internalization of the thin ideal and maternal, media, and peer influences. *International Journal of Eating Disorders*, *48*(8), 1166–1169. https://doi.org/10.1002/eat.22432

Daniels, E. A., Zurbriggen, E. L., & Monique Ward, L. (2020). Becoming an object: A review of self-objectification in girls. *Body Image, 33,* 278–299. https://doi.org/10.1016/j.bodyim.2020.02.016

Davis, D. S., Sbrocco, T., & Williams, J. (2009). Understanding body image in African American and Caucasian first-graders: A partnership with the YMCA. *Progress in Community Health Partnerships, 3*(4), 277–286. https://doi.org/10.1353/cpr.0.0092

Davison, K. K., & Birch, L. L. (2002). Processes linking weight status and self-concept among girls from ages 5 to 7 years. *Developmental Psychology, 38*(5), 735–748. https://doi.org/10.1037/0012-1649. 38.5.735

de Valle, M. K., Gallego-García, M., Williamson, P., & Wade, T. D. (2021). Social media, body image, and the question of causation: Meta-analyses of experimental and longitudinal evidence. *Body Image, 39,* 276–292. https://doi.org/10.1016/j.bodyim.2021.10.001

Deci, E. L., & Ryan, R. M. (2000). The "what" and "why" of goal pursuits: Human needs and the self determination of behavior. *Psychological Inquiry, 11*(4), 227–268. https://doi.org/10.1207/ S15327965PLI1104_01

DeJesus, J. M., Gelman, S. A., Viechnicki, G. B., Appugliese, D. P., Miller, A. L., Rosenblum, K. L., & Lumeng, J. C. (2018). An investigation of maternal food intake and maternal food talk as predictors of child food intake. *Appetite, 127,* 356–363. https://doi.org/10.1016/ j.appet.2018.04.018

DeJesus, J. M., Kinzler, K. D., & Shutts, K. (2018). Food cognition and nutrition knowledge. In J. C. Lumeng & J. O. Fisher (Eds.), *Pediatric food preferences and eating behaviors* (pp. 271–288). Academic Press. https://doi.org/10.1016/B978-0-12-811716-3.00014-2

DeJesus, J. M., Shutts, K., & Kinzler, K. D. (2018). Mere social knowledge impacts children's consumption and categorization of foods. *Developmental Science, 21*(5), Article e12627. https://doi.org/10.1111/ desc.12627

Demo, D. H. (1992). The self-concept over time: Research issues and directions. *Annual Review of Sociology, 18*(1), 303–326. https://doi.org/ 10.1146/annurev.so.18.080192.001511

Devine, R. T., & Lecce, S. (Eds.). (2021). *Theory of mind in middle childhood and adolescence: Integrating multiple perspectives.* Routledge.

Diener, E., & Chan, M. Y. (2011). Happy people live longer: Subjective well-being contributes to health and longevity. *Applied Psychology: Health and Well-Being, 3*(1), 1–43. https://doi.org/10.1111/j.1758-0854.2010.01045.x

Dion, K., Berscheid, E., & Walster, E. (1972). What is beautiful is good. *Journal of Personality and Social Psychology, 24*(3), 285–290. https://doi.org/10.1037/h0033731

Dittmar, H., Halliwell, E., & Ive, S. (2006). Does Barbie make girls want to be thin? The effect of experimental exposure to images of dolls on the body image of 5- to 8-year-old girls. *Developmental Psychology, 42*(2), 283–292. https://doi.org/10.1037/0012-1649.42.2.283

Dixey, R., Sahota, P., Atwal, S., & Turner, A. (2001). "Ha ha, you're fat, we're strong"; a qualitative study of boys' and girls' perception of fatness, thinness, social pressures and health using focus groups. *Health Education, 101*(5), 206–216. https://doi.org/10.1108/EUM0000000005644

Dixon, R. S., Gill, J. M. W., & Adair, V. A. (2003). Exploring paternal influences on the dieting behaviors of adolescent girls. *Eating Disorders, 11*(1), 39–50. https://doi.org/10.1080/10640260390167474

Dodge, J., Clunie, L., Harary, R., Chapman, K., Ziegler-Sullivan, U., Kraft, S., & Stevens, T. (Executive Producers). (2013–present). *Paw patrol* [TV series]. Nickelodeon Productions.

Dohnt, H. K., & Tiggemann, M. (2005). Peer influences on body dissatisfaction and dieting awareness in young girls. *British Journal of Developmental Psychology, 23*(1), 103–116. https://doi.org/10.1348/026151004X20658

Dohnt, H. K., & Tiggemann, M. (2006). Body image concerns in young girls: The role of peers and media prior to adolescence. *Journal of Youth and Adolescence, 35*(2), 135–145. https://doi.org/10.1007/s10964-005-9020-7

Dohnt, H. K., & Tiggemann, M. (2008). Promoting positive body image in young girls: An evaluation of 'Shapesville.' *European Eating Disorders Review, 16*(3), 222–233. https://doi.org/10.1002/erv.814

Downey, G., & Feldman, S. I. (1996). Implications of rejection sensitivity for intimate relationships. *Journal of Personality and Social Psychology, 70*(6), 1327–1343. https://doi.org/10.1037/0022-3514.70.6.1327

Dweck, C. S. (2017). The journey to children's mindsets—and beyond. *Child Development Perspectives, 11*(2), 139–144. https://doi.org/10.1111/cdep.12225

Edmonds, A. (2012). Body image in non-Western societies. In T. Cash (Ed.), *The encyclopedia of body image and human appearance* (pp. 238–242). Elsevier Press. https://doi.org/10.1016/B978-0-12-384925-0.00036-5

Edwards, J. S. A., & Hartwell, H. H. (2002). Fruit and vegetables—Attitudes and knowledge of primary school children. *Journal of Human Nutrition and Dietetics, 15*(5), 365–374. https://doi.org/10.1046/j.1365-277X.2002.00386.x

Elavsky, S. (2010). Longitudinal examination of the exercise and self-esteem model in middle-aged women. *Journal of Sport & Exercise Psychology, 32*(6), 862–880. https://doi.org/10.1123/jsep.32.6.862

Else-Quest, N. M., Higgins, A., Allison, C., & Morton, L. C. (2012). Gender differences in self-conscious emotional experience: A meta-analysis. *Psychological Bulletin, 138*(5), 947–981. https://doi.org/10.1037/a0027930

Emery, L. F., Walsh, C., & Slotter, E. B. (2015). Knowing who you are and adding to it: Reduced self-concept clarity predicts reduced self-expansion. *Social Psychological and Personality Science, 6*(3), 259–266. https://doi.org/10.1177/1948550614555029

Emmons, R. A. (2007). *Thanks! How the new science of gratitude can make you happier.* Houghton Mifflin Company.

Fardouly, J., Slater, A., Parnell, J., & Diedrichs, P. C. (2023). Can following body positive or appearance neutral Facebook pages improve young women's body image and mood? Testing novel social media micro-interventions. *Body Image, 44*, 136–147. https://doi.org/10.1016/j.bodyim.2022.12.008

Farr, R. H. (2017). Does parental sexual orientation matter? A longitudinal follow-up of adoptive families with school-age children. *Developmental Psychology, 53*(2), 252–264. https://doi.org/10.1037/dev0000228

Farr, R. H., Bruun, S. T., & Patterson, C. J. (2019). Longitudinal associations between coparenting and child adjustment among lesbian, gay, and heterosexual adoptive parent families. *Developmental Psychology, 55*(12), 2547–2560. https://doi.org/10.1037/dev0000828

Farrow, C., Haycraft, E., & Meyer, C. (2011). Similarities between eating attitudes among friendship groups in childhood: The moderating role of child anxiety. *Journal of Pediatric Psychology, 36*(10), 1144–1152. https://doi.org/10.1093/jpepsy/jsp105

Feher, A., Smith, M. M., Saklofske, D. H., Plouffe, R. A., Wilson, C. A., & Sherry, S. B. (2020). The big three perfectionism scale–short form (BTPS-SF): Development of a brief self-report measure of multidimensional perfectionism. *Journal of Psychoeducational Assessment, 38*(1), 37–52. https://doi.org/10.1177/0734282919878553

Festinger, L. (1954). A theory of social comparison processes. *Human Relations, 7*(2), 117–140. https://doi.org/10.1177/001872675400700202

Firme, J. N., de Almeida, P. C., dos Santos, E. B., Zandonadi, R. P., Raposo, A., & Botelho, R. B. A. (2023). Instruments to evaluate food neophobia in children: An integrative review with a systematic approach. *Nutrients, 15*(22), 4769. https://doi.org/10.3390/nu15224769

Flavell, J. H., Everett, B. A., Croft, K., & Flavell, E. R. (1981). Young children's knowledge about visual perception: Further evidence for the Level 1–Level 2 distinction. *Developmental Psychology, 17*(1), 99–103. https://doi.org/10.1037/0012-1649.17.1.99

Frazier, B. N., Gelman, S. A., Kaciroti, N., Russell, J. W., & Lumeng, J. C. (2012). I'll have what she's having: The impact of model characteristics on children's food choices. *Developmental Science, 15*(1), 87–98. https://doi.org/10.1111/j.1467-7687.2011.01106.x

Frederick, D. A., Crerand, C. E., Brown, T. A., Perez, M., Best, C. R., Cook-Cottone, C. P., Compte, E. J., Convertino, L., Gordon, A. R., Malcarne, V. L., Nagata, J. M., Parent, M. C., Pennesi, J.-L., Pila, E., Rodgers, R. F., Schaefer, L. M., Thompson, J. K., Tylka, T. L., & Murray, S. B. (2022). Demographic predictors of body image satisfaction: The U.S. Body Project I. *Body Image, 41*, 17–31. https://doi.org/10.1016/j.bodyim.2022.01.011

Fredrickson, B. L., & Roberts, T. A. (1997). Objectification theory: Toward understanding women's lived experiences and mental health risks. *Psychology of Women Quarterly, 21*(2), 173–206. https://doi.org/10.1111/j.1471-6402.1997.tb00108.x

Frost, R. O., Marten, P., Lahart, C., & Rosenblate, R. (1990). The dimensions of perfectionism. *Cognitive Therapy and Research, 14*(5), 449–468. https://doi.org/10.1007/BF01172967

Funder, D. C. (Ed.). (1999). *Personality judgment: A realistic approach to person perception.* Elsevier.

Funder, D. C. (2019). *The personality puzzle* (8th ed.). W. W. Norton & Company.

Gallagher, P., Yancy, W. S., Jr., Denissen, J. J. A., Kühnel, A., & Voils, C. I. (2013). Correlates of daily leisure-time physical activity in a community sample: Narrow personality traits and practical barriers. *Health Psychology, 32*(12), 1227–1235. https://doi.org/10.1037/a0029956

Gallagher, P., Yancy, W. S., Jr., Jeffreys, A. S., Coffman, C. J., Weinberger, M., Bosworth, H. B., & Voils, C. I. (2013). Patient self-efficacy and spouse perception of spousal support are associated with lower patient weight: Baseline results from a spousal support behavioral intervention. *Psychology, Health & Medicine, 18*(2), 175–181. https://doi.org/10.1080/13548506.2012.715176

Gamble, S. D. (1943). The disappearance of foot-binding in Tinghsien. *American Journal of Sociology, 49*(2), 181–183. https://doi.org/10.1086/219351

Gerwig, G. (Director). (2023). *Barbie* [Film]. Mattel Films.

Ghosh, T., & Periasamy, A. (2019). Comparative positive psychological attributes among sportswomen of group & individual sports and non-sportswomen. *International Journal of Physiology, Nutrition, and Physical Education*, 19–24.

Gibbons, F. X., & Buunk, B. P. (1999). Individual differences in social comparison: Development of a scale of social comparison orientation. *Journal of Personality and Social Psychology, 76*(1), 129–142. https://doi.org/10.1037/0022-3514.76.1.129

Gifford-Smith, M. E., & Brownell, C. A. (2003). Childhood peer relationships: Social acceptance, friendships, and peer networks. *Journal of School Psychology, 41*(4), 235–284. https://doi.org/10.1016/S0022-4405(03)00048-7

Gillison, F. B., Lorenc, A. B., Sleddens, E. F. C., Williams, S. L., & Atkinson, L. (2016). Can it be harmful for parents to talk to their child about their weight? A meta-analysis. *Preventive Medicine, 93*, 135–146. https://doi.org/10.1016/j.ypmed.2016.10.010

Gingras, J., Fitzpatrick, J., & McCargar, L. (2004). Body image of chronic dieters: Lowered appearance evaluation and body satisfaction. *Journal of the American Dietetic Association, 104*(10), 1589–1592. https://doi.org/10.1016/j.jada.2004.07.025

Goel, N. J., Thomas, B., Boutté, R. L., Kaur, B., & Mazzeo, S. E. (2021). Body image and eating disorders among South Asian American women: What are we missing? *Qualitative Health Research, 31*(13), 2512–2527. https://doi.org/10.1177/10497323211036896

Gollwitzer, P. M., & Sheeran, P. (2006). Implementation intentions and goal achievement: A meta-analysis of effects and processes. *Advances in Experimental Social Psychology, 38*, 69–119. https://doi.org/10.1016/S0065-2601(06)38002-1

Gosling, S. D., Rentfrow, P. J., & Swann, W. B., Jr. (2003). A very brief measure of the Big-Five personality domains. *Journal of Research in Personality, 37*(6), 504–528. https://doi.org/10.1016/S0092-6566(03)00046-1

Goswami, U. (Ed.). (2010). *The Wiley-Blackwell handbook of childhood cognitive development*. Blackwell Publishing, Ltd. https://doi.org/10.1002/9781444325485

Grabe, S., & Hyde, J. S. (2006). Ethnicity and body dissatisfaction among women in the United States: A meta-analysis. *Psychological Bulletin, 132*(4), 622–640. https://doi.org/10.1037/0033-2909.132.4.622

Grabe, S., Ward, L. M., & Hyde, J. S. (2008). The role of the media in body image concerns among women: A meta-analysis of experimental and correlational studies. *Psychological Bulletin, 134*(3), 460–476. https://doi.org/10.1037/0033-2909.134.3.460

Greenhalgh, J., Dowey, A. J., Horne, P. J., Fergus Lowe, C., Griffiths, J. H., & Whitaker, C. J. (2009). Positive- and negative peer modelling effects on young children's consumption of novel blue foods. *Appetite, 52*(3), 646–653. https://doi.org/10.1016/j.appet.2009.02.016

Griffith, J. M., Clark, H. M., Haraden, D. A., Young, J. F., & Hankin, B. L. (2021). Affective development from middle childhood to late adolescence: Trajectories of mean-level change in negative and positive affect. *Journal of Youth and Adolescence, 50*(8), 1550–1563. https://doi.org/10.1007/s10964-021-01425-z

Groesz, L. M., Levine, M. P., & Murnen, S. K. (2002). The effect of experimental presentation of thin media images on body satisfaction: A meta-analytic review. *International Journal of Eating Disorders, 31*(1), 1–16. https://doi.org/10.1002/eat.10005

Gu, X., Chen, S., & Zhang, X. (2019). Physical literacy at the start line: Young children's motor competence, fitness, physical activity, and fitness knowledge. *Journal of Teaching in Physical Education, 38*(2), 146–154. https://doi.org/10.1123/jtpe.2018-0069

Hall, J. C. (2017). No longer invisible: Understanding the psychosocial impact of skin color stratification in the lives of African American women. *Health & Social Work, 42*(2), 71–78. https://doi.org/10.1093/hsw/hlx001

Handford, C. M., Rapee, R. M., & Fardouly, J. (2018). The influence of maternal modeling on body image concerns and eating disturbances in preadolescent girls. *Behaviour Research and Therapy, 100,* 17–23. https://doi.org/10.1016/j.brat.2017.11.001

Hanley, A. W., de Vibe, M., Solhaug, I., Gonzalez-Pons, K., & Garland, E. L. (2019). Mindfulness training reduces neuroticism over a 6-year longitudinal randomized control trial in Norwegian medical and psychology students. *Journal of Research in Personality, 82,* Article 103859. https://doi.org/10.1016/j.jrp.2019.103859

Harriger, J. A. (2015). Age differences in body size stereotyping in a sample of preschool girls. *Eating Disorders, 23*(2), 177–190. https://doi.org/10.1080/10640266.2014.964610

Harriger, J. A., Schaefer, L. M., Kevin Thompson, J., & Cao, L. (2019). You can buy a child a curvy Barbie doll, but you can't make her like it: Young girls' beliefs about Barbie dolls with diverse shapes and sizes. *Body Image, 30,* 107–113. https://doi.org/10.1016/j.bodyim.2019.06.005

Hart, K. H., Bishop, J. A., & Truby, H. (2002). An investigation into school children's knowledge and awareness of food and nutrition. *Journal of Human Nutrition and Dietetics, 15*(2), 129–140. https://doi.org/10.1046/j.1365-277X.2002.00343.x

Hart, L. M., Damiano, S. R., Cornell, C., & Paxton, S. J. (2015). What parents know and want to learn about healthy eating and body image in preschool children: A triangulated qualitative study with parents and Early Childhood Professionals. *BMC Public Health, 15,* Article 596. https://doi.org/10.1186/s12889-015-1865-4

Harter, S. (2006). The development of self-esteem. In M. H. Kernis (Ed.), *Self-esteem issues and answers: A sourcebook of current perspectives* (pp. 144–150). Psychology Press.

Hartup, W. W. (1984). The peer context in childhood. In W. A. Collins (Ed.), *Development during middle childhood: The years from six to twelve* (pp. 240–282). National Academy Press.

Hatano, G., & Inagaki, K. (1994). Young children's naive theory of biology. *Cognition, 50*(1–3), 171–188.

Hausenblas, H. A., & Fallon, E. A. (2006). Exercise and body image: A meta-analysis. *Psychology & Health, 21*(1), 33–47. https://doi.org/10.1080/14768320500105270

Hayes, S., & Tantleff-Dunn, S. (2010). Am I too fat to be a princess? Examining the effects of popular children's media on young girls' body image. *British Journal of Developmental Psychology, 28*(2), 413–426. https://doi.org/10.1348/026151009X424240

Heffer, T., Good, M., Daly, O., MacDonell, E., & Willoughby, T. (2019). The longitudinal association between social-media use and depressive symptoms among adolescents and young adults: An empirical reply to Twenge et al. (2018). *Clinical Psychological Science, 7*(3), 462–470. https://doi.org/10.1177/2167702618812727

Heilman, M. E., & Saruwatari, L. R. (1979). When beauty is beastly: The effects of appearance and sex on evaluations of job applicants for managerial and nonmanagerial jobs. *Organizational Behavior and Human Performance, 23*(3), 360–372. https://doi.org/10.1016/0030-5073(79)90003-5

Helgeson, V. S., & Mickelson, K. D. (1995). Motives for social comparison. *Personality and Social Psychology Bulletin, 21*(11), 1200–1209. https://doi.org/10.1177/01461672952111008

Henning, T., Holman, M., Ismael, L., Yu, K. Y., Williams, L., Shelton, S. J., & Perez, M. (2022). Examination of hair experiences among girls with Black/African American identities. *Body Image, 42*, 75–83. https://doi.org/10.1016/j.bodyim.2022.05.009

Henrich, J., Heine, S. J., & Norenzayan, A. (2010). The weirdest people in the world? *Behavioral and Brain Sciences, 33*(2–3), 61–83. https://doi.org/10.1017/s0140525x0999152x

Herbozo, S., Tantleff-Dunn, S., Gokee-Larose, J., & Thompson, J. K. (2004). Beauty and thinness messages in children's media: A content analysis. *Eating Disorders, 12*(1), 21–34. https://doi.org/10.1080/10640260490267742

Higgins, E. T., Klein, R., & Strauman, T. (1985). Self-concept discrepancy theory: A psychological model for distinguishing among different aspects of depression and anxiety. *Social Cognition, 3*(1), 51–76. https://doi.org/10.1521/soco.1985.3.1.51

Holub, S. C., Musher-Eizenman, D. R., Persson, A. V., Edwards-Leeper, L. A., Goldstein, S. E., & Miller, A. B. (2005). Do preschool children understand what it means to "diet," and do they do it? *International Journal of Eating Disorders, 38*(1), 91–93. https://doi.org/10.1002/eat.20143

Holub, S. C., Tan, C. C., & Patel, S. L. (2011). Factors associated with mothers' obesity stigma and young children's weight stereotypes.

Journal of Applied Developmental Psychology, 32(3), 118–126. https://doi.org/10.1016/j.appdev.2011.02.006

Hunger, J. M., & Tomiyama, A. J. (2014). Weight labeling and obesity: A longitudinal study of girls aged 10 to 19 years. *JAMA Pediatrics, 168*(6), 579–580. https://doi.org/10.1001/jamapediatrics.2014.122

Hutchinson, D. M., & Rapee, R. M. (2007). Do friends share similar body image and eating problems? The role of social networks and peer influences in early adolescence. *Behaviour Research and Therapy, 45*(7), 1557–1577. https://doi.org/10.1016/j.brat.2006.11.007

Inagaki, K., & Hatano, G. (2006). Young children's conception of the biological world. *Current Directions in Psychological Science, 15*(4), 177–181. https://doi.org/10.1111/j.1467-8721.2006.00431.x

Ivtzan, I., Gardner, H. E., & Smailova, Z. (2011). Mindfulness meditation and curiosity: The contributing factors to wellbeing and the process of closing the self-discrepancy gap. *International Journal of Wellbeing, 1*(3), 316–327. https://doi.org/10.5502/ijw.v1i3.2

Jaakkola, R. O., & Slaughter, V. (2002). Children's body knowledge: Understanding 'life' as a biological goal. *British Journal of Developmental Psychology, 20*(3), 325–342. https://doi.org/10.1348/026151002320620352

Jansen, E., Mulkens, S., & Jansen, A. (2010). How to promote food consumption in children: Visual appeal versus restriction. *Appetite, 54*(3), 599–602. https://doi.org/10.1016/j.appet.2010.02.012

Jarry, J. L., Dignard, N. A. L., & O'Driscoll, L. M. (2019). Appearance investment: The construct that changed the field of body image. *Body Image, 31*, 221–244. https://doi.org/10.1016/j.bodyim.2019.09.001

Jellinek, R. D., Myers, T. A., & Keller, K. L. (2016). The impact of doll style of dress and familiarity on body dissatisfaction in 6- to 8-year-old girls. *Body Image, 18*(18), 78–85. https://doi.org/10.1016/j.bodyim.2016.05.003

Jiménez-Loaisa, A., Beltrán-Carrillo, V. J., González-Cutre, D., & Jennings, G. (2020). Healthism and the experiences of social, healthcare and self-stigma of women with higher-weight. *Social Theory & Health, 18*, 410–424. https://doi.org/10.1057/s41285-019-00118-9

Jorm, A. F. (1989). Modifiability of trait anxiety and neuroticism: A meta-analysis of the literature. *Australian & New Zealand Journal of Psychiatry, 23*(1), 21–29. https://doi.org/10.3109/00048678909062588

Kaestner, R., & Xu, X. (2006). Effects of Title IX and sports participation on girls' physical activity and weight. In K. Bolin & J. Cawley (Eds.), *Advances in health economics and health services research: Vol. 17. The economics of obesity* (pp. 79–111). Emerald Group Publishing Limited. https://doi.org/10.1016/S0731-2199(06)17004-1

Kalish, C. (1997). Preschoolers' understanding of mental and bodily reactions to contamination: What you don't know can hurt you, but cannot sadden you. *Developmental Psychology, 33*(1), 79–91. https://doi.org/10.1037/0012-1649.33.1.79

Karazsia, B. T., Murnen, S. K., & Tylka, T. L. (2017). Is body dissatisfaction changing across time? A cross-temporal meta-analysis. *Psychological Bulletin, 143*(3), 293–320. https://doi.org/10.1037/bul0000081

Karraker, K. H., Vogel, D. A., & Lake, M. A. (1995). Parents' gender-stereotyped perceptions of newborns: The Eye of the Beholder revisited. *Sex Roles, 33*(9/10), 687–701. https://doi.org/10.1007/BF01547725

Kawamura, K. (2012). Body image among Asian Americans. In T. F. Cash (Ed.), *The encyclopedia of body image and human appearance* (pp. 95–102). Elsevier Press. https://doi.org/10.1016/B978-0-12-384925-0.00039-0

Kennedy, M. A., Templeton, L., Gandhi, A., & Gorzalka, B. B. (2004). Asian body image satisfaction: Ethnic and gender differences across Chinese, Indo-Asian, and European-descent students. *Eating Disorders, 12*(4), 321–336. https://doi.org/10.1080/10640260490521415

Killen, M., & Smetana, J. G. (2015). Origins and development of morality. In W. Damon (Ed.), *Handbook of child psychology and developmental science: Vol. 3. Socioemotional processes* (7th ed., pp. 701–749). John Wiley & Sons. https://doi.org/10.1002/9781118963418.childpsy317

Kinsaul, J. A., Curtin, L., Bazzini, D., & Martz, D. (2014). Empowerment, feminism, and self-efficacy: Relationships to body image and disordered eating. *Body Image, 11*(1), 63–67. https://doi.org/10.1016/j.bodyim.2013.08.001

Knopf, A. (2018). Don't harm children by shaming them for obesity; stigma doesn't work, says AAP. *The Brown University Child and Adolescent Behavior Letter, 34*(1), 1–7. https://doi.org/10.1002/cbl.30263

Kostanski, M., & Gullone, E. (2007). The impact of teasing on children's body image. *Journal of Child and Family Studies, 16*(3), 307–319. https://doi.org/10.1007/s10826-006-9087-0

Kranz, D. (2023). On the attribution of parental competence: Parents' behavior matters, not their sexual orientation. *Journal of Child and Family Studies, 32*(4), 1121–1137. https://doi.org/10.1007/s10826-022-02335-9

Kross, E. (2021). *Chatter: The voice in our head, why it matters, and how to harness it.* Crown.

Kuhn, M. H., & McPartland, T. S. (1954). An empirical investigation of self-attitudes. *American Sociological Review, 19*(1), 68–76. https://doi.org/10.2307/2088175

Lagattuta, K. H., & Kramer, H. J. (2021). Advanced theory of mind in middle childhood and adulthood: Inferring mental states and emotions from life history. In R. T. Devine & S. Lecce (Eds.), *Theory of mind in middle childhood and adolescence: Integrating multiple perspectives* (pp. 15–36). Routledge. https://doi.org/10.4324/9780429326899-3

Landers, D. M., & Arent, S. M. (2007). Physical activity and mental health. In G. Tennenbaum & R. C. Eklund (Eds.), *Handbook of sport psychology* (3rd ed., pp. 467–491). John Wiley & Sons. https://doi.org/10.1002/9781118270011.ch21

Langlois, J. H., Kalakanis, L., Rubenstein, A. J., Larson, A., Hallam, M., & Smoot, M. (2000). Maxims or myths of beauty? A meta-analytic and theoretical review. *Psychological Bulletin, 126*(3), 390–423. https://doi.org/10.1037/0033-2909.126.3.390

Lanigan, J. D. (2011). The substance and sources of young children's healthy eating and physical activity knowledge: Implications for obesity prevention efforts. *Child: Care, Health and Development, 37*(3), 368–376. https://doi.org/10.1111/j.1365-2214.2010.01191.x

Lansford, J. E. (2022). Annual research review: Cross-cultural similarities and differences in parenting. *Journal of Child Psychology and Psychiatry, 63*(4), 466–479. https://doi.org/10.1111/jcpp.13539

Lapan, C., & Boseovski, J. J. (2017). When peer performance matters: Effects of expertise and traits on children's self-evaluations after social comparison. *Child Development, 88*(6), 1860–1872. https://doi.org/10.1111/cdev.12941

Larson, R. W., Moneta, G., Richards, M. H., & Wilson, S. (2002). Continuity, stability, and change in daily emotional experience across adolescence. *Child Development, 73*(4), 1151–1165. https://doi.org/10.1111/1467-8624.00464

Lazuka, R. F., Wick, M. R., Keel, P. K., & Harriger, J. A. (2020). Are we there yet? Progress in depicting diverse images of beauty in Instagram's body positivity movement. *Body Image, 34*, 85–93. https://doi.org/10.1016/j.bodyim.2020.05.001

Leahey, T. M., Crowther, J. H., & Mickelson, K. D. (2007). The frequency, nature, and effects of naturally occurring appearance-focused social comparisons. *Behavior Therapy, 38*(2), 132–143. https://doi.org/10.1016/j.beth.2006.06.004

Leaper, C. (2015). Gender and social-cognitive development. In L. S. Liben, U. Müller, & R. M. Lerner (Eds.), *Handbook of child psychology and developmental science: Vol. 2. Cognitive processes* (pp. 806–853). John Wiley & Sons. https://doi.org/10.1002/9781118963418.childpsy219

Leary, M. R. (2004). *The curse of the self: Self-awareness, egotism, and the quality of human life.* Oxford University Press. https://doi.org/10.1093/acprof:oso/9780195172423.001.0001

Leary, M. R., & Baumeister, R. F. (2000). The nature and function of self-esteem: Sociometer theory. In M. P. Zanna (Ed.), *Advances in experimental social psychology* (Vol. 32, pp. 1–62). Academic Press. https://doi.org/10.1016/S0065-2601(00)80003-9

León, M. P., González-Martí, I., & Contreras-Jordán, O. R. (2021). What do children think of their perceived and ideal bodies? Understandings of body image at early ages: A mixed study. *International Journal of Environmental Research and Public Health, 18*(9), Article 4871. https://doi.org/10.3390/ijerph18094871

Lev-Ari, L., Baumgarten-Katz, I., & Zohar, A. H. (2014). Mirror, mirror on the wall: How women learn body dissatisfaction. *Eating Behaviors, 15*(3), 397–402. https://doi.org/10.1016/j.eatbeh.2014.04.015

Liechty, J. M., Clarke, S., Birky, J. P., Harrison, K., & the STRONG Kids Team. (2016). Perceptions of early body image socialization in families: Exploring knowledge, beliefs, and strategies among mothers of preschoolers. *Body Image, 19*, 68–78. https://doi.org/10.1016/j.bodyim.2016.08.010

Liechty, T., Freeman, P. A., & Zabriskie, R. B. (2006). Body image and beliefs about appearance: Constraints on the leisure of college-age and middle-age women. *Leisure Sciences, 28*(4), 311–330. https://doi.org/10.1080/01490400600745845

Lin, K. L., & Raval, V. V. (2020). Understanding body image and appearance management behaviors among adult women in South Korea within a sociocultural context: A review. *International Perspectives in Psychology: Research, Practice, Consultation, 9*(2), 96–122. https://doi.org/10.1037/ipp0000124

Linardon, J., Anderson, C., Messer, M., Rodgers, R. F., & Fuller-Tyszkiewicz, M. (2021). Body image flexibility and its correlates: A meta-analysis. *Body Image, 37,* 188–203. https://doi.org/10.1016/j.bodyim.2021.02.005

Livesley, W. J., & Bromley, D. B. (1973). *Person perception in childhood and adolescence.* John Wiley & Sons.

Lombardo, C., Battagliese, G., Lucidi, F., & Frost, R. O. (2012). Body dissatisfaction among pre-adolescent girls is predicted by their involvement in aesthetic sports and by personal characteristics of their mothers. *Eating and Weight Disorders, 17*(2), e116–e127. https://doi.org/10.1007/BF03325335

Lopez, N. V., Schembre, S., Belcher, B. R., O'Connor, S., Maher, J. P., Arbel, R., Margolin, G., & Dunton, G. F. (2018). Parenting styles, food-related parenting practices, and children's healthy eating: A mediation analysis to examine relationships between parenting and child diet. *Appetite, 128,* 205–213. https://doi.org/10.1016/j.appet.2018.06.021

Luo, Y., Parish, W. L., & Laumann, E. O. (2005). A population-based study of body image concerns among urban Chinese adults. *Body Image, 2*(4), 333–345. https://doi.org/10.1016/j.bodyim.2005.09.003

MacNeill, L. P., & Best, L. A. (2015). Perceived current and ideal body size in female undergraduates. *Eating Behaviors, 18,* 71–75. https://doi.org/10.1016/j.eatbeh.2015.03.004

Maestripieri, D., Klimczuk, A. C. E., Traficonte, D. M., & Wilson, M. C. (2014). A greater decline in female facial attractiveness during middle age reflects women's loss of reproductive value. *Frontiers in Psychology, 5,* Article 179. https://doi.org/10.3389/fpsyg.2014.00179

Manago, A. M., Ward, L. M., Lemm, K. M., Reed, L., & Seabrook, R. (2015). Facebook involvement, objectified body consciousness, body shame, and sexual assertiveness in college women and men. *Sex Roles, 72*(1–2), 1–14. https://doi.org/10.1007/s11199-014-0441-1

Mao, Y., Zhao, J., Xu, Y., & Xiang, Y. (2021). How gratitude inhibits envy: From the perspective of positive psychology. *PsyCh Journal*, *10*(3), 384–392. https://doi.org/10.1002/pchj.413

Marcovitch, S., Boseovski, J. J., Knapp, R. J., & Kane, M. J. (2010). Goal neglect and working memory capacity in 4- to 6-year-old children. *Child Development*, *81*(6), 1687–1695. https://doi.org/10.1111/j.1467-8624.2010.01503.x

Markus, H. R., & Kitayama, S. (1991). Culture and the self: Implications for cognition, emotion, and motivation. *Psychological Review*, *98*(2), 224–253. https://doi.org/10.1037/0033-295X.98.2.224

Marsh, H. W., Ellis, L. A., & Craven, R. G. (2002). How do preschool children feel about themselves? Unraveling measurement and multi-dimensional self-concept structure. *Developmental Psychology*, *38*(3), 376–393. https://doi.org/10.1037/0012-1649.38.3.376

Martin, C. L., Andrews, N. C., England, D. E., Zosuls, K., & Ruble, D. N. (2017). A dual identity approach for conceptualizing and measuring children's gender identity. *Child Development*, *88*(1), 167–182. https://doi.org/10.1111/cdev.12568

Martin, C. L., Eisenbud, L., & Rose, H. (1995). Children's gender-based reasoning about toys. *Child Development*, *66*(5), 1453–1471. https://doi.org/10.2307/1131657

Martz, D. M., Petroff, A. B., Curtin, L., & Bazzini, D. G. (2009). Gender differences in fat talk among American adults: Results from the Psychology of Size Survey. *Sex Roles*, *61*, 34–41. https://doi.org/10.1007/s11199-009-9587-7

Master, A., Cheryan, S., Moscatelli, A., & Meltzoff, A. N. (2017). Programming experience promotes higher STEM motivation among first-grade girls. *Journal of Experimental Child Psychology*, *160*, 92–106. https://doi.org/10.1016/j.jecp.2017.03.013

Maunder, R., & Monks, C. P. (2019). Friendships in middle childhood: Links to peer and school identification, and general self-worth. *British Journal of Developmental Psychology*, *37*(2), 211–229. https://doi.org/10.1111/bjdp.12268

Mbilishaka, A. M., Clemons, K., Hudlin, M., Warner, C., & Jones, D. (2020). Don't get it twisted: Untangling the psychology of hair discrimination within Black communities. *American Journal of Orthopsychiatry*, *90*(5), 590–599. https://doi.org/10.1037/ort0000468

McCabe, M. P., & Ricciardelli, L. A. (2003). Body image and strategies to lose weight and increase muscle among boys and girls. *Health Psychology*, *22*(1), 39–46. https://doi.org/10.1037/0278-6133.22.1.39

McComb, C. A., Vanman, E. J., & Tobin, S. J. (2023). A meta-analysis of the effects of social media exposure to upward comparison targets on self-evaluations and emotions. *Media Psychology*, *26*(5), 612–635. https://doi.org/10.1080/15213269.2023.2180647

McHale, S. M., Shanahan, L., Updegraff, K. A., Crouter, A. C., & Booth, A. (2004). Developmental and individual differences in girls' sex-typed activities in middle childhood and adolescence. *Child Development*, *75*(5), 1575–1593. https://doi.org/10.1111/j.1467-8624.2004.00758.x

McKinley, N. M. (2006). The developmental and cultural contexts of objectified body consciousness: A longitudinal analysis of two cohorts of women. *Developmental Psychology*, *42*(4), 679–687. https://doi.org/10.1037/0012-1649.42.4.679

McKinley, N. M., & Hyde, J. S. (1996). The objectified body consciousness scale: Development and validation. *Psychology of Women Quarterly*, *20*(2), 181–215. https://doi.org/10.1111/j.1471-6402.1996.tb00467.x

McLoughlin, N., & Over, H. (2017). Young children are more likely to spontaneously attribute mental states to members of their own group. *Psychological Science*, *28*(10), 1503–1509. https://doi.org/10.1177/0956797617710724

Merwin, R. M., Nikolaou, P., Moskovich, A. A., Babyak, M., Smith, P. J., & Karekla, M. (2023). Change in body image flexibility and correspondence with outcomes in a digital early intervention for eating disorders based on acceptance and commitment therapy. *Body Image*, *44*, 131–135. https://doi.org/10.1016/j.bodyim.2022.12.010

Meyer, M., & Gelman, S. A. (2016). Gender essentialism in children and parents: Implications for the development of gender stereotyping and gender-typed preferences. *Sex Roles*, *75*(9–10), 409–421. https://doi.org/10.1007/s11199-016-0646-6

Michela, J. L., & Contento, I. R. (1984). Spontaneous classification of foods by elementary school-aged children. *Health Education Quarterly*, *11*(1), 57–76. https://doi.org/10.1177/109019818401100103

Miller, W. R., & Rollnick, S. (2002). *Motivational interviewing: Preparing people for change* (2nd ed.). Guilford Press.

Mills, C. M., & Keil, F. C. (2008). Children's developing notions of (im)partiality. *Cognition, 107*(2), 528–551. https://doi.org/10.1016/j.cognition.2007.11.003

Mills, J. S., Minister, C., & Samson, L. (2022). Enriching sociocultural perspectives on the effects of idealized body norms: Integrating shame, positive body image, and self-compassion. *Frontiers in Psychology, 13*, Article 983534. https://doi.org/10.3389/fpsyg.2022.983534

Mingoia, J., Hutchinson, A. D., Wilson, C., & Gleaves, D. H. (2017). The relationship between social networking site use and the internalization of a thin ideal in females: A meta-analytic review. *Frontiers in Psychology, 8*, Article 1351. https://doi.org/10.3389/fpsyg.2017.01351

Mishra, A., Craddock, N., Chan, J., Elwyn, R., Cerea, S., Tan, W. Q., Bin Haamed, H., & Turk, F. (2023). "You can't be too skinny. You can't be too fat. I don't know what you are supposed to be.": A qualitative focus group study exploring body image expectations of South Asian women in the UK. *Body Image, 46*, 123–138. https://doi.org/10.1016/j.bodyim.2023.05.005

Moradi, B., & Huang, Y. P. (2008). Objectification theory and psychology of women: A decade of advances and future directions. *Psychology of Women Quarterly, 32*(4), 377–398. https://doi.org/10.1111/j.1471-6402.2008.00452.x

Murnen, S. K. (2011). Gender and body images. In T. F. Cash & L. Smolak (Eds.), *Body image: A handbook of science, practice, and prevention* (pp. 173–179). Guilford Press.

Musher-Eizenman, D. R., Holub, S. C., Edwards-Leeper, L., Persson, A. V., & Goldstein, S. E. (2003). The narrow range of acceptable body types of preschoolers and their mothers. *Journal of Applied Developmental Psychology, 24*(2), 259–272. https://doi.org/10.1016/S0193-3973(03)00047-9

Musher-Eizenman, D. R., Holub, S. C., Miller, A. B., Goldstein, S. E., & Edwards-Leeper, L. (2004). Body size stigmatization in preschool children: The role of control attributions. *Journal of Pediatric Psychology, 29*(8), 613–620. https://doi.org/10.1093/jpepsy/jsh063

Myers, T. A., & Crowther, J. H. (2009). Social comparison as a predictor of body dissatisfaction: A meta-analytic review. *Journal of Abnormal Psychology, 118*(4), 683–698. https://doi.org/10.1037/a0016763

Neff, K. D. (2003). The development and validation of a scale to measure self-compassion. *Self and Identity, 2*(3), 223–250. https://doi.org/10.1080/15298860309027

Neff, K. D. (2011). Self-compassion, self-esteem, and well-being. *Social and Personality Psychology Compass, 5*(1), 1–12. https://doi.org/10.1111/j.1751-9004.2010.00330.x

Nelson, T. D., Jensen, C. D., & Steele, R. G. (2011). Weight-related criticism and self-perceptions among preadolescents. *Journal of Pediatric Psychology, 36*(1), 106–115. https://doi.org/10.1093/jpepsy/jsq047

Nerini, A., Matera, C., & Stefanile, C. (2016). Siblings' appearance-related commentary, body dissatisfaction, and risky eating behaviors in young women. *European Review of Applied Psychology/Revue Européenne de Psychologie Appliquée, 66*(6), 269–276. https://doi.org/10.1016/j.erap.2016.06.005

Nguyen, S. P., & McCullough, M. B. (2009). Making sense of what is healthy for you: Children's and adults' evaluative categories of food. In S. J. Ellsworth & R. C. Schuster (Eds.), *Appetite and nutritional assessment* (pp. 176–187). Nova Science Publishers, Inc.

Nichter, M., & Vuckovic, N. (1994). Fat talk: Body image among adolescent girls. In N. Sault (Ed.), *Many mirrors* (pp. 109–131). Rutgers University Press.

Niveau, N., New, B., & Beaudoin, M. (2021). Self-esteem intervention in adults: A systematic review and meta-analysis. *Journal of Research in Personality, 94*, Article 104131. https://doi.org/10.1016/j.jrp.2021.104131

Noh, J. W., Kwon, Y. D., Yang, Y., Cheon, J., & Kim, J. (2018). Relationship between body image and weight status in east Asian countries: Comparison between South Korea and Taiwan. *BMC Public Health, 18*(1), 814. https://doi.org/10.1186/s12889-018-5738-5

Noom, M. J., Deković, M., & Meeus, W. (2001). Conceptual analysis and measurement of adolescent autonomy. *Journal of Youth and Adolescence, 30*(5), 577–595. https://doi.org/10.1023/A:1010400721676

Norton, L., Parkinson, J., Harris, N., Darcy, M., & Hart, L. (2023). Parental food communication and child eating behaviours: A systematic literature review. *Health Promotion Journal of Australia, 34*(2), 366–378. https://doi.org/10.1002/hpja.604

Norwood, K. J., & Foreman, V. S. (2014). The ubiquitousness of colorism: Then and now. In K. J. Norwood (Ed.), *Color matters: Skin tone bias and the myth of a post-racial America* (pp. 9–28). Routledge.

O'Brien, K. S., Latner, J. D., Ebneter, D., & Hunter, J. A. (2013). Obesity discrimination: The role of physical appearance, personal ideology, and anti-fat prejudice. *International Journal of Obesity, 37*(3), 455–460. https://doi.org/10.1038/ijo.2012.52

O'Dea, J. A. (2012). Body image and self-esteem. In T. F. Cash (Ed.), *Encyclopedia of body image and human appearance* (pp. 141–147). Elsevier Academic Press. https://doi.org/10.1016/B978-0-12-384925-0.00021-3

Oliver, K. K., & Thelen, M. H. (1996). Children's perceptions of peer influence on eating concerns. *Behavior Therapy, 27*(1), 25–39. https://doi.org/10.1016/S0005-7894(96)80033-5

Oliver, M., Schofield, G. M., & Kolt, G. S. (2007). Physical activity in preschoolers: Understanding prevalence and measurement issues. *Sports Medicine, 37*(12), 1045–1070. https://doi.org/10.2165/00007256-200737120-00004

Onetti, W., Fernández-García, J. C., & Castillo-Rodríguez, A. (2019). Transition to middle school: Self-concept changes. *PLOS ONE, 14*(2), Article e0212640. https://doi.org/10.1371/journal.pone.0212640

Oyserman, D., Elmore, K., & Smith, G. (2012). Self, self-concept, and identity. In J. Tangney & M. Leary (Eds.), *The handbook of self and identity* (2nd ed., pp. 69–104). Guilford Press.

Ozbek, S., Greville, J., & Hooper, N. (2023). The thin-ideal across two cultural contexts: The role of body image inflexibility and the fear of negative evaluation. *Psychology of Popular Media.* Advance online publication. https://doi.org/10.1037/ppm0000464

Park, L. E. (2007). Appearance-based rejection sensitivity: Implications for mental and physical health, affect, and motivation. *Personality and Social Psychology Bulletin, 33*(4), 490–504. https://doi.org/10.1177/0146167206296301

Park, N., Kee, K. F., & Valenzuela, S. (2009). Being immersed in social networking environment: Facebook groups, uses and gratifications, and social outcomes. *Cyberpsychology & Behavior, 12*(6), 729–733. https://doi.org/10.1089/cpb.2009.0003

Parrett, M. (2015). Beauty and the feast: Examining the effect of beauty on earnings using restaurant tipping data. *Journal of Economic Psychology, 49*, 34–46. https://doi.org/10.1016/j.joep.2015.04.002

Patton, T. O. (2006). Hey girl, am I more than my hair? African American women and their struggles with beauty, body image, and hair. *NWSA Journal, 18*(2), 24–51. https://www.jstor.org/stable/4317206

Paxton, S. J., & Damiano, S. R. (2017). The development of body image and weight bias in childhood. *Advances in Child Development and Behavior, 52,* 269–298. https://doi.org/10.1016/bs.acdb.2016.10.006

Pellizzer, M. L., & Wade, T. D. (2023). Developing a definition of body neutrality and strategies for an intervention. *Body Image, 46,* 434–442. https://doi.org/10.1016/j.bodyim.2023.07.006

Peretz-Lange, R., & Kibbe, M. M. (2024). "Shape bias" goes social: Children categorize people by weight rather than race. *Developmental Science, 27*(2), Article e13454. https://doi.org/10.1111/desc.13454

Perez, M., Kroon Van Diest, A. M., Smith, H., & Sladek, M. R. (2018). Body dissatisfaction and its correlates in 5- to 7-year-old girls: A social learning experiment. *Journal of Clinical Child and Adolescent Psychology, 47*(5), 757–769. https://doi.org/10.1080/15374416.2016.1157758

Perry, D. G., Pauletti, R. E., & Cooper, P. J. (2019). Gender identity in childhood: A review of the literature. *International Journal of Behavioral Development, 43*(4), 289–304. https://doi.org/10.1177/016502541811129

Petersen, T. L., Møller, L. B., Brønd, J. C., Jepsen, R., & Grøntved, A. (2020). Association between parent and child physical activity: A systematic review. *The International Journal of Behavioral Nutrition and Physical Activity, 17*(1), 67. https://doi.org/10.1186/s12966-020-00966-z

Phares, V., Steinberg, A. R., & Thompson, J. K. (2004). Gender differences in peer and parental influences: Body image disturbance, self-worth, and psychological functioning in preadolescent children. *Journal of Youth and Adolescence, 33*(5), 421–429. https://doi.org/10.1023/B:JOYO.0000037634.18749.20

Phinney, J. S., & Ong, A. D. (2007). Conceptualization and measurement of ethnic identity: Current status and future directions. *Journal of Counseling Psychology, 54*(3), 271–281. https://doi.org/10.1037/0022-0167.54.3.271

Pine, K. J. (2001). Children's perceptions of body shape: A thinness bias in pre-adolescent girls and associations with femininity. *Clinical Child*

Psychology and Psychiatry, *6*(4), 519–536. https://doi.org/10.1177/1359104501006004006

Pont, S. J., Puhl, R., Cook, S. R., Slusser, W., the Section on Obesity, & the Obesity Society. (2017). Stigma experienced by children and adolescents with obesity. *Pediatrics*, *140*(6), Article e20173034. https://doi.org/10.1542/peds.2017-3034

Pronovost, M. A., & Scott, R. M. (2022). The influence of language input on 3-year-olds' learning about novel social categories. *Acta Psychologica*, *230*, Article 103729. https://doi.org/10.1016/j.actpsy.2022.103729

Puhl, R. M., & Heuer, C. A. (2009). The stigma of obesity: A review and update. *Obesity*, *17*(5), 941–964. https://doi.org/10.1038/oby.2008.636

Puhl, R. M., & Latner, J. D. (2007). Stigma, obesity, and the health of the nation's children. *Psychological Bulletin*, *133*(4), 557–580. https://doi.org/10.1037/0033-2909.133.4.557

Puhl, R. M., & Lessard, L. M. (2020). Weight stigma in youth: Prevalence, consequences, and considerations for clinical practice. *Current Obesity Reports*, *9*(4), 402–411. https://doi.org/10.1007/s13679-020-00408-8

Puhl, R. M., Lessard, L. M., Foster, G. D., & Cardel, M. I. (2022). A comprehensive examination of the nature, frequency, and context of parental weight communication: Perspectives of parents and adolescents. *Nutrients*, *14*(8), Article 1562. https://doi.org/10.3390/nu14081562

Pyszczynski, T., Greenberg, J., Solomon, S., Arndt, J., & Schimel, J. (2004). Why do people need self-esteem? A theoretical and empirical review. *Psychological Bulletin*, *130*(3), 435–468. https://doi.org/10.1037/0033-2909.130.3.435

Quiñones, I. C., Herbozo, S., & Haedt-Matt, A. A. (2022). Body dissatisfaction among ethnic subgroups of Latin women: An examination of acculturative stress and ethnic identity. *Body Image*, *41*, 272–283. https://doi.org/10.1016/j.bodyim.2022.03.006

Quittkat, H. L., Hartmann, A. S., Düsing, R., Buhlmann, U., & Vocks, S. (2019). Body dissatisfaction, importance of appearance, and body appreciation in men and women over the lifespan. *Frontiers in Psychiatry*, *10*, 864. https://doi.org/10.3389/fpsyt.2019.00864

Raihani, N. J., & Smith, S. (2015). Competitive helping in online giving. *Current Biology*, *25*(9), 1183–1186. https://doi.org/10.1016/j.cub.2015.02.042

Raman, L. (2014). Children's and adults' understanding of the impact of nutrition on biological and psychological processes. *British Journal of Developmental Psychology, 32*(1), 78–93. https://doi.org/10.1111/bjdp.12024

Rancaño, K., Eliasziw, M., Puhl, R., Skeer, M., & Must, A. (2021). Exposure to negative weight talk from family members is associated with weight bias internalization in children. *Current Developments in Nutrition, 5*(2), 1241. https://doi.org/10.1093/cdn/nzab055_051

Rex-Lear, M., Jensen-Campbell, L. A., & Lee, S. (2019). Young and biased: Children's perception of overweight peers. *Journal of Applied Biobehavioral Research, 24*(3), Article e12161. https://doi.org/10.1111/jabr.12161

Rhode, D. L. (2010). *The beauty bias: The injustice of appearance in life and law.* Oxford University Press.

Rhodes, M., Leslie, S. J., Bianchi, L., & Chalik, L. (2018). The role of generic language in the early development of social categorization. *Child Development, 89*(1), 148–155. https://doi.org/10.1111/cdev.12714

Riboli, G., Borlimi, R., & Caselli, G. (2022). A qualitative approach—Delineates changes on pubertal body image after menarche. *International Journal of Adolescence and Youth, 27*(1), 111–124. https://doi.org/10.1080/02673843.2022.2032219

Ricciardelli, L. A., & McCabe, M. P. (2001). Children's body image concerns and eating disturbance: A review of the literature. *Clinical Psychology Review, 21*(3), 325–344. https://doi.org/10.1016/S0272-7358(99)00051-3

Ricciardelli, L. A., McCabe, M. P., Holt, K. E., & Finemore, J. (2003). A biopsychosocial model for understanding body image and body change strategies among children. *Journal of Applied Developmental Psychology, 24*(4), 475–495. https://doi.org/10.1016/S0193-3973(03)00070-4

Rice, K., Prichard, I., Tiggemann, M., & Slater, A. (2016). Exposure to Barbie: Effects on thin-ideal internalisation, body esteem, and body dissatisfaction among young girls. *Body Image, 19*, 142–149. https://doi.org/10.1016/j.bodyim.2016.09.005

Rich, M. K., & Cash, T. F. (1993). The American image of beauty: Media representations of hair color for four decades. *Sex Roles, 29*(1–2), 113–124. https://doi.org/10.1007/BF00289999

Riniolo, T. C., Johnson, K. C., Sherman, T. R., & Misso, J. A. (2006). Hot or not: Do professors perceived as physically attractive receive higher student evaluations? *Journal of General Psychology, 133*(1), 19–35. https://doi.org/10.3200/GENP.133.1.19-35

Rivero, A., Killoren, S. E., Kline, G., & Campione-Barr, N. (2022). Negative messages from parents and sisters and Latina college students' body image shame. *Body Image, 42,* 98–109. https://doi.org/10.1016/j.bodyim.2022.05.011

Robert-McComb, J. J., & Massey-Stokes, M. (2014). Body image concerns throughout the lifespan. In J. J. Robert-McComb, R. L. Norman, & M. Zumwalt (Eds.), *The active female* (2nd ed., pp. 3–23). Springer. https://doi.org/10.1007/978-1-4614-8884-2_1

Robinson, E., & Sutin, A. R. (2017). Parents' perceptions of their children as overweight and children's weight concerns and weight gain. *Psychological Science, 28*(3), 320–329. https://doi.org/10.1177/0956797616682027

Rodgers, R. F., Damiano, S. R., Wertheim, E. H., & Paxton, S. J. (2017). Media exposure in very young girls: Prospective and cross-sectional relationships with BMIz, self-esteem and body size stereotypes. *Developmental Psychology, 53*(12), 2356–2363. https://doi.org/10.1037/dev0000407

Rodgers, R. F., Laveway, K., Campos, P., & de Carvalho, P. H. B. (2023). Body image as a global mental health concern. *Global Mental Health, 10,* Article e9. https://doi.org/10.1017/gmh.2023.2

Rodgers, R. F., Paxton, S. J., & Wertheim, E. H. (2021). #Take idealized bodies out of the picture: A scoping review of social media content aiming to protect and promote positive body image. *Body Image, 38,* 10–36. https://doi.org/10.1016/j.bodyim.2021.03.009

Rodgers, R. F., Wertheim, E. H., Damiano, S. R., & Paxton, S. J. (2020). Maternal influences on body image and eating concerns among 7- and 8-year-old boys and girls: Cross-sectional and prospective relations. *International Journal of Eating Disorders, 53*(1), 79–84. https://doi.org/10.1002/eat.23166

Rodgers, R. F., Wertheim, E. H., Paxton, S. J., Tylka, T. L., & Harriger, J. A. (2022). #Bopo: Enhancing body image through body positive social media—Evidence to date and research directions. *Body Image, 41,* 367–374. https://doi.org/10.1016/j.bodyim.2022.03.008

Rogers Wood, N. A., & Petrie, T. A. (2010). Body dissatisfaction, ethnic identity, and disordered eating among African American women. *Journal of Counseling Psychology, 57*(2), 141–153. https://doi.org/10.1037/a0018922

Rosenberg, M. (1965). *Society and the adolescent self-image.* Princeton University Press. https://doi.org/10.1515/9781400876136

Rousseau, A., & Eggermont, S. (2018). Media ideals and early adolescents' body image: Selective avoidance or selective exposure? *Body Image, 26,* 50–59. https://doi.org/10.1016/j.bodyim.2018.06.001

Rudiger, J. A., & Winstead, B. A. (2013). Body talk and body-related co-rumination: Associations with body image, eating attitudes, and psychological adjustment. *Body Image, 10*(4), 462–471. https://doi.org/10.1016/j.bodyim.2013.07.010

Runfola, C. D., Von Holle, A., Trace, S. E., Brownley, K. A., Hofmeier, S. M., Gagne, D. A., & Bulik, C. M. (2013). Body dissatisfaction in women across the lifespan: Results of the UNC-SELF and Gender and Body Image (GABI) studies. *European Eating Disorders Review, 21*(1), 52–59. https://doi.org/10.1002/erv.2201

Russell, R. (2011). Why cosmetics work. In R. B. Adams, Jr., N. Ambady, K. Nakayama, & S. Shimojo (Eds.), *The science of social vision* (pp. 186–204). Oxford University Press.

Sahlan, R. N., Saunders, J. F., & Fitzsimmons-Craft, E. E. (2021). Body-, eating-, and exercise-related social comparison behavior and disordered eating in college women in the U.S. and Iran: A cross-cultural comparison. *Eating Behaviors, 40,* 101451. https://doi.org/10.1016/j.eatbeh.2020.101451

Salomon, I., & Brown, C. S. (2021). That selfie becomes you: Examining taking and posting selfies as forms of self-objectification. *Media Psychology, 24*(6), 847–865. https://doi.org/10.1080/15213269.2020.1817091

Sandoval, C. M., Martz, D. M., Bazzini, D. G., Webb, R. M., Hinkle, M. M., & Francis, L. (2022). Does fat talk affect relationship and sexual satisfaction? Adults' perceptions of fat talk in a fictional romantic relationship. *Eating Behaviors, 45,* Article 101603. https://doi.org/10.1016/j.eatbeh.2022.101603

Sandoz, E. K., Wilson, K. G., Merwin, R. M., & Kate Kellum, K. (2013). Assessment of body image flexibility: The Body Image-Acceptance and Action Questionnaire. *Journal of Contextual Behavioral Science*, *2*(1–2), 39–48. https://doi.org/10.1016/j.jcbs.2013.03.002

Schaefer, L. M., & Thompson, J. K. (2014). The development and validation of the Physical Appearance Comparison Scale-Revised (PACS-R). *Eating Behaviors*, *15*(2), 209–217. https://doi.org/10.1016/j.eatbeh. 2014.01.001

Schult, C. A., & Wellman, H. M. (1997). Explaining human movements and actions: Children's understanding of the limits of psychological explanation. *Cognition*, *62*(3), 291–324. https://doi.org/10.1016/ S0010-0277(96)00786-X

Schultz, C. M., & Danford, C. M. (2016). Children's knowledge of eating: An integrative review of the literature. *Appetite*, *107*, 534–548. https:// doi.org/10.1016/j.appet.2016.08.120

Schultz, C. M., & Danford, C. A. (2021). What obese and healthy weight preschoolers believe and know about food. *Cognitive Development*, *57*, Article 101000. https://doi.org/10.1016/j.cogdev.2020.101000

Schwartz, M. B., & Puhl, R. (2003). Childhood obesity: A societal problem to solve. *Obesity Reviews*, *4*(1), 57–71. https://doi.org/10.1046/j.1467-789X.2003.00093.x

Shaffer, D. R., Crepaz, N., & Sun, C. R. (2000). Physical attractiveness stereotyping in cross-cultural perspective: Similarities and differences between Americans and Taiwanese. *Journal of Cross-Cultural Psychology*, *31*(5), 557–582. https://doi.org/10.1177/0022022100031005002

Shannon, A., & Mills, J. S. (2015). Correlates, causes, and consequences of fat talk: A review. *Body Image*, *15*, 158–172. https://doi.org/10.1016/ j.bodyim.2015.09.003

Sheeran, P., Maki, A., Montanaro, E., Avishai-Yitshak, A., Bryan, A., Klein, W. M. P., Miles, E., & Rothman, A. J. (2016). The impact of changing attitudes, norms, and self-efficacy on health-related intentions and behavior: A meta-analysis. *Health Psychology*, *35*(11), 1178–1188. https://doi.org/10.1037/hea0000387

Shtulman, A., Share, I., Silber-Marker, R., & Landrum, A. R. (2020). OMG GMO! Parent–child conversations about genetically modified foods. *Cognitive Development*, *55*, 100895. https://doi.org/10.1016/j.cogdev. 2020.100895

Siegal, M. (1988). Children's knowledge of contagion and contamination as causes of illness. *Child Development*, *59*(5), 1353–1359. https:// doi.org/10.2307/1130497

Siegel, J. A., Ramseyer Winter, V., & Cook, M. (2021). "It really presents a struggle for females, especially my little girl": Exploring fathers' experiences discussing body image with their young daughters. *Body Image, 36*, 84–94. https://doi.org/10.1016/j.bodyim.2020.11.001

Skoog, T., & Stattin, H. (2014). Why and under what contextual conditions do early-maturing girls develop problem behaviors? *Child Development Perspectives, 8*(3), 158–162. https://doi.org/10.1111/cdep.12076

Slater, A., Cole, N., & Fardouly, J. (2019). The effect of exposure to parodies of thin-ideal images on young women's body image and mood. *Body Image, 29*, 82–89. https://doi.org/10.1016/j.bodyim.2019.03.001

Slater, A., Halliwell, E., Jarman, H., & Gaskin, E. (2017). More than just child's play? An experimental investigation of the impact of an appearance-focused internet game on body image and career aspirations of young girls. *Journal of Youth and Adolescence, 46*(9), 2047–2059. https://doi.org/10.1007/s10964-017-0659-7

Slater, A., & Tiggemann, M. (2006). The contribution of physical activity and media use during childhood and adolescence to adult women's body image. *Journal of Health Psychology, 11*(4), 553–565. https://doi.org/10.1177/1359105306065016

Slater, A., & Tiggemann, M. (2011). Gender differences in adolescent sport participation, teasing, self-objectification and body image concerns. *Journal of Adolescence, 34*(3), 455–463. https://doi.org/10.1016/j.adolescence.2010.06.007

Slater, A., & Tiggemann, M. (2014). Media matters for boys too! The role of specific magazine types and television programs in the drive for thinness and muscularity in adolescent boys. *Eating Behaviors, 15*(4), 679–682. https://doi.org/10.1016/j.eatbeh.2014.10.002

Slater, A., & Tiggemann, M. (2016). Little girls in a grown up world: Exposure to sexualized media, internalization of sexualization messages, and body image in 6–9 year-old girls. *Body Image, 18*, 19–22. https://doi.org/10.1016/j.bodyim.2016.04.004

Slaughter, V., & Ting, C. (2010). Development of ideas about food and nutrition from preschool to university. *Appetite, 55*(3), 556–564. https://doi.org/10.1016/j.appet.2010.09.004

Slevec, J. H., & Tiggemann, M. (2011). Predictors of body dissatisfaction and disordered eating in middle-aged women. *Clinical Psychology Review, 31*(4), 515–524. https://doi.org/10.1016/j.cpr.2010.12.002

Smolak, L. (2004). Body image in children and adolescents: Where do we go from here? *Body Image, 1*(1), 15–28. https://doi.org/10.1016/S1740-1445(03)00008-1

Snyder, M. (1987). *Public appearances, private realities: The psychology of self-monitoring.* W. H. Freeman/Times Books/Henry Holt & Co.

Snyder, M., & Gangestad, S. (1986). On the nature of self-monitoring: Matters of assessment, matters of validity. *Journal of Personality and Social Psychology, 51*(1), 125–139. https://doi.org/10.1037/0022-3514.51.1.125

Spencer, R. A., Rehman, L., & Kirk, S. F. L. (2015). Understanding gender norms, nutrition, and physical activity in adolescent girls: A scoping review. *The International Journal of Behavioral Nutrition and Physical Activity, 12*, Article 6. https://doi.org/10.1186/s12966-015-0166-8

Spiel, E. C., Paxton, S. J., & Yager, Z. (2012). Weight attitudes in 3- to 5-year-old children: Age differences and cross-sectional predictors. *Body Image, 9*(4), 524–527. https://doi.org/10.1016/j.bodyim.2012.07.006

Stewart, J. E., II. (1985). Appearance and punishment: The attraction-leniency effect in the courtroom. *The Journal of Social Psychology, 125*(3), 373–378. https://doi.org/10.1080/00224545.1985.9922900

Stice, E., & Agras, W. S. (1998). Predicting onset and cessation of bulimic behaviors during adolescence: A longitudinal grouping analysis. *Behavior Therapy, 29*(2), 257–276. https://doi.org/10.1016/S0005-7894(98)80006-3

Stoeber, J., & Janssen, D. P. (2011). Perfectionism and coping with daily failures: Positive reframing helps achieve satisfaction at the end of the day. *Anxiety, Stress, & Coping, 24*(5), 477–497. https://doi.org/10.1080/10615806.2011.562977

Sullivan, L. A., & Harnish, R. J. (1990). Body image: Differences between high and low self-monitoring males and females. *Journal of Research in Personality, 24*(3), 291–302. https://doi.org/10.1016/0092-6566(90)90022-X

Tam, K.-P., Leung, A. K.-Y., & Chiu, C.-Y. (2008). On being a mindful authoritarian: Is need for cognition always associated with less punitiveness? *Political Psychology, 29*(1), 77–91. https://doi.org/10.1111/j.1467-9221.2007.00613.x

Tatangelo, G., McCabe, M., Mellor, D., & Mealey, A. (2016). A systematic review of body dissatisfaction and sociocultural messages related to the body among preschool children. *Body Image, 18*, 86–95. https://doi.org/10.1016/j.bodyim.2016.06.003

Tatangelo, G. L., & Ricciardelli, L. A. (2017). Children's body image and social comparisons with peers and the media. *Journal of Health Psychology*, 22(6), 776–787. https://doi.org/10.1177/1359105315615409

Tatlow-Golden, M., Hennessy, E., Dean, M., & Hollywood, L. (2013). 'Big, strong and healthy.' Young children's identification of food and drink that contribute to healthy growth. *Appetite*, 71, 163–170. https://doi.org/10.1016/j.appet.2013.08.007

Taylor, M. G. (1996). The development of children's beliefs about social and biological aspects of gender differences. *Child Development*, 67(4), 1555–1571. https://doi.org/10.2307/1131718

Taylor, M. G., Rhodes, M., & Gelman, S. A. (2009). Boys will be boys; cows will be cows: Children's essentialist reasoning about gender categories and animal species. *Child Development*, 80(2), 461–481. https://doi.org/10.1111/j.1467-8624.2009.01272.x

Thelen, M. H., & Cormier, J. F. (1995). Desire to be thinner and weight control among children and their parents. *Behavior Therapy*, 26(1), 85–99. https://doi.org/10.1016/S0005-7894(05)80084-X

Thompson, R. A., & Lagattuta, K. H. (2006). Feeling and understanding: Early emotional development. In K. McCartney & D. Phillips (Eds.), *Blackwell handbook of early childhood development* (pp. 317–337). Blackwell Publishing. https://doi.org/10.1002/9780470757703.ch16

Tiberio, S. S., Kerr, D. C., Capaldi, D. M., Pears, K. C., Kim, H. K., & Nowicka, P. (2014). Parental monitoring of children's media consumption: The long-term influences on body mass index in children. *JAMA Pediatrics*, 168(5), 414–421. https://doi.org/10.1001/jamapediatrics.2013.5483

Tiggemann, M. (2015). Considerations of positive body image across various social identities and special populations. *Body Image*, 14, 168–176. https://doi.org/10.1016/j.bodyim.2015.03.002

Tiggemann, M., & Lowes, J. (2002). Changes in ratings of figure preference in girls ages five to seven years. *Perceptual and Motor Skills*, 94(2), 424. https://doi.org/10.2466/pms.2002.94.2.424

Tiggemann, M., & McCourt, A. (2013). Body appreciation in adult women: Relationships with age and body satisfaction. *Body Image*, 10(4), 624–627. https://doi.org/10.1016/j.bodyim.2013.07.003

Tiggemann, M., & Slater, A. (2014). Contemporary girlhood: Maternal reports on sexualized behaviour and appearance concern in 4–10 year-old girls. *Body Image, 11*(4), 396–403. https://doi.org/10.1016/j.bodyim.2014.06.007

Tiggemann, M., & Zaccardo, M. (2015). "Exercise to be fit, not skinny": The effect of fitspiration imagery on women's body image. *Body Image, 15*, 61–67. https://doi.org/10.1016/j.bodyim.2015.06.003

Todorov, A., Pakrashi, M., & Oosterhof, N. (2009). Evaluating faces on trustworthiness after minimal time exposure. *Social Cognition, 27*(6), 813–833. https://doi.org/10.1521/soco.2009.27.6.813

Trekels, J., & Eggermont, S. (2017). Aspiring to have the looks of a celebrity: Young girls' engagement in appearance management behaviors. *European Journal of Pediatrics, 176*(7), 857–863. https://doi.org/10.1007/s00431-017-2918-8

Trottier, K., MacDonald, D. E., McFarlane, T., Carter, J., & Olmsted, M. P. (2015). Body checking, body avoidance, and the core cognitive psychopathology of eating disorders: Is there a unique relationship? *Advances in Eating Disorders, 3*(3), 288–299. https://doi.org/10.1080/21662630.2015.1053819

Tucker, K. L., Martz, D. M., Curtin, L. A., & Bazzini, D. G. (2007). Examining "fat talk" experimentally in a female dyad: How are women influenced by another woman's body presentation style? *Body Image, 4*(2), 157–164. https://doi.org/10.1016/j.bodyim.2006.12.005

Turnage, B. F. (2004). Influences on adolescent African American females' global self-esteem. *Journal of Ethnic & Cultural Diversity in Social Work, 13*(4), 27–45. https://doi.org/10.1300/J051v13n04_02

Tylka, T. L. (2011). Positive psychology perspectives on body image. In T. F. Cash & L. Smolak (Eds.), *Body image: A handbook of science, practice, and prevention* (2nd ed., pp. 56–64). Guilford Press.

Tylka, T. L. (2019). Body appreciation. In T. L. Tylka & N. Piran (Eds.), *Handbook of positive body image and embodiment: Constructs, protective factors, and interventions* (pp. 22–32). Oxford University Press. https://doi.org/10.1093/med-psych/9780190841874.003.0003

Tylka, T. L., & Wood-Barcalow, N. L. (2015a). The Body Appreciation Scale-2: Item refinement and psychometric evaluation. *Body Image, 12*, 53–67. https://doi.org/10.1016/j.bodyim.2014.09.006

Tylka, T. L., & Wood-Barcalow, N. L. (2015b). What is and what is not positive body image? Conceptual foundations and construct definition. *Body Image, 14*, 118–129. https://doi.org/10.1016/j.bodyim.2015.04.001

Valutis, S. A., Goreczny, A. J., Abdullah, L., Magee, E., & Wister, J. A. (2009). Weight preoccupation, body image dissatisfaction, and self-efficacy in female undergraduates. *Journal of Psychiatry, Psychology and Mental Health, 3*(1), 1–11.

Vartanian, L. R. (2009). When the body defines the self: Self-concept clarity, internalization, and body image. *Journal of Social and Clinical Psychology, 28*(1), 94–126. https://doi.org/10.1521/jscp.2009.28.1.94

Vartanian, L. R. (2012). Self-discrepancy theory and body image. In T. F. Cash (Ed.), *Encyclopedia of body image and human appearance* (pp. 711–717). Elsevier Academic Press. https://doi.org/10.1016/B978-0-12-384925-0.00112-7

Voges, M. M., Giabbiconi, C. M., Schöne, B., Waldorf, M., Hartmann, A. S., & Vocks, S. (2019). Gender differences in body evaluation: Do men show more self-serving double standards than women? *Frontiers in Psychology, 10*, Article 544. https://doi.org/10.3389/fpsyg.2019.00544

Vohs, K. D., & Baumeister, R. F. (Eds.). (2016). *Handbook of self-regulation: Research, theory, and applications*. Guilford Press.

Vonk, R. (2006). Improving self-esteem. In M. Kernis (Ed.), *Self-esteem: Issues and answers* (pp. 178–187). Psychology Press.

Wade, T. D., & Tiggemann, M. (2013). The role of perfectionism in body dissatisfaction. *Journal of Eating Disorders, 1*, Article 2. https://doi.org/10.1186/2050-2974-1-2

Walker, D. C., & Murray, A. D. (2012). Body image behaviors: Checking, fixing, and avoiding. In T. F. Cash (Ed.), *Encyclopedia of body image and human appearance* (pp. 166–172). Elsevier Science. https://doi.org/10.1016/B978-0-12-384925-0.00025-0

Walton, G. M., Paunesku, D., & Dweck, C. S. (2012). Expandable selves. In M. R. Leary & J. P. Tangney (Eds.), *Handbook of self and identity* (2nd ed., pp. 141–154). Guilford Press.

Warburton, V. E., Beaumont, L. C., & Bishop, K. C. M. (2022). Pre-adolescent children's understanding of health and being healthy: A multidimensional perspective from the UK. *Health Education, 122*(5), 519–534. https://doi.org/10.1108/HE-10-2021-0135

Wijayaratne, S., Westberg, K., Reid, M., & Worsley, A. (2022). Developing food literacy in young children in the home environment. *International Journal of Consumer Studies, 46*(4), 1165–1177. https://doi.org/10.1111/ijcs.12750

Wilks, M., & Bloom, P. (2022). Children prefer natural food, too. *Developmental Psychology, 58*(9), 1747–1758. https://doi.org/10.1037/dev0001387

Wilson, M., & Russell, K. (1996). *Divided sisters: Bridging the gap between Black women and White women.* Anchor Books.

Winn, L., & Cornelius, R. (2020). Self-objectification and cognitive performance: A systematic review of the literature. *Frontiers in Psychology, 11*, 20. https://doi.org/10.3389/fpsyg.2020.00020

Wiseman, N., Harris, N., & Lee, P. (2016). Lifestyle knowledge and preferences in preschool children: Evaluation of the Get up and Grow healthy lifestyle education programme. *Health Education Journal, 75*(8), 1012–1024. https://doi.org/10.1177/0017896916648726

Wood-Barcalow, N. L., Alleva, J. M., & Tylka, T. L. (2024). Revisiting positive body image to demonstrate how body neutrality is not new. *Body Image, 50*, 101741. https://doi.org/10.1016/j.bodyim.2024.101741

Wood-Barcalow, N. L., Tylka, T. L., & Augustus-Horvath, C. L. (2010). "But I like my body": Positive body image characteristics and a holistic model for young-adult women. *Body Image, 7*(2), 106–116. https://doi.org/10.1016/j.bodyim.2010.01.001

Worobey, J., & Worobey, H. S. (2014). Body-size stigmatization by preschool girls: In a doll's world, it is good to be "Barbie." *Body Image, 11*(2), 171–174. https://doi.org/10.1016/j.bodyim.2013.12.001

Yeung, S. P., & Wong, W. I. (2018). Gender labels on gender-neutral colors: Do they affect children's color preferences and play performance? *Sex Roles, 79*(5–6), 260–272. https://doi.org/10.1007/s11199-017-0875-3

Zeinstra, G. G., Koelen, M. A., Kok, F. J., & de Graaf, C. (2007). Cognitive development and children's perceptions of fruit and vegetables; a qualitative study. *The International Journal of Behavioral Nutrition and Physical Activity, 4*(1), Article 30. https://doi.org/10.1186/1479-5868-4-30

Zelazo, P. D., Craik, F. I., & Booth, L. (2004). Executive function across the life span. *Acta Psychologica, 115*(2–3), 167–183. https://doi.org/10.1016/j.actpsy.2003.12.005

Zelazo, P. D., Müller, U., Frye, D., Marcovitch, S., Argitis, G., Boseovski, J., Chiang, J. K., Hongwanishkul, D., Schuster, B. V., & Sutherland, A. (2003). The development of executive function in early childhood. *Monographs of the Society for Research in Child Development, 68*(3), vii–137. https://doi.org/10.1111/j.0037-976x.2003.00260.x

INDEX

ABOUT THE AUTHORS

Janet Boseovski, PhD, is a professor of psychology at the University of North Carolina at Greensboro. Her research focuses on social and cognitive development in early to late childhood, and her work has been published in leading scientific journals. Dr. Boseovski is an associate editor of the journal *Social Development* and serves on the board of directors of the Greensboro Science Center and the Jean Piaget Society for the Study of Knowledge and Development. She enjoys speaking with parenting groups, teachers, and science educators about human development and writing about developmental science for the public. Visit https://www.duck-lab.com/ and https://www.psychologytoday.com/us/blog/head-start-for-healthy-body-image.

Ashleigh Gallagher, PhD, is a senior lecturer in the Department of Psychology at the University of North Carolina at Greensboro. Her research and teaching interests are in the areas of emotion, culture, and gender, and she enjoys applying psychology beyond academic contexts. She has experience working in public policy and has coauthored a book on the opportunities available to researchers outside of the academy (*The Portable PhD: Taking Your Psychology Career Beyond Academia*, American Psychological Association, 2020).